Macromedia®
Director® 8
Shockwave Studio
Illustrated Introductory

Steven M. Johnson

COURSE
TECHNOLOGY
™
THOMSON LEARNING

Australia • Canada • Mexico • Singapore • Spain • United Kingdom • United States

COURSE TECHNOLOGY

THOMSON LEARNING

Macromedia® Director® 8 Shockwave Studio—Illustrated Introductory
is published by Course Technology.

Managing Editor:
Nicole Jones Pinard

Product Manager:
Rebecca Berardy

Associate Product Manager:
Emeline Elliot

Production Editor:
Jennifer Goguen

Developmental Editor:
Barbara Waxer

Composition House:
GEX, Inc.

QA Manuscript Reviewer:
Jeff Schwartz, Ashlee Welz

Text Designer:
Joseph Lee, Black Fish Design

Cover Designer:
Doug Goodman, Doug Goodman Designs

Macromedia® Director® 8 Shockwave Studio and Macromedia® Fireworks® 3 are registered trademarks of Macromedia, Inc.

Some of the images used in this book are the property of Atlas Image [or Atlas Image mosaic] obtained as part of the Two Micron All Sky Survey (2MASS), a joint project of the University of Massachusetts and the Infrared Processing and Analysis Center/California Institute of Technology, funded by the National Aeronautics and Space Administration and the National Science Foundation; and material was also created by STScI under contract for NASA.

For permission to use material from this text or product, contact us by

- Web: www.thomsonrights.com
- Phone: 1-800-730-2214
- Fax: 1-800-730-2215

ISBN 0-619-01772-4 (packaged with 30-day trial software)

ISBN 0-619-04568-X (packaged with 120-day trial software)

Exciting New Products

Try out Illustrated's New Product Line: Multimedia Tools

Multimedia tools teach students how to create text, graphics, video, animations, and sound, all of which can be incorporated for use in printed materials, Web pages, CD-ROMs, and multimedia presentations.

New Titles

- Adobe Photoshop 5.5—Illustrated Introductory (0-7600-6337-0)
- Adobe Illustrator 8.0—Illustrated Introductory (0-619-01750-3)
- Macromedia Director 8 Shockwave Studio—Illustrated Introductory (0-619-01772-4)
- Macromedia Director 8 Shockwave Studio—Illustrated Complete (0-619-01779-1)
- Multimedia Concepts—Illustrated Introductory (0-619-01765-1)
- Macromedia Shockwave 8—Illustrated Essentials (0-7600-6398-2)

Master Microsoft Office 2000

Master Microsoft Office 2000 applications with the Illustrated series. With *Microsoft Office 2000—Illustrated Introductory*, students will learn the basics of Microsoft Office 2000 Professional Edition. *Microsoft Office 2000—Illustrated Second Course* focuses on the more advanced skills of Office 2000 applications, and it includes coverage of all of the software in the Premium Edition.

Illustrated also offers individual application books on Access, Excel, Word, and PowerPoint 2000. Each book covers basic to advanced skills for the application and meets Microsoft Office User Specialist (MOUS) Expert certification.

Other titles include:

- Microsoft Access 2000—Illustrated Introductory, Complete, and Second Course
- Microsoft Publisher 2000—Illustrated Essentials
- Microsoft Publisher 2000—Illustrated Introductory
- Microsoft Outlook 2000—Illustrated Essentials
- Microsoft FrontPage 2000—Illustrated Introductory and Complete
- Microsoft FrontPage 2000—Illustrated Essentials
- Microsoft Office 2000—Illustrated Introductory and Second Course
- Microsoft Office 2000—Illustrated Brief
- Microsoft PowerPoint 2000—Illustrated Brief and Introductory
- Microsoft Word 2000—Illustrated Introductory, Complete, and Second Course
- Microsoft PhotoDraw (version 2) —Illustrated Essentials
- Microsoft Excel 2000—Illustrated Introductory, Complete, and Second Course

Check Out Computer Concepts

Computer Concepts—Illustrated Brief and Introductory, Third Edition is the quick and visual way to learn cutting-edge computer concepts. The third edition has been updated to include advances to the Internet and multimedia, changes to the industry, and an introduction to e-commerce and security.

Create Your Ideal Course Package with CourseKits™

If one book doesn't offer all the coverage you need, create a course package that does. With Course Technology's CourseKits—our mix-and-match approach to selecting texts—you have the freedom to combine products from more than one series. When you choose any two or more Course Technology products for one course, we'll discount the price and package them together so your students can pick up one convenient bundle at the bookstore.

Preface

Welcome to *Macromedia Director 8 Shockwave Studio—Illustrated Introductory*. This highly visual book offers users a hands-on introduction to Macromedia Director 8 Shockwave Studio and also serves as an excellent reference for future use.

This book is a member of Illustrated's **Multimedia Tools** series. These books teach students how to create text, graphics, video, animations, and sound for use in print publications, CD-ROM products, and Web-based applications. Check out books on Photoshop and Illustrator for more multimedia curriculum.

▶ Organization and Coverage

This text is organized into eight units with one appendix. In these units students learn how to create a movie; create, modify, and manage cast members; create and modify sprites; add navigation and user interaction; add audio and video; and prepare and deliver movies. The appendix at the back of the book gives more in depth coverage of the skills taught in the lessons.

▶ About this Approach

What makes the Illustrated approach so effective at teaching software skills? It's quite simple. Each skill is presented on two facing pages, with the step-by-step instructions on the left page, and large screen illustrations on the right. Students can focus on a single skill without having to turn the page. This unique design makes information extremely accessible and easy to absorb, and provides a great reference for after the course is over. This hands-on approach also makes it ideal for both self-paced or instructor-led classes.

Each lesson, or "information display," contains the following elements:

Each 2-page spread focuses on a single skill.

Clear step-by-step directions explain how to complete the specific task, with what students are to type in green. When students follow the numbered steps, they quickly learn how each procedure is performed and what the results will be.

Concise text that introduces the basic principles discussed in the lesson. Procedures are easier to learn when concepts fit into a framework.

Director 8

Saving and Unlinking a Cast

You can use the Save button on the toolbar to save a movie, save an External Cast, or save both. When you select the Stage window before you save, Director saves the movie and all linked Cast windows; when you select an unlinked External Cast window, Director saves just the External Cast. Before you can use external cast members in a movie, you need to link the External Cast to the movie. After you link an External Cast to the current movie, Director opens that Cast whenever you open the movie. When you unlink an External Cast from a movie, the Cast is not available the next time you open the movie unless you open the Cast and relink it. When you make changes to an External Cast that is not linked to your movie, you need to save the External Cast. Director doesn't save changes to an External Cast when you save the movie, because the External Cast is not recognized as being part of the movie file. When you want to save an unlinked External Cast, you can select the External Cast window and use the Save button on the toolbar. Once you save an unlinked External Cast, you can use the Save All button on the toolbar to save the unlinked External Cast and the current movie. Remember to include the External Cast file when you distribute and package a movie. ▰ Jean saves the External Cast and the movie.

Steps

QuickTip
To save an External Cast with a new name, click the Cast window, click File on the menu bar, then click Save As.

1. Click the **title bar** in the Space Graphics Cast window, then click the **Save button** 🖫 on the toolbar
   The Save Cast "Space Graphics" dialog box opens.

2. Navigate to the drive and folder where your Project Files are located, then click **Save**
   The Space Graphics cast and the SpaceWorks Game Promo are saved. The External Cast file is saved with a .cst extension (Win).

3. Click **Modify** on the menu bar, point to **Movie**, then click **Casts**
   The Movie Casts dialog box opens, as shown in Figure D-21.

4. Click **Space Graphics** in the text box, then click **Remove**

5. Click **OK**
   Since a cast member in the Space Graphics cast is used in the movie, a warning dialog box opens, asking if you want to remove the Cast and remove the cast member from the movie.

QuickTip
To link an External Cast to the current movie, click Modify on the menu bar, point to Movie, click Casts, click Link, double-click the External Cast file, then click OK.

6. Click **Cancel**
   The Space Graphics Cast remains linked to the movie. Figure D-22 shows the Director window. The next time you open this movie, Director looks in the specified path in Cast Properties and opens the Cast.

7. Click the **Close button** in the Space Graphics Cast window
   The Space Graphics Cast window closes. The Cast window is still linked to the movie—it's just not open.

QuickTip
To open a linked Cast, click Window on the menu bar, point to Cast, then click a Cast name.

8. Click the **Score Window button** 🖽 on the toolbar
   The Score window opens.

9. Click **File** on the Menu bar, click **Exit** (Win) or **Quit** (Mac) then if asked to save your work, click **Yes** (Win) or **Save** (Mac)
   Director closes.

▶ DIRECTOR D-18   MANAGING AND MODIFYING CAST MEMBERS

Hints as well as trouble-shooting advice, right where you need it — next to the step itself.

Every lesson features large-size, full-color representations of what the students' screen should look like after completing the numbered steps.

FIGURE D-21: Movie Casts dialog box

List of linked Casts

Movie Casts
Internal
Space Graphics

OK
Cancel

Internal Cast cannot be removed

Click button to create a new Cast

New...   Link...   Remove   Help

Click button to link an External Cast

FIGURE D-22: Director window with linked External Cast

Cast member from External Cast

External Cast linked to the movie

CLUES TO USE

Creating a cast library

If you save an unlinked External Cast in the Libs folder in the Director folder, you create a cast library. A **cast library** is a special type of unlinked external cast. When you drag a cast member from an External Cast library to the Stage or Score, Director copies the cast member to one of the movie's Internal Casts. Libraries are useful for storing any type of commonly used cast members, especially behaviors. Unlike an External Cast, a library cannot be linked to a movie.

MANAGING AND MODIFYING CAST MEMBERS   DIRECTOR D-19

Clues to Use boxes provide concise information that either expands on one component of the major lesson skill or describes an independent task that is in some way related to the major lesson skill.

The page numbers are designed like a road map. D indicates the fourth unit, and 19 indicates the page within the unit.

Additional Features

The two-page lesson format featured in this book provides the new user with a powerful learning experience. Additionally, this book contains the following features:

▶ **Trial Software**
At the back of this book, you will find a CD containing a trial version of Macromedia Director 8 Shockwave Studio and Macromedia Fireworks 3 for both Macintosh and Windows operating systems. Students can use this software to gain additional practice using the software away from the classroom. *Note:* The trial software will cease operating after a limited number of days. Check the Read Me on the CD for more information.

▶ **Dual Platform**
The units in this book can be completed either on a Macintosh or on a Windows platform. The steps are written for both operating systems, with Mac and PC tips and trouble-shooting advice in the margin.

▶ **Real-World Case**
The case study used throughout the textbook, a fictitious company called SpaceWorks, is designed to be "real-world" in nature and introduces the kinds of activities that students will encounter when working with Director. With a real-world case, the process of solving problems will be more meaningful to students.

▶ **End-of-Unit Material**
Each unit concludes with a Concepts Review that tests students' understanding of what they learned in the unit. The Concepts Review is followed by a Skills Review, which provides students with additional hands-on practice of the skills. The Skills Review is followed by Independent Challenges, which pose case problems for students to solve. At least one Independent Challenge in each unit asks students to use the World Wide Web to solve the problem as indicated by a Web Work icon. The Visual Workshops that follow the Independent Challenges help students develop critical thinking skills. Students are shown completed Web pages or screens and are asked to recreate them from scratch.

Director 8

V

Instructor's Resource Kit

The Instructor's Resource Kit is Course Technology's way of putting the resources and information needed to teach and learn effectively into your hands. With an integrated array of teaching and learning tools that offers you and your students a broad range of technology-based instructional options, we believe this kit represents the highest quality and most cutting edge resources available to instructors today. Many of these resources are available at **www.course.com**. The resources available with this book are:

Course Test Manager Designed by Course Technology, this Windows-based software helps you design, administer, and print tests and pre-tests. A full-featured program, Course Test Manager also has an online testing component that allows students to take tests at the computer and have their exams automatically graded.

Instructor's Manual Available as an electronic file, the Instructor's Manual is quality-assurance tested and includes unit overviews, detailed lecture topics for each unit with teaching tips, an Upgrader's Guide, solutions to all lessons and end-of-unit material, and extra Independent Challenges. The Instructor's Manual is available on the Instructor's Resource Kit CD-ROM or you can download it from **www.course.com**.

Course Faculty Online Companion You can browse this textbook's password-protected site to obtain the Instructor's Manual, Solution Files, Project Files, and any updates to the text. Contact your Customer Service Representative for the site address and password.

Project Files Project Files contain all of the data that students will use to complete the lessons and end-of-unit material. A Readme file includes instructions for using the files. Adopters of this text are granted the right to install the Project Files on any standalone computer or network. The Project Files are available on the Instructor's Resource Kit CD-ROM, the Review Pack, and can also be downloaded from **www.course.com**.

Solution Files Solution Files contain every file students are asked to create or modify in the lessons and end-of-unit material. A Help file on the Instructor's Resource Kit includes information for using the Solution Files.

Figure Files The figures in the text are provided on the Instructor's Resourse Kit CD to help you illustrate key topics or concepts. You can create traditional overhead transparencies by printing the figure files. Or you can create electronic slide shows by using the figures in a presentation program such as PowerPoint.

Student Online Companion This book features its own Online Companion where students can go to access Web sites that will help them complete the Web Work Independent Challenges. Because the Web is constantly changing, the Student Online Companion will provide the reader with current updates regarding links referenced in the book.

Brief Contents

Contents

Contents

SpaceWorks Promotion

Schematic Flowchart

Managing and Modifying Cast Members

Contents

Adding Audio, Video, and Other Media

DIRECTOR G-1

Contents

Appendix DIRECTOR AP-1

Read This Before You Begin

Project Files

To complete the lessons and end-of-unit material in this book, students need to obtain the necessary project files. Please refer to the instructions on the front inside cover for various methods of getting these files. Once obtained, the user selects where to store the files, such as to the hard disk drive, network server, or Zip disk. Depending on where you store the files, you might need to relink any external files, such as a video clip, associated with a Director project file. When you open a project file, Director will ask you the location of the external file.

Director Settings

Each time you start Director, the program remembers previous settings, such as program preferences, open or closed windows, and Control Panel options, to name a few. When you start Director, your initial screen might look different than the ones in this book. For the purposes of this book, make sure the following settings in Director are in place before you start each unit:

- Toolbar and Tool Palette on the Windows menu are turned on.

- Stage window, Score window, Cast window, and Property Inspector on the Windows menu are turned on.

- Cast window is set to Thumbnail view; click the Cast View Style button in the Cast window, if necessary.

- Loop Playback on the Control menu is turned off.

- Tempo Mode and Actual Tempo Mode on the Control Panel are set to fps (frames per second).

- Show Info on Sprite Overlay submenu on the View menu is turned off.

- Snap to Grid and Snap to Guide on the Guides and Grid tab in the Property Inspector are turned on.

- On the Guides and Grid tab in the Property Inspector—Guide: Visible is turned on, and Grid: Visible is turned off.

Director for Windows and Macintosh

This book is written for the Windows version and the Macintosh version of Macromedia Director 8 Shockwave Studio. Both versions of the software are virtually the same, but there are a few platform differences. When there are differences between the two versions of the software, steps written specifically for the Windows version end with the notation (Win) and steps for the Macintosh version end with the notation (Mac). In instances where the lessons are split between the two operating systems, a line divides the page and is accompanied by Mac and Win icons.

Free Trial Software

Included on a CD with this book is the Macromedia® Director® 8 Shockwave Studio and Macromedia® Fireworks® 3 Trial Software. The trial software is for students' use away from the classroom, and it should not be used in a classroom lab because it will expire after a limited number of days. Please check the CD for more information.

Installation instructions for the CD-ROM are included below.

Windows: Insert the CD in the CD-ROM drive, open Windows Explorer, select the CD-ROM drive, double-click director8trial.exe or fireworks3.exe in the right pane of Windows Explorer, then follow the on-screen instructions to complete the installation.

Macintosh: Insert the CD in the CD-ROM drive, double-click the CD icon titled Director 8 Tryout, double-click the VISE Fireworks 3 Trial Installer or the StuffIt Install D8Trial.sea icon, then follow the on-screen instructions to complete the installation.

Getting

Started with Director 8

Objectives

► **Understand Director basics**
► **Start Director 8**
► **View the Director window**
► **Open and save a movie**
► **Work with Director windows**
► **View the score**
► **Play a movie**
► **Get Help**
► **Close a movie and exit Director**

Macromedia Director 8 Shockwave Studio is a multimedia program that lets you easily create animations, movies, interactive training, marketing presentations, technical simulations, and multiuser games. This unit introduces you to basic Director skills. First, you'll learn how to start Director and identify Director window elements. Then, you'll learn how to open and save a movie, how to move around the different Director windows, and how to get help. Finally, you'll learn how to play and close a movie and exit Director. ✐— Jean Young is an instructional designer at SpaceWorks Interactive, a small educational game company dedicated to teaching people about space exploration and technology. She wants to use her instructional design background and Director to create visual presentations and interactive training. As a novice multimedia developer, Jean gets started learning Director basics.

Understanding Director Basics

Director 8 is a software program that allows you to create your own software. It's often referred to as an **authoring tool** or a **development platform**. Director allows you to use a combination of graphics, images, digital video, sound, text, and animation, known as **multimedia**, and includes user feedback and navigation, known as **interactivity**, to develop virtually any type of software you want to deliver. Thus, the term **interactive multimedia** is often applied to the software produced with Director. With Director, you can create fully self-contained, self-running interactive multimedia software for distribution on CD-ROM or over the Internet on the World Wide Web, or Web. Since Director is available in both Macintosh and Windows versions, it's relatively easy to produce software that runs on both platforms. ✒ Jean is new to the product and the process of developing software, so she wants to learn the basic steps to developing interactive multimedia software with Director, as shown in Figure A-1, and listed below.

Step 1: Plan the project carefully
Creating a movie can take a long time; it's worth the effort to plan carefully. You need to figure out the goal of the project, the look and feel of your production, its length and size, how it will interact with the viewer, and how it will be distributed and for whom.

Step 2: Assemble the media elements in the Cast
Media elements include graphics, images, digital videos, animations, sounds, and text. You can create new media elements in Director or import ones that have already been developed and store them in the **Cast**. Director provides several tools for creating elements, including a paint tool and text creation tools. You can import elements from a variety of sources.

Step 3: Position the media elements on the Stage and sequence them in the Score
You use the Stage to create the look and feel for your production; you use the Stage and Score together to arrange the media elements from the Cast in space and time. The **Stage** is the viewing area for the visual elements of a Director movie, and the Score is the timeline you use to organize what happens when and where.

Step 4: Add interactive behaviors and scripting
If you want, you can add interactive behaviors and scripting to your production. Interactive behaviors can include buttons, arrows, or other navigation elements that move the viewer to different parts of the movie or the Internet. **Scripting** allows you to extend the functionality of your movie beyond what is possible using the Stage and Score. In Director, scripts are written in Lingo, a Director-specific programming language. To help you get started scripting and save you some time, Director comes with ready-made scripts called **behaviors**.

Step 5: Preview and test the movie with the Control Panel
After you create your movie, you use the Control Panel to preview and test the movie to make sure it runs the way you want it to. The Control Panel allows you to play, stop, rewind, and step through your movie. As needed, make refinements and adjustments in the Score.

Step 6: Package the movie as a stand-alone projector file, or save the movie as a Shockwave file for use over the Internet
When the movie runs the way you want it to, you can package your production as a stand-alone projector movie that viewers can run from a CD-ROM or hard drive. When you distribute your movie in projector form, viewers can run the movie without using Director. Viewers can't change the movies; they can only play them back. Or, you can save your production as a Shockwave movie that viewers can play back on a Web page, using a Web browser.

FIGURE A-1: Developing interactive software with Director

Step 1: Plan the project

Step 2: Assemble the media elements in the Cast

Step 6: Package or save the movie

Step 5: Preview and test the movie with the Control Panel

Step 3: Position the media elements on the Stage, and sequence them in the Score

Step 4: Add interactive behaviors and scripting

CLUES TO USE

Royalty-free distribution

All software created with Director can be freely sold and distributed, without having to pay Macromedia a royalty for the privilege. That may be something you take for granted, but some development platforms actually have licensing agreements stipulating that you have to pay in order to market anything created with the product. Macromedia doesn't require you to pay any fees, but they do ask that you place a special "Made with Macromedia" logo, shown in Figure A-2, on your software packaging. The logo is included with the project files that accompany this book.

FIGURE A-2: Made with Macromedia logo

Director 8

Starting Director

If Director is not yet installed on your computer, you must first install it according to the instructions that come with the program. After Director is installed, you can start the program in several ways, depending on the platform you are using. When you start Director, the computer displays a splash screen and then the Director window. Director displays a set of blank windows ready for you to create a new **file**, which is a collection of information stored together as an individual unit. A file in Director is called a **movie**. Jean can develop interactive multimedia software using Director on the Windows or Macintosh platform, but she will need to learn some aspects of each version in order to create final software for distribution on both Windows and Macintosh computers.

WIN

1. Click the Start button 🎬Start **on the taskbar**
The Start button is on the left side of the taskbar and is used to start programs on your computer.

2. Point to Programs, then point to Macromedia Director 8
The Programs menu lists all the programs, including Macromedia Director, that are installed on your computer, as shown in Figure A-3. Your Programs menu might look different, depending on the programs you have installed.

Trouble?

If Director doesn't open, check the software documentation for the required minimum configuration of hardware and operating system software.

3. Click Director 8
The Director program opens, displaying the work area for a new file.

MAC

1. Double-click the hard drive icon
The Start button is on the left side of the taskbar and is used to start programs on your computer.

2. Double-click the Macromedia Director folder
The Macromedia Director folder opens, displaying the program icon and associated files that come with the product, as shown in Figure A-4.

3. Double-click the Director 8 program icon
The Director program opens, displaying the work area for a new file.

FIGURE A-3: Starting Director (Windows)

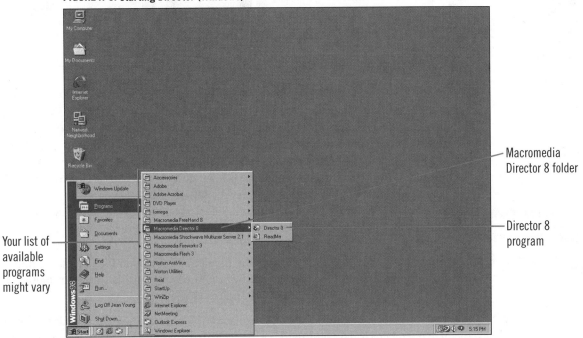

Your list of available programs might vary

Macromedia Director 8 folder

Director 8 program

FIGURE A-4: Starting Director (Macintosh)

Director 8 program icon

Starting Director and opening a movie

You can start Director and open a movie at the same time. Simply double-click the Director file icon in Windows Explorer (Win) or in a Macintosh folder (Mac). You can identify a Director movie in Windows Explorer by the .dir file extension (Win), or in a Macintosh folder by the type of file icon 📄 (Mac). A **file extension** is a three-letter extension at the end of a filename that identifies the file type for the operating system. You will not see a document's file extension in Windows Explorer if your system is set up to hide it. If you want to show file extensions in Windows, open My Computer, click View on the menu bar, click Folder Options, click the View tab, click the Hide file extensions for known file types check box to deselect it, then click OK. The Macintosh doesn't use file extensions.

Director 8

Viewing the Director Window

When you start Director, five main windows of varying sizes appear in the Director window: the Stage, the Score, the Cast, the Property Inspector, and the Control Panel. Depending on your installation, not all of these windows may appear, or additional ones may be visible. The windows are placed in different locations, depending on the size of your monitor. If you do not see the Control Panel, it may be behind the larger Score and Stage windows, or it may be closed. You'll do the bulk of your work in Director with these five windows. If you can't see the window you want to use, you can use the Window menu to display it. Jean takes some time to familiarize herself with the elements of the Director window. Refer to your screen and Figure A-5 as you locate the elements of the Director window described below.

Details

Trouble?

The size and location of your windows might differ.

The program window **title bar** displays the filename of the open file (the name doesn't appear on your title bar, because the file has not been named yet) and the program name, Director 8. The title bar also contains a Close button and resizing buttons.

A **menu** is a list of commands that you use to accomplish certain tasks. You've already used the Start menu to open Director. A **command** is a directive that accesses a feature of a program. Director has its own set of menus, which are located on the menu bar along the top of the program window.

The **menu bar** organizes commands into groups of related operations. Each group is listed under the name of the menu, such as "File" or "Help." You can choose a menu command by clicking it. See Table A-1 for examples of items on a typical menu.

The **toolbar** contains buttons for the most frequently used commands. Clicking a button on a toolbar is often faster than clicking a menu and then clicking a command. When you position the mouse pointer over a button, a **ScreenTip** appears.

The **Tool palette** contains a set of tools you can use to create shapes, such as lines, rectangles, rounded rectangles, and ellipses, and to create simple buttons, such as radio, check box, and command buttons. You can fill shapes with a color, pattern, or custom tile. The shapes and buttons you create in Director are saved as media elements in the Cast.

The **Stage window** title bar displays the movie name and the zoom factor. Notice that the default values are Untitled Stage (100%). The Stage is the visible portion of a movie, on which you determine where your media elements appear. You can define the properties of your Stage, such as its size and color.

The **Cast window** is the storage area that contains your media elements, such as graphics, images, digital videos, sounds, animations, text, color palettes, film loops, and scripts. The media elements in the Cast window are called **cast members**. In the Cast window you can view your cast members as a list or as thumbnails. You can create your own cast members, and you can import existing media to include in your cast. You can also open or create Cast windows to organize sets of cast members. When you open Director with a new movie, the Cast window is called **Internal Cast**.

The **Score window** organizes and controls media elements over a linear timeline, in rows called **channels** and in columns called **frames**. The Score displays a movie's timeline and monitors the playback frame by frame. A frame represents a single point in a movie. The Score includes special channels that control the movie's tempo, sound, transitions, and color palettes.

The **Property Inspector** provides a convenient way to view and change attributes of any selected object or multiple objects in your movie. Once you select an object, relevant category tabs and associated fields for it appear on the Property Inspector.

The **Control Panel** provides VCR-type control over the playback of your movie, including Rewind, Stop, and Play buttons. You can also modify volume, tempo, and playback settings.

FIGURE A-5: Director window

- Title bar
- Toolbar
- Tool palette
- Stage window
- Score window
- Control Panel
- Menu bar
- Cast window
- Property Inspector

TABLE A-1: Typical items on a menu

item	description	example
Dimmed command	A menu command that is not currently available	Undo Ctrl+Z
Ellipsis	Indicates that this menu command opens a dialog box that allows you to select from several options	Save As...
Triangle	Indicates that this menu command opens a cascading menu containing an additional list of menu commands	Zoom ▶
Keyboard shortcut	An alternative to using the mouse for executing a menu command	Paste Ctrl+V
Underlined letter	Pressing the underlined letter while also pressing [Alt] (Win) or [Command] (Mac) executes the menu command	Print Ctrl+P

Unit A
Director 8

Opening and Saving a Movie

A movie is the product you create using Director. When you start Director, the program displays a set of blank windows. You can insert new information to create a new movie and save the result as a file, or you can open an existing movie and save the file with any changes. To prevent any accidental changes to the original movie, you can save the movie with a new name. This makes a copy of the movie, so you can make changes to the new movie and leave the original file unaltered. Throughout this book, you will be instructed to open a file from a drive and folder where your Project Files are located, to use the Save As command to create a copy of the file with a new name, and then to modify the new file by following the lesson steps. Saving the files with new names keeps your original Project Files intact, in case you need to start the lesson over or wish to repeat an exercise. ✒ Jean wants to open an existing Director movie to learn more about using Director windows. She opens an existing movie and saves it with a new name before making any changes to it.

Steps 1 2 3 4

QuickTip

To open Director 5, 6, and 7 movies, click Xtras on the menu bar, click Update Movies, select one of the Action options, select one of the Backup Folder options, click OK, select the movies and casts you want to update, then click Update.

QuickTip

Use the List View 🖿 or Details View 🖿 button (Win) in the Open and Save As dialog boxes to display the list of files and folders with more or less information. Details View on the Macintosh is in the operating system.

QuickTip

To open the last saved version of your current movie, click File on the menu bar, then click Revert.

1. **Click the Open button 🖼 on the toolbar**
   The Open dialog box opens. In this dialog box, you locate and choose the file you wish to open. The file Jean wants to open is stored in your Project Files.

2. **Click the Look in list arrow, then click the drive and folder where your Project Files are located**
   A file appears in the file list, as shown in Figure A-6. You can select a file in the file list or type the name of the file you want in the File name text box.

3. **In the file list, click MD A-1, then click Open**
   The MD A-1 file opens.

4. **Click File on the menu bar, then click Save As**
   The Save Movie dialog box opens, as shown in Figure A-7. The Save As command allows you to save an existing document under a new name and also in a different folder or drive location.

5. **Make sure that the Save in list box displays the folder where your Project Files are located**

6. **In Windows, if MD A-1 is not already selected, click in the File name text box, then select the entire filename by dragging the mouse pointer over it**
   In Director, as in most other Windows programs, you must select text in order to modify it. When you **select** text, the selection appears **highlighted** (white text on a dark background) to indicate that it has been selected. Any action you now take will be performed on the selected text.

7. **Type SpaceWorks Promo as the new filename**
   The text you type replaces the selected text. It's a good idea to use descriptive names for your files so you can identify their contents more easily.

8. **Click Save**
   The file is saved under the new name, SpaceWorks Promo, in the same folder and drive location as the MD A-1 file. The original MD A-1 file automatically closes, and the new filename appears in the title bar of the Director, Score, and Stage windows.

FIGURE A-6: Open dialog box

Available files and folders appear here

The selected filename will appear here

Click list arrow to display a list of available drives

Click button to determine the view

Click button to select a file from the Internet

FIGURE A-7: Save Movie dialog box

Your list of files might be different

Type the new filename here

Current drive or folder (yours might differ)

About saving files

Until you save them, the movies you create are stored in the computer's random access memory (RAM). **RAM** is a temporary storage space that is erased when the computer is turned off. To store a document permanently, you must save it as a file to a disk. You can save files to a **floppy disk** or other **removable media** that you insert into the disk drive of your computer (usually drive A, B, D, or E [Win] or an icon [Mac]), to a **hard disk**, which is built into the computer (usually drive C [Win] or an icon [Mac]), **or to a server**, which is a computer on a network. This book assumes that you will save all of your files to your Project Files, which your instructor has provided to you. Windows and Macintosh let you save files using names that have up to 255 characters, including spaces.

Director 8

Working with Director Windows

With Director you work with several windows at one time. This means that the Director window can easily become cluttered with open windows. To organize the Director window, sometimes it is necessary to change the size of a window, move it to a different location, or close it altogether. Each window, except the Control Panel, is surrounded by a standard border that you can drag to change the size of the window. The Control Panel is a **windoid**, a window that can be moved but not resized. Each window has one or more buttons in the upper-right corner that allow you to close it or change its size. In addition to using the resizing buttons, you can also drag the mouse pointer to resize a window. Table A-2 shows the different mouse pointer shapes that appear when resizing windows. To open a window, you can use the Windows menu or a shortcut key. Jean doesn't see the Control Panel in her Director window, so she opens it and moves it out of the way. She also resizes the Stage and Score windows to make more room to see other windows.

Steps

QuickTip

You can use keyboard shortcuts located on the right side of the Windows menu to quickly open and close Director windows; for the Control Panel window, press [Ctrl][2] (Win) or [Command][2] (Mac).

1. Click **Window** on the menu bar

The Window menu appears, displaying the available View commands, as shown in Figure A-8. On a menu, a **check mark** identifies a feature that is currently selected (that is, the feature is enabled or on). To disable (turn off) the feature, you click the command again to remove the check mark. A menu can contain several checkmarked features. A **bullet mark** also indicates that an option is enabled, but a menu can contain only one bullet-marked feature per menu section. To disable a command with a bullet mark next to it, you must select a different bullet option on the menu in the section.

2. On the Window menu, click **Control Panel**, if turned off (no check mark)

The Control Panel opens and appears in front of the other Director windows. The Control Panel window is active, unlike other Director windows.

3. Click the **title bar** on the Cast window

The Cast window is now **active** (the color of the title bar changes from gray to blue); this means that any actions you perform will take place in this window. At times, you may want to close a window.

QuickTip

You can use buttons on the toolbar to quickly open and close many Director windows; for the Property Inspector window, click the Property Inspector button ⓘ to toggle the window open and closed.

4. Click **File** on the menu bar, click **Close**, then click the **Close button** in the Property Inspector window

The Cast and Property Inspector windows no longer appear in the Director window. When you close a window, you can open the window again at any time. When you reopen a window, it appears in the same position in which it was last closed. You'll open these windows again later.

5. Position the **mouse pointer** on the Control Panel window title bar, then click and drag the **title bar** to an empty area of the Director window

The window moves to a new location.

6. Position the mouse pointer on the lower-right corner of the **Stage window** until the pointer changes to ↖, then drag the **border** to the right to expand the window, as shown in Figure A-9

The window is now resized equally on each side. You can also resize a window's height or width by dragging any border.

QuickTip

You can also double-click the title bar of a window to switch between maximizing and restoring the size of a window.

7. Click the **Maximize button** ▫ in the Stage window

The Stage window takes up the entire screen. Notice that the Control Panel window is still visible.

8. Click the **Restore button** ▣ in the Stage window

The **Restore button** returns a window to its previous size. The Restore button only appears when a window is maximized.

FIGURE A-8: Window menu

Check mark means the Stage window is turned on

Bullet means the Cast window is turned on

Keyboard shortcut to open and close a window

Window menu in Director

FIGURE A-9: Director window

Control Panel is a windoid

Resizing mouse pointer

TABLE A-2: Mouse pointer shapes that appear when resizing windows

mouse pointer shape	use to
↔	Drag the right or left edge of a window to change its width
↕	Drag the top or bottom edge of a window to change its height
↙ or ↘	Drag any corner of a window to proportionally change its size

Director 8

Viewing the Score

While the movie is displayed in the Stage window, the Cast window stores the media elements, or cast members that play in the movie. The Score window is where you instruct the cast members where to appear on the stage, what to do, and where to exit, as shown in Figure A-10. The Score window resembles a spreadsheet with lots of individual cells divided into rows and columns. The rows are used as channels; the columns are used as frames. Each column has a number associated with it; they are marked off in shaded, five-column intervals, and each channel begins with either a number or a distinctive icon, called a **marker**. When you first view the Score window, all the channels might not be visible. The upper channels are called the **effects channels**. You can display and hide the effects channels using the Hide/Show Effects Channels arrows on the right side of the window. Jean takes some time to familiarize herself with the elements of the Score window. Refer to your screen and Figure A-11 as you locate the elements of the Score window described below.

Details

The Score window contains seven channel types, each designed to hold different types of data. These channels and other features are described below.

Trouble?

If the effects channels are not visible, you can display them by clicking the Hide/Show Effects Channels arrows on the right side of the Score window.

 The **tempo channel** is used to adjust the speed, or time, of the movie as it plays. The tempo determines how many frames per second are displayed in the movie.

 The **palette channel** sets the available colors for the movie.

 The **transition channel** allows you to set screen transitions, such as fades, wipes, dissolves, and zooms.

 The two **sound channels** are used to add music, sound effects, and voice-overs.

 The **behavior channel**, or **script channel**, provides a place to write frame scripts. **Frame scripts** provide one way to add interactivity and extended functionality to a movie.

 The **frame channel**, or **timeline**, is the shaded channel that contains the numbers 5, 10, 15, 20, and so on. These numbers identify the frame number. An individual frame represents a single point in a movie.

 The **playback head** is the object in the frame channel that moves through the Score, indicating the frame that is currently displayed on the Stage.

 The **sprite channels** are the numbered channels at the bottom of the Score window. You use these channels to assemble and synchronize all the cast members in the Cast window. A **sprite** is a representation of a cast member that has been placed on the Stage or in the Score. Director provides 1000 available sprite channels.

FIGURE A-10: Cast, Score, and Stage interaction

Cast

Score

Stage

FIGURE A-11: Score window

Tempo channel
Palette channel
Transition channel
Sound channels
Behavior channel

Sprite channels

Click arrows to hide or show Effects channels

Playback head

Click button to display Zoom menu

Sprite   Cell   Frame   Frame channel (Timeline)

Understanding the playback head and channels

As Director plays a movie, the playback head moves from left to right across the frame channel in the Score window. As the playback head enters a frame, Director draws the sprites (representations of cast members) that it finds in the sprite channels for that frame. When the playback head moves to another frame, Director redraws the stage with the sprites in the frames it enters. When sprites change or move from frame to frame, animation effects are created. When drawing each frame on the stage, Director draws the contents of each sprite channel starting with channel 1, and the remaining channels overdraw the lower-numbered channels wherever they might overlap. As a result, the highest-numbered sprite will always be visible, and the lower-numbered sprites will be visible only if no higher-numbered sprite appears at the same location. For this reason, the background image is usually kept in sprite channel 1, the lowest-numbered sprite.

Director 8

Playing a Movie

The Control Panel gives you control over the playback of your Director movie and displays important information about your movie's performance. You can use the buttons on the Control Panel, as described in Table A-3, to play a movie or to monitor the speed, or **tempo**, at which it plays. As you play your movie, the playback head automatically moves through your Score. The playback head moves through the Score to show the frame currently displayed on the Stage. A frame in the Score represents a single point in a movie; it is similar in theory to a frame in a traditional celluloid film. To go to a specific frame number, you can enter a number in the frame counter. You can also click any frame in the Score to move the playback head to that frame, and you can drag the playback head backward or forward through frames. You can also set the number of frames displayed per second (fps) to control the movie's playback speed. ✎ Jean uses the Control Panel to play a movie.

QuickTip

You can also access many of the same commands on the Control Panel using the Control menu.

1. Click the **Play button** ▶ on the Control Panel

The movie plays on the Stage, and the playback head moves from frame to frame through the Score.

2. Before the end of the movie, click the **Stop button** ■ on the Control Panel

The movie stops in the Stage window, and the playback head stops in the Score window, as shown in Figure A-12.

QuickTip

The Play, Stop, and Rewind buttons are also available on the main toolbar in Director.

3. Click the **Rewind button** ◀ on the Control Panel

The playback head moves all the way to the first frame of the movie, and the frame number on the Control Panel displays 1.

4. Click the **Step Forward button** ▶ on the Control Panel 10 times

The playback head in the Score window moves forward one frame at a time, the movie in the Stage window plays forward, and the frame number in the Control Panel increases by one each time you click the button.

5. Click the **Step Backward button** ◀ on the Control Panel 6 times

The playback head moves back one frame at a time, the movie in the Stage window plays backward, and the frame number in the Control Panel decreases by one each time you click the button.

6. Click **number 1** on the frame channel in the Score window

The playback head moves to frame 1. Notice that the Score and Control Panel windows also display frame 1 settings.

Controlling and monitoring tempo in the Control Panel

Tempo mode displays the playback rate that Director is currently attempting to achieve. If you have specified a tempo in the Score's tempo channel, it will be displayed here; otherwise, Director's default of 15 **frames per second (fps)** will be displayed. Click the Tempo Mode button fps. on the Control Panel to reveal the **seconds per frame (spf)**. The spf rate is a little more accurate, since it times a frame's duration right down to the millisecond—but unless you need the accuracy, the distinction is really a matter of taste. **Actual Tempo** documents the real speed of playback.

It's often enlightening to compare and contrast the number displayed here with the set tempo above it. You can click the Actual Tempo Mode button fps. on the Control Panel to display three additional modes: Seconds Per Frame, Running Total, and Estimated Total. Running Total calculates the total time elapsed since the beginning of your movie, and Estimated Total does the same thing, but with a little more accuracy. Director will use the last setting change you made the next time you create a new movie or open an existing movie.

FIGURE A-12: **Control Panel**

The Rewind, Stop, and Play buttons also appear on the toolbar

Click timeline to move the playback head to frame 1

Current frame number with the playback head

Click button to play the movie

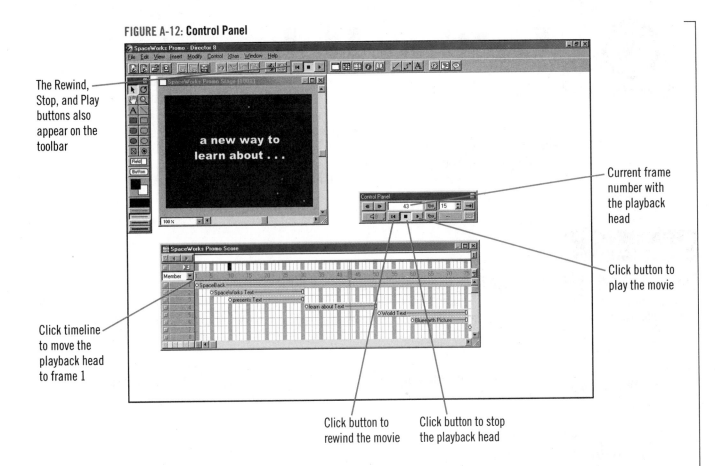

Click button to rewind the movie

Click button to stop the playback head

TABLE A-3: **Control Panel buttons**

button	name	function
◀|	**Step Backward**	Moves the playback head backward one frame
|▶	**Step Forward**	Moves the playback head forward one frame
43	**Frame**	Displays the current location of the playback head in the Score; you can jump to a specific frame number by typing that number in this box and then pressing Enter (Win) or Return (Mac)
fps	**Tempo Mode**	Displays the playback type (frames per second or seconds per frame) of the movie
15	**Tempo**	Displays the playback rate that Director is currently attempting to achieve
⟳	**Loop Playback**	Indicates whether playback stops at the end of the Score or continuously repeats until further notice (On/Off)
🔊	**Volume**	Lets you temporarily lower the volume or mute your movie while keeping your soundtracks intact; this control is useful when you continually play a movie and do not want to hear the audio
◀	**Rewind**	Moves the playback head all the way to the first frame of the movie
■	**Stop**	Stops the playback entirely
▶	**Play**	Starts the playback
fps	**Actual Tempo Mode**	Displays the actual playback type, running time total, or estimated total
15	**Actual Tempo**	Documents the real speed of playback
▭	**Selected Frames Only**	Limits playback to the frames highlighted in the Score; this control is useful when you're working on a single section of a larger movie

Director 8

Getting Help

When you have a question about how to do something in Director, you can usually find the answer with a few clicks of your mouse. Director provides an extensive Help system that you can access for definitions, explanations, and useful tips. Help system information is displayed in a separate window. You can resize the Help window and set it to display on-screen so you can refer to it as you work. You can also access **context-sensitive help** that specifically relates to what you are doing; when you are working in a dialog box, you can click the Help button [?], and then click any item to get more information about the item (Win). Jean decides to use Help to find out about Director basics.

QuickTip

You can also press [F1] to open the Director 8 Help dialog box.

1. Click **Help** on the menu bar, then click **Director Help**

The Help Topics: Director 8 Help dialog box opens, with the Contents tab in front. The Contents tab provides you with a list of Help categories. Each book icon has several "chapters" (topics) that you can see by clicking the book icon or the name of the Help category next to the book.

2. Click the **Contents tab** (if necessary), then double-click the **Director Basics** category

A list of Help topics underneath the Director Basics category appears, as shown in Figure A-13. To collapse a category, you double-click the open category.

QuickTip

To print a Help topic, click the Print button on the window bar.

3. Double-click the **Director basics: Overview** topic

The Director basics: Overview topic window opens, as shown in Figure A-14. Read the information on the Director basics. You can move back and forth between Help topics you have already visited by clicking the Back button and the Forward button on the Help toolbar.

4. Click the **Index button** on the Help toolbar

QuickTip

The Find tab helps you locate the topic you need, using keywords. You can find a topic by entering a keyword in the text box, clicking List Topics, selecting a topic, and then clicking Display.

The Help Topics: Director 8 Help dialog box opens, with the Index tab in front. The Index tab provides you with an alphabetical list of all the Help topics that are available, much like an index at the end of a book. You can find out about any Director feature by either entering the topic in the text box, or by scrolling down to the topic for which you want help, selecting a topic, and then clicking Display.

5. Type **stage**

As you type each letter, relevant topics scroll in the list box below the text box. Information about the Stage now appears, as shown in Figure A-15.

6. Click **Display**

The Introducing the Director workspace topic window opens.

7. Read about the Help topic, click the **Close button** in the Help window, then click the **Close button** in the Help Topics: Director 8 Help dialog box, if necessary

Keeping a Help window open while working

In Windows, you can keep any Help window open while working in Director. To keep the Help window open, click Help on the menu bar, locate and open a Help topic, click Options on the Director 8 Help window menu bar, point to Keep on Top, then click On Top. Once you change the option, you can click the Director 8 taskbar button. You will be able to work on any open window, and the Help window will remain visible. You might want to resize the Help window so that it does not obscure your view of a Director window.

FIGURE A-13: Help Topics: Director 8 Help window

Double-click topic to display Topic window

Director 8 Help Topics

Double-click category to expand or hide a Help category

Close button

FIGURE A-14: Director basics: Overview Help topic

Help window navigation buttons

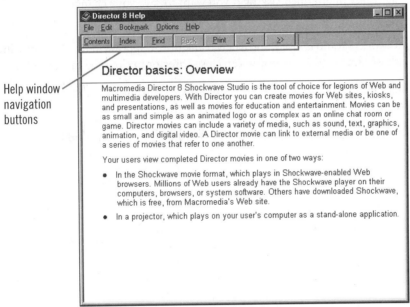

FIGURE A-15: Director 8 Help window with Index tab

Type initial characters for topic here

List of available topics

Director 8

Director 8

Closing a Movie and Exiting Director

After you work on a movie, you can close the movie by saving it, by creating a new movie, by opening an existing movie, or by exiting Director. You should save the movie before closing it. Creating a new movie or opening an existing movie closes the current movie but leaves the Director window open. Exiting Director closes the current movie and the Director window. You can use the Exit command on the File menu to close a movie and exit Director, or you can use the Close button on the Director window title bar, as shown in Figure A-16. Unlike the Close command in other Windows programs, the Close command on the File menu doesn't close the movie file; it only closes the active Director window. Table A-4 describes the different methods to close a movie. ✐ Jean is finished reviewing Director, so she closes the Spaceworks Promo movie and exits Director.

Steps 1 2 3 4

QuickTip

If you saved your movie before opening a new one, the previous movie closes immediately and a new blank movie appears.

QuickTip

You can also close a movie and exit Director by clicking the Close button on the Director window title bar.

1. **Click the New Movie button** ▣ **on the toolbar**
   An alert box might open, asking if you want to save your changes.

2. **If asked to save your work, click Yes (Win) or Save (Mac)**
   Spaceworks Promo is saved, and a new blank movie appears in the Director window. When you finish working with a movie, you can close Director to close the movie and exit the program.

3. **Click File on the menu bar, then click Exit (Win) or Quit (Mac)**
   If you didn't perform any actions, Director closes.

4. **If asked to save your work, click No (Win) or Don't Save (Mac)**
   Director closes.

TABLE A-4: How to close a movie

command	function
Create a new movie	Closes the current movie and creates a blank Stage, Score, and Cast in the Director window
Open an existing movie	Closes the current movie and opens a movie in the Director window
Exit Director	Closes the current movie, closes the Director window, and returns you to the desktop

FIGURE A-16: Exiting Director using the File menu

Close button

Close active window in Director window

Exit command

CLUES TO USE

Using the Director Support Center on the Web

The Director Support Center Web site contains the latest information on Director, plus additional topics, examples, tips, and updates, explaining how to get the most out of the program. Click Help on the menu bar, click Web Links, then click the Director Support Center Web site link. Figure A-17 shows the Director Support Center Web site. Because this site is continually updated, your screen might look different. To find additional sites on the Web with Director information, you can use a search engine.

FIGURE A-17: Director Support Center Web site

Director 8

Practice

► Concepts Review

Label each of the elements of the screen shown in Figure A-18.

FIGURE A-18

Match each of the terms with the statement that describes its function.

6. Tempo channel   a. ⏱
7. Sprite channel   b. ▦
8. Palette channel   c. ▶◀
9. Sound channel   d. 1
10. Script channel   e. ▤
11. Transition channel   f. ◄1

Select the best answer from the following list of choices.

12. What type of program is Director?
    a. Authoring tool
    b. Word-processing program
    c. Spreadsheet program
    d. Graphics program

13. A file is a:
   a. Collection of information stored separately.
   b. Collection of programs stored separately.
   c. Collection of information stored together.
   d. Collection of programs stored together.

14. The file extension for a Director movie in Windows is:
   a. .mov
   b. .dir
   c. .mve
   d. .dtr

15. The Tool palette in Director contains:
   a. Shapes.
   b. Buttons.
   c. All of the above.
   d. None of the above.

16. Which window is considered NOT to be a main window in Director?
   a. Property Inspector
   b. Movie Inspector
   c. Score
   d. Control Panel

17. Which window in Director can't be resized?
   a. Score
   b. Stage
   c. Control Panel
   d. Cast

18. Channels appear in which window in Director?
   a. Score
   b. Stage
   c. Control Panel
   d. Cast

19. In which window in Director can you change the tempo of a movie?
   a. Score
   b. Stage
   c. Control Panel
   d. Cast

20. Which command closes a movie?
   a. Open
   b. New
   c. Exit or Quit
   d. All of the above

▶ Skills Review

1. **Understand Director basics.**
   a. Write down the basic steps to developing interactive multimedia software with Director, without referring to the unit material.
   b. Compare your results with Figure A-1.

2. **Start Director.**
   a. Click the Start button, point to Programs, point to Macromedia Director 8, then click Director 8 (Win).
   b. Double-click the hard drive icon, double-click the Macromedia Director folder, then double-click the Director 8 program icon (Mac).

3. **View the Director window.**
   a. Identify and write down elements in the Director window, without referring to the unit material.
   b. Compare your results with Figure A-5.

4. **Open and save a movie.**
   a. Click the Open button on the toolbar.
   b. Open the Project File MD A-1 from the drive and folder where your Project Files are located.
   c. Click File on the menu bar, then click Save As.
   d. Save it as *SpaceWorks Promo2* where your Project Files are stored.

Director 8

5. Work with Director windows.

   a. Click Window on the menu bar, then click Control Panel, if turned off (no check mark).

   b. Click Window on the menu bar, then click Cast.

   c. Click Window on the menu bar, point to Inspectors, then click Property.

   d. Drag the Control Panel to an empty area of the Director window.

   e. Click the Maximize button in the Stage window.

   f. Click the Restore button in the Stage window.

6. View the Score.

   a. Identify and write down elements in the Score window, without referring to the unit material.

   b. Compare your results with Figure A-11.

7. Play a movie.

   a. Click the Play button on the Control Panel.

   b. Before the end of the movie, click the Stop button on the Control Panel.

   c. Click the Rewind button on the Control Panel.

   d. Click the number 50 on the frame channel in the Score window.

   e. Click the Step Forward button on the Control Panel 10 times.

8. Get Help.

   a. Click Help on the menu bar, then click Director Help.

   b. Click the Contents tab (if necessary), then double-click the Director Basics category.

   c. Double-click the Cast window topic.

   d. Click the Find button on the Help toolbar. (*Hint:* If the Find Setup Wizard opens, click the Maximize search capabilities option button, click Next, then click Finish.)

   e. Type **movie**, then click Movie in the text box below.

   f. Click the topic About Channels in the Score, then click Display.

   g. Click the Close button in the Director 8 Help window.

9. Close a movie and exit Director.

   a. Click the Close button on the Director window title bar.

   b. If asked to save your work, click Yes (Win) or Save (Mac).

► Independent Challenges

1. You are new to Director and want to learn how to use the product. Director 8 provides extensive online Help. At any time, you can select Director Help from the Help menu and get the assistance you need. Use the Help options to learn about the topics listed below.

   To complete this independent challenge:

   a. Locate and read the Help information on increasing or decreasing your view of the Stage.

   b. Locate and read the Help information on sprites.

   c. Locate and read the Help information on the playback head.

   d. Locate and read the Help information on the Control Panel.

   e. Locate and read the Help information on the Director Support Center.

   f. Print one or more of the Help topics you located.

   g. Close the Director Help window.

2. You have an opportunity to become the multimedia expert at your new job. First, you decide to take a Director class. The instructor asks you to open a sample file that comes with Director. The sample and instructional movies that are installed with the Director program are typically located in a subfolder inside the Director 8 folder.

To complete this independent challenge:

a. Display the Open dialog box.

b. Locate the My_Tutorial folder. For the typical Director 8 installation, the folder is located in the Programs Files folder, Macromedia folder, Director 8 folder, and Learning folder (Win) or Director 8 and Learning folder (Mac).

c. Open the chat.dir file (Win) or chat file (Mac).

d. Open the Control Panel, if turned off, and display the Stage window to play the movie.

e. Play the movie until it reaches frame 25.

f. Print the Screen. (For Windows, use the Windows Paint program. Press the Print Screen key to make a copy of the screen, start the Paint program by clicking Start, pointing to Programs, pointing to Accessories, then clicking Paint, click Edit on the menu bar, click Paste to paste the screen into Paint, then click Yes to paste the large image if necessary. Click File on the menu bar, click Print, click Print or OK in the dialog box, then exit Paint. For the Macintosh, use the SimpleText program. Hold and press the Command, Shift, and 3 keys to make a copy of the screen, double-click the document Picture 1 located on your hard drive, click File on the menu bar, click Print, then click Print in the dialog box.)(*Note*: When you create a new document with a copy of the screen and a document Picture 1 already exists, the Macintosh names the new document Picture 2.)

g. Exit Director and don't save the movie.

3. Your boss has sent your entire department to a class on Director 8. After completing the first tutorial, the instructor asks you to open the completed tutorial file that comes with Director, play the movie, and save the file so you can take it back to the office. The sample and instructional movies that are installed with the Director program are typically located in a subfolder inside the Director 8 folder.

To complete this independent challenge:

a. Display the Open dialog box.

b. Locate the Completed_Tutorials folder. For the typical Director 8 installation, the folder is located in the Programs Files folder, Macromedia folder, Director 8 folder, and Learning folder (Win) or Director 8 folder and Learning folder (Mac).

c. Open the fun.dir file (Win) or fun file (Mac).

d. Open the Control Panel, if turned off.

e. Play the movie.

f. Print the screen. (See Independent Challenge 2, Step f for screen-printing instructions.)

g. Save the movie as *Fun Tutorial* in the drive and folder where your Project Files are located.

h. Exit Director.

4. You prefer using keyboard shortcuts instead of menu commands. Director 8 provides additional Help on the Web. You want to locate a document on the Director Support Center Web site that contains Director 8 keyboard shortcuts. You need an Internet connection to complete this task.

To complete this independent challenge:

a. Open Web Links.

b. Display the Director 8 Keyboard Shortcut Web page.

c. Print the Web page.

d. If possible, download the appropriate file for keyboard shortcuts for Win or Mac, then print it out.

e. Close the Web browser.

f. Close the Director Help window.

g. Exit Director.

Director 8

▶ Visual Workshop

Recreate the screen shown in Figure A-19. Print the screen. (See Independent Challenge 2, Step f for screen-printing instructions.) Your Control Panel settings might vary.

FIGURE A-19

Creating
a Movie

Objectives

- ► **Plan a movie**
- ► **Set up a movie**
- ► **Import cast members**
- ► **Create and name cast members**
- ► **Create sprites**
- ► **Sequence and modify sprites**
- ► **Create animation using keyframes**
- ► **Print a movie**

Director's built-in media tools and visual production methods make it easy to create your own movie. In this unit, you'll learn how to plan a movie, and then create it step by step. To begin, you'll start Director to create a blank new movie and set movie properties, import media elements that have already been developed, and then use Director to create new ones. To create a movie, you'll position the media elements on the Stage, sequence them in the Score, and add some animation. Finally, you'll preview the results and print frames from your movie. After learning Director basics, Jean wants to create a movie that promotes the company.

Planning a Movie

Director 8

Creating a movie can take a long time; it's worth the effort to plan carefully. The tendency for most first-time Director developers is to start creating a movie without carefully planning the project. Before you begin, you need to develop and follow a plan. Otherwise, you'll spend a lot of time during the project fixing or completely changing parts of the movie, which could have been avoided from the beginning. Planning a movie involves determining its purpose, identifying the audience, logically developing the content and organizing the structure of the content, developing the layout and design, and identifying the delivery computer system. ✎ Jean definitely doesn't want to spend time redoing her project, so she carefully plans the SpaceWorks Interactive promotional movie.

Details

When you want to create a movie, it's important to accomplish the following:

Determine the purpose

Is it for training? Promotion? Sales? Marketing? The consumer market? The answer will determine the types of features you may want to include or exclude in the movie. You need to make sure that what you produce is in line with the purpose of the project.

QuickTip

To change a computer monitor's resolution, right-click the desktop, click Properties, click the Settings tab, drag the Screen area slider, then click OK (Win), or click the Apple menu, point to Control Panel, click Monitors & Sound, click the Monitor icon, click a resolution, then click the Close button (Mac).

Identify the audience

How you create your movie will depend on how you classify the intended audience. If the intended audience consists of novice computer users, you will have to concentrate on making the navigational controls and layout as simple to use as possible. If the users are experienced computer users, you can include more advanced features and interactions.

Develop the content and organize the structure

The most beneficial planning tools for the multimedia developer are the script and schematic flowchart. The script tells the story of your movie production in text form, as shown in Figure B-1. Just as in the movies, a script is used to describe each section, to list audio or video, and to provide a basis for the text that will appear on-screen or will be read by a voice-over talent. Schematic flowcharts are the best way to sketch out the navigational structure of a movie and make sure that each of the sections is properly connected, as shown in Figure B-2. Once you have the script and schematic flowchart mapped out on paper, you will quickly see the correlation between what you have developed and what you will begin to set up in Director.

Develop the layout and design of the movie

The storyboard tells the story of your movie in visual form. It helps you design the layout of each screen in your movie. The storyboard follows the script and develops visual frames of the movie's main transitional points, which help you develop the Director media elements that you will use to create your movie. A storyboard can take a long time to develop, but the media elements you assemble and create in the process will shorten the overall development time.

Identify the delivery computer system to be used for playback

Some computers are more up to date than others. You need to determine the minimum computer hardware and software requirements in which your movie will be delivered. The hardware and software requirements will determine what types of media you can use and how the movie will play back. Some hardware requirements you need to consider are the CPU (central processing unit), which determines the speed with which your computer can compute data and other types of information; RAM (system memory), which determines how fast files load and how smoothly they run; sound cards, which determine whether you can use sound files; video cards, which determine the quality and speed of the graphic and video display; and monitor resolution, which determines the color display, size, and overall look of your movie. Some software requirements you need to consider are the delivery platform—Macintosh, PC, or both (cross-platform)—and operating system (Windows 95/98/2000 or Macintosh OS 7/8/9). Each platform and operating system will determine which types of image files will work on which types of systems.

FIGURE B-1: Project-planning script

Script

Project: SpaceWorks Promotion

Scene	Text	Graphics	Audio	Video	Animation	Navigation	Transition
1	SpaceWorks	SpaceWorks Background	None	None	None	None	None
1	presents	None	None	None	Text fly from bottom	None	Scene 2
2	a new way to learn about …	None	None	None	None	None	Scene 3
3	your World	Blue Earth	None	None	None	Buttons	Scene 1 or 4
4	None	Mwm Logo	None	None	None	None	None

FIGURE B-2: Project-planning schematic flowchart

Computer requirements for developing and playing a movie

Developing a movie requires a computer with an increased level of hardware and software capabilities. The minimum requirements to develop Director movies are an Intel Pentium II 200 processor running Windows 95/98 or NT version 4.0 or later, or a Power PC 180 Macintosh running System 8.1 or later, 32 MB of installed RAM plus 100 MB of available disk space, a sound card, a color monitor, and a CD-ROM drive. The increased CPU requirements provide the necessary speed to preview and test your movie on the Stage. For the playback computer with a slower CPU (Intel Pentium 166 processor running Windows 95/98 or NT 4.0 or later[Win], or a Power PC 120 Macintosh running System 8.1 or later [Mac]), the movie is optimized to achieve the same results. The additional disk space requirements provide the necessary storage space to store large media elements, such as graphics, animation, video, and sound. For the playback computer, the movie is distributed on CD-ROM or the Web, where the available disk space exceeds the requirements.

Unit B

Director 8

Setting Up a Movie

When you start Director, it displays the Director window with a set of blank windows ready for you to create a new movie. Before you start, however, you need to first set up the movie properties. You set movie properties at the beginning of the project in order to make basic decisions about how your movie looks and operates. You use the Property Inspector's Movie tab to specify movie properties settings that affect the entire movie, such as how colors are defined, the size and location of the Stage, the number of channels in the Score, copyright information, and font mapping. These settings apply only to the current movie unless you set Director preferences to apply to every movie. ✒️ Based on the project plans, Jean modifies the movie properties for the company's promotional movie. Before Jean makes any changes, she starts Director to create a blank work area for a new movie and saves it with an appropriate filename.

Steps

QuickTip

Your initial settings in Director windows may be different.

1. Start **Director**

Director opens, displaying the work area for a new movie.

2. Click **File** on the menu bar, click **Save As**, navigate to the drive and folder where your Project Files are located, type **SpaceWorks Promotion** in the File name text box (Win) or Saving Movie field (Mac), then click **Save**

Trouble?

If the Property Inspector is not open, click Window on the menu bar, point to Inspectors, then click Property. If necessary, click the Expander arrow ▶ to display all of the window.

3. Click the **Stage window**, then click the **Movie tab** in the Property Inspector

The Movie tab on the Property Inspector appears, as shown in Figure B-3. The Movie tab appears only if you do *not* have an object selected on the Stage or in the Score. Table B-1 describes the movie properties available in the Property Inspector. For additional information about these movie properties, click the Help button 🔘 in the Property Inspector.

4. Click the **Movie Palette list arrow** 🔽, then click **Web 216**, if necessary

The Web 216 movie palette provides you with a set of Web-safe colors that will ensure that your colors will be properly displayed on the Web. This palette remains selected until Director encounters a different palette setting in the palette channel.

QuickTip

To display a ScreenTip, point to an icon in the Property Inspector.

5. Click the **Color box** next to the Stage Fill Color

The Color box displays the color last selected in Director. A pop-up color palette appears, displaying the current color palette, as shown in Figure B-4. Because the RGB option is selected, the color palette is based on RGB colors. Notice that you may have to hold down the mouse button a bit longer than usual to display the color palette.

6. Click the **first black color box** in the first row of the pop-up color palette, as shown in Figure B-4

The Stage Fill Color changes to black, and the RGB color value in the text box to the right changes to #000000 (black).

7. Click the **Save button** 💾 on the toolbar

All the changes you made to the movie since the last time you saved it are saved. This includes changes to the Property Inspector settings. It's a good idea to frequently save your work in case of power failure or other computer problems.

Working with color palettes

Director comes with two color palette displays. One is a pop-up color palette, and the other is a color palette window. The pop-up color palette provides quick access to colors in the color palette, while the color palette window allows you to select or create a color palette, define new colors, or change foreground, background, and fill colors. To display the pop-up color palette, click the Color box. To close it, click a color or click an empty area of the screen. To open the color window, double-click the Color box or click Window on the menu bar, then click Color Palettes.

FIGURE B-3: Property Inspector window

Movie palette
Stage size
Stage location
Stage fill color
Color box
Score channels
Click expander arrow to display rest of window

FIGURE B-4: Movie tab with pop-up color palette

RGB color palette
Click the black color box here

TABLE B-1: Movie properties in the Property Inspector

movie property	allows you to
Movie Palette	Set the default color palette for your movie
Stage Size	Change the size of the Stage by choosing a monitor size from the pop-up menu, or by entering values into the Width and Heights text boxes
Stage Location	Select a stage location, either Centered, Upper Left, or Other; you enter values (in pixels) in the Left and Top text boxes to specify how far away you want the Stage to be from the top-left corner of the screen
Stage Fill Color	Select the color of the stage from a pop-up color palette
Color Box	Select the color palette for your movie, either RGB (assign all color values as absolute RGB values) or Palette Index (assign color according to its position in the current palette)
Score Channels	Set the number of channels available for sprites in the Score
Expander Arrow	Expand or collapse the Property Inspector window to display all settings
Remap Palettes If Needed	Remap different color palettes associated with cast members displayed on the Stage to a common color palette that Director creates
Enable Edit Shortcuts	Cut, copy, and paste Editable text boxes while a movie is playing
About, Copyright	Specify About and Copyright information for your movie
Save	Save current font map settings in a specific text file
Load	Load font map settings from a file

Importing Cast Members

If you have already developed animations and multimedia content, images, sounds, video, or text in other programs, you can import these media elements into the active Cast Window. Table AP-1 provides a summary of the formats and objects that you can import into Director. As Director imports images into a Cast window, the program checks that the images are compatible with the current movie property settings. If an incompatibility arises, Director prompts you on how to resolve it. ⟍⟍⟍ Jean imports media elements provided by the art department at SpaceWorks Interactive.

1. Click the **Import button** 🖻 on the toolbar

The Import Files into "Internal" dialog box opens.

QuickTip

To import one file, click the file, then click Import. To import more than one file at once, click the file and click Add until you're done adding to the list, then click Import.

2. Click the **Look in list arrow** ▼, click the drive and folder where your Project Files are located, then double-click the **Media folder**

A list of the files and folders appears in the File List, as shown in Figure B-5. You can select files individually or as a group and import them into the active Cast window.

3. Click **Add All**

All the files in the Media folder appear in the File List. The selected files will be imported into the active Cast window according to the order of the files in the File List from top to bottom. The top file in the list will be imported into the next available location in the Cast window. You can change the import order by selecting a file and clicking Move Up or Move Down.

Trouble?

If your monitor is set to 32 bits, the same color depth as the graphic, the Image Options dialog box may not appear. Skip steps 5 and 6.

4. Click **Import**

The Image Options dialog box opens, as shown in Figure B-6, indicating that the graphic you are importing has a different color depth from the system into which you're importing. The number of colors that a graphic or a computer system can display is called **color depth**. Your computer monitor and the images you import into a movie can have different color depths. If your computer monitor is set to a higher color depth than 8 bits, the Stage setting in this dialog box will be a higher number, such as 16 bits.

Trouble?

If you don't change an image to the Stage color depth when you import it, you might experience color flashes or conflicts when the image appears on the Stage.

5. In the Color Depth area, click the **Stage (8 bits) option button** or **Stage (16 bits) option button**

This value reflects the color depth set for your system, so an 8-bit or 16-bit stage setting reflects an 8-bit or 16-bit monitor setting. In most cases, you should transform images with higher color depth settings to the lower setting listed next to the Stage option button so that the color depth setting for the Stage and the image will match.

6. Click the **Same Settings for Remaining Images check box** to select it, then click **OK**

The Select Format dialog box opens, indicating that the image you are importing can be imported using multiple formats. The Animated GIF format is selected.

7. Click **OK**

All the files in the file list appear in the Cast window. In the Cast window, you can view the cast in either List view or Thumbnail view. You can click the Cast View Style button in the Cast window to switch between the two views.

8. If List view appears in the Cast window, click the **Cast View Style button** 🗒 in the Cast window to change to Thumbnail view

The Cast window appears in Thumbnail view with all the files from the file list, as shown in Figure B-7. To change the default Cast window view to Thumbnail view, click File on the menu bar, point to Preferences, click Cast, click the Apply to All Casts check box, click the Thumbnail option button, click Save As Default, then click OK.

FIGURE B-5: Import Files into "Internal" dialog box

List of media files

Click button to add files one at a time

Files selected for import will appear here

Click button to import files

Click button to specify a URL for the file

Click buttons to change the order of the imported files

FIGURE B-6: Image Options dialog box

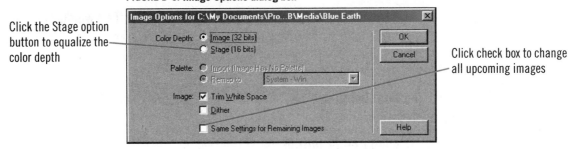

Click the Stage option button to equalize the color depth

Click check box to change all upcoming images

FIGURE B-7: Cast window

Click button to display cast member properties

Click button to change the view of cast members

Imported media files as cast members

CLUES TO USE

Understanding color depth

The higher the color depth value, the greater the number of colors that can be displayed, which necessitates greater system memory. An image with a 1-bit color depth appears only in black and white; similarly, a monitor with a 1-bit color depth setting displays only black-and-white images. The most common color depth display settings are: 2-bit, which displays 4 colors; 4-bit, which displays 16 colors; 8-bit, which displays 256 colors; 16-bit, which displays 32,768 colors; and 24-bit and 32-bit, both of which display 16.7 million colors.

Creating and Naming Cast Members

You can create new media elements in Director or import ones that have already been developed. Director provides several tools for creating media elements, including a paint tool and text creation tools. The text tool provides standard text-formatting controls in a window that resembles a word-processing program. When you create or import a media element, it is stored in the Cast window. A Cast window can contain up to 32,000 cast members, each one represented by a thumbnail image and identified by its position number and an optional name. A small icon in the lower-right corner of each cast member identifies its type. Table AP-1 identifies each cast member by its icon. You can name a new cast member or rename an existing one. You can also copy, paste, delete, duplicate, relocate, and modify a cast member. Any changes you make to a cast member are reflected in its appearance on the Stage. You don't have to use every cast member in your movie; however, saving your movie with all of the unused cast members increases the file size. ⟍⟍⟍ Jean has already imported images in the Cast window and now wants to create text cast members in Director.

QuickTip

You can also use the Text tool **A** on the Tool palette to create a cast member on the Stage.

1. Click the **Text Window button** **A** on the toolbar

   The Text window opens, displaying Text 4 on the title bar. The number 4 indicates that this cast member will be stored in location number 4 in the Cast window.

2. Position the **mouse pointer** on the bottom-right corner of the **Text window** until the pointer changes to ⟍, then drag the **border** to the dimension shown in Figure B-8

   The Text window expands. The Text window provides standard text-formatting controls in a window that resembles a word-processing program.

QuickTip

To change the Font color, select the text, click Modify on the menu bar, click Font, click the Color box, click a color, then click OK.

3. Click the **Font list arrow** ▼, scroll if necessary, click **Arial Black**, click the **Size list arrow** ▼, then click **36**

4. Click the **Align Center button** ▤ in the Text Window

   The font attributes are set for the text cast member, and the insertion point (blinking cursor) appears in the Text window.

Trouble?

If the text doesn't fit on one line, drag the black bar in the top-right corner of the text box until the text fits.

5. Type **SpaceWorks**

   The text appears in the Text window with the font attributes you set. The last set font color selected appears in the Text window; your font color might be different from the black color used here. If you make a mistake, press Backspace (Win) or Delete (Mac) to delete the incorrect text, then retype the text.

6. Click the **Cast Member Name text box**, type **SpaceWorks Text**, then press **Enter** (Win) or **Return** (Mac)

   The new name appears in the Text title bar, in the Property Inspector Name text box, and as cast member 4 in the Cast window.

7. Click the **New Cast Member button** ➕ in the Text window

   A blank Text window entitled Text 5 appears. The Text window retains the formatting attributes from the previous Text window.

QuickTip

To display a text cast member not currently open in the Text window, click the Next Cast Member button ▸ or the Previous Cast Member button ◂.

8. Click the **Size list arrow**, click **18**, type **presents**, click the **Cast Member Name text box**, type **Presents Text**, then press **Enter** (Win) or **Return** (Mac)

9. Click the **Close button** in the Text window

   The Text window closes and the new cast member, Presents Text, is stored as cast member 5 in the Cast window, as shown in Figure B-9.

FIGURE B-8: Text window

Click buttons to view other text cast members

Click button to create a new cast member

Cast member name text box

Text area

Cast member number

Formatting toolbar

Ruler

Drag black bar to resize text box

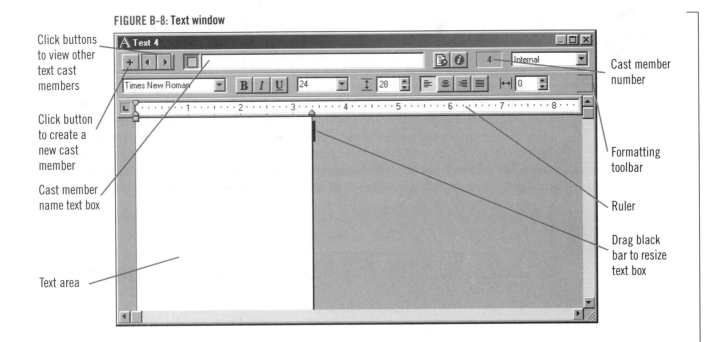

FIGURE B-9: Cast window with text cast members

Name of selected cast member

Cast member type

Cast member number

New text cast members

CLUES TO USE

Changing text alignment

In the Text window, you can change the alignment for each paragraph in a text cast member. A paragraph is a new section of text. To create a new paragraph in the Text window, press [Enter] (Win) or [Return](Mac). You can align paragraph text relative to the margins in the Text window. Although you can vary the width and placement of the margins, the right margin cannot exceed the length of the text cast member. By default, text is left-aligned ▤, or flush with the left margin. However, you can also right-align text ▤ flush with the right margin, center text ▤ between the margins, or justify text ▤ so that both the left and right edges are evenly aligned. To align multiple paragraphs, you need to select the paragraphs, then select an alignment option.

Creating Sprites

A sprite is an object that consists of a cast member and a set of properties and behaviors. The properties and behaviors control how, where, and when cast members appear in a movie. You can create sprites by placing cast members either on the Stage or in the Score—regardless of where you create the sprite, it will appear in both locations. You can create different sprites from a single cast member. You use the Stage to control *where* a sprite appears, and you use the Score to control *when* it appears. Sprites appear on the Stage, layered according to the corresponding channel in the Score. Sprites in higher-numbered channels appear in front of sprites in lower-numbered channels. ✒️ Jean adds sprites to the Stage and in the Score to create a movie.

Steps 1234

1. Resize the Stage, Score, and Cast windows to match the windows in Figure B-10

2. Click **cast member 3** (Space Background) in the Cast window
   When you position the mouse pointer over a selected cast member, the arrow changes to a 🖑.

QuickTip
You can use the playback head to locate the frame number.

3. Drag the **cast member** from the Cast window to **frame 1, channel 1** in the Score, as shown in Figure B-10
   When you drag a cast member in the Score, an outline of the sprite appears, indicating the current location of the sprite when you release the mouse. Each new sprite you create has a default duration of 28 frames, called the **span duration**. The range of frames in which the sprite appears is called the **sprite span**. You can change the duration of the sprite at any time. Placing a sprite over a range of frames indicates when the sprite appears during the movie. When you place a cast member (space background) in the Score, the sprite appears in the center of the Stage with a selection rectangle. Attached to the bottom of the sprite selection rectangle is the Sprite Overlay panel. The **Sprite Overlay panel** displays important sprite properties directly on the Stage.

4. Click **frame 5** in the frame channel to move the playback head to frame 5
   When you add a cast member to the Stage, it will be placed in frame 5.

5. Drag **cast member 4** (SpaceWorks Text) from the Cast window to the upper-center of the Stage, then click the **gray area around the Stage** or an **empty area of the Stage** to deselect the sprite
   The sprite appears on the Stage and in channel 2 in the Score, starting at frame 5. Use the outline of the image to determine when it is positioned in the right location; you can always adjust it again if necessary.

6. Drag **cast member 5** (Presents Text) from the Cast window to the Stage below cast member 4 (SpaceWorks Text), then click the **gray area around the Stage** or an **empty area of the Stage** to deselect the sprite
   Your screen should be similar to Figure B-11.

Trouble?
If the playback loop is turned on, click the Stop button ◼ on the toolbar.

7. Click the **Rewind button** ◀ on the toolbar, then click the **Play button** ▶ on the toolbar
   The movie plays on the Stage and the playback head moves frame to frame through the Score until it reaches the end of the longest sprite. The movie shows the text appearing in default colors above the background, then the background disappears.

FIGURE B-10: Score window with a new sprite

New sprite on
the Stage

Sprite Overlay panel

New sprite in Score

Sprite span

FIGURE B-11: Stage and Score windows with new sprites

New sprites

CLUES TO USE

Changing sprite preferences

You can use the Sprite Preferences dialog box to control the way sprites appear and behave in the Score and on the Stage. You can change sprite options that control Stage selection, span defaults, and span duration. To change preferences for sprites, click File on the menu bar, point to Preferences, then click Sprite. With Stage selection, you can customize how you select a sprite on the Stage; you can select the entire span of the sprite or only the current frame in the sprite. With span defaults, you can determine the appearance and behavior of sprites you'll create in the future. With span duration, you can determine the length of sprites in frames, indicating either a specified amount or the visible width of the Score window.

Unit B

Director 8

Sequencing and Modifying Sprites

You can reposition sprites on the Stage and make other changes to them without affecting the original cast members. To move or edit a sprite, you must select it first. You use the Arrow tool on the Tool palette to select one or more sprites. You can also select a certain frame or range of frames within a sprite instead of the entire sprite. The first frame in a sprite is called a **keyframe** and the last frame is called an **end frame**. A keyframe is denoted in a sprite by a circle, while an end frame is denoted by a small bar. The line that connects the circle and the small bar is called the **sprite bar**. Jean takes some time to familiarize herself with the elements of the Score window.

1. Click **anywhere** in the **Space Background sprite** in channel 1 in the Score
   The sprite is highlighted in the Score and on the Stage.

Trouble?

If the Score window is not wide enough, you can resize it or drag the playback head to the edge of the window and scroll.

2. Position the mouse pointer over the **end frame** in the Space Background sprite in channel 1, then drag the **end frame** to **frame 75**
   The sprite in channel 1 is extended to frame 75, denoting the new end of the movie. The previous end was at frame 32. Notice that the sprite outline is not visible while you drag the end frame.

3. Position the mouse pointer over the **Presents Text sprite** in channel 3 (approximately over the frame number, not over the keyframe or end frame), then drag the **sprite** so that the keyframe starts at **frame 10**
   An outline surrounds the sprite as you drag it. The sprite is repositioned in the Score, as shown in Figure B-12.

4. Drag the **end frame** for the SpaceWorks Text sprite in channel 2 back to **frame 30**, then drag the **end frame** for the Presents Text sprite in channel 3 back to **frame 30**
   Now both sprites finish their appearance in the movie at the same time.

5. Click the **SpaceWorks Text sprite** in the sprite bar, press and hold **[Shift]**, then click the **Presents Text sprite** within the sprite bar to select both sprites
   The SpaceWorks Text sprite and Presents Text sprite are selected. You can also drag a selection rectangle in the Score to select all the sprites in an area. Right now, the text color of each of the sprites on the Stage is the default color with which Director opened. These colors may not show up well against a space background. You can use tools on the Tool palette which are similar to those found in drawing programs, to change the color of the sprites, as shown in Figure B-13.

6. Click the **Foreground Color box** on the Tool palette, then click the **large white color box** at the end of the second row on the pop-up color palette
   The text color of the sprites changes to white and blends in with the white background. If the Tool palette is not open, click Window on the menu bar, then click Tool Palette.

7. Click and hold the **Background Color box** on the Tool palette, click the **large black color box** at the beginning of the first row on the pop-up color palette, then click the **gray area around the Stage** to deselect the sprites
   The background of the sprite changes to black to match the space background and the white text is visible, as shown in Figure B-14.

Trouble?

If the playback loop is turned on, click the Stop button ■ on the toolbar.

8. Click the **Rewind button** ◄◄ on the toolbar, then click the **Play button** ► on the toolbar
   The movie plays on the Stage and the playback head moves frame to frame through the Score until it reaches the end. The movie shows the text appearing in white, then disappearing.

FIGURE B-12: Sprite repositioned in the Score

Keyframe

Sprite bar

Sprite repositioned in the Score

End frame

FIGURE B-13: Tool palette

Arrow — Rotate and skew
Hand — Magnifying glass
Text — Line
Filled shapes — Shapes
Check box — Radio
Field
Push
Foreground Color box — Background Color box
Pattern
Line styles

FIGURE B-14: Stage window with new foreground and background colors

Background color of the text changes to black

Foreground color of the text changes to white

Creating Animation Using Keyframes

The simplest way to make a sprite move from one position to another is through tweening. In traditional animation, tweening describes the process in which an animator draws all the frames *in between* the frames where major changes take place in order to create the impression of movement. To tween the animation, you need to set the frames in the Score that correspond to the major change points on the Stage where the sprite will move to and from. The major change point frames are the keyframes in the animation. A keyframe is the first frame in a sprite (the starting point for the animation) and the selected frames in the Score where a sprite appears in a new location or changes appearance in some other way. As you place keyframes in the sprite, Director automatically tweens the sprites between the keyframes. You can set many keyframes in a sprite. ◆▬▬ Jean wants to sequence a sprite in the Score to create an animation.

1. Click frame 10 in channel 3

The first frame in the text sprite is selected in the Score to indicate the start position for the animation. A sprite's first frame is a keyframe. Selecting the keyframe of the sprite lets Director know you want to make a change to the sprite in this frame.

2. In the Stage window, press and hold [Shift], then drag the Presents Text sprite in a straight path to the gray area at the bottom of the Stage

The text sprite is moved on the Stage to its start position for the animation, as shown in Figure B-15.

3. Click frame 20 in channel 3

A keyframe is selected in the Score to indicate the end point for the animation. Selecting frame 20 for a keyframe makes the animation take place in frames 10 through 20. After frame 20, the line of text will remain in place.

4. Click Insert on the menu bar, then click Keyframe

Director places a keyframe indicator in the sprite. After every keyframe, Director inserts a sprite label in the sprite so you can identify what appears after the keyframe, as shown in Figure B-16.

5. Press and hold [Shift], then drag the Presents Text sprite in a straight path from the gray area at the bottom of the Stage to an area below the SpaceWorks text

A white vertical line appears as you move the text sprite on the Stage to its end point for the animation, as shown in Figure B-17.

6. Click the Rewind button ◄◄ on the toolbar, then click the Play button ▶ on the toolbar

The movie plays on the Stage and the playback head moves frame to frame through the Score until it reaches the end. The movie shows the text animated—"presents" moves up the screen and stops beneath Spaceworks.

7. Click the Save button 🖫 on the toolbar

All the changes you made to the movie since the last time you saved it are saved.

QuickTip

When you press and hold [Shift] as you move a sprite, the object is constrained horizontally or vertically to move in a straight line right to left or up and down, respectively.

Trouble?

If the playback loop is turned on, click the Stop button ■ on the toolbar.

FIGURE B-15: **Start position for animation**

Start position for animation on the Stage

Start position for animation in Score

FIGURE B-16: **Score window with a keyframe indicator**

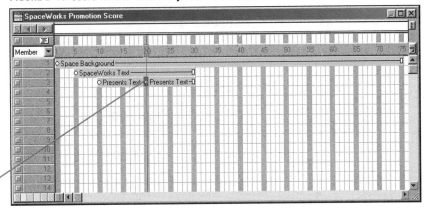

Keyframe indicator

FIGURE B-17: **Stage window with an animation**

Animation end position

Animation path

Animation start position

Director 8

Printing a Movie

Sometimes the best way to review different parts of your movie content and mark changes is to print it out. You can print a movie in a variety of ways. You can print an image of the Stage in standard or storyboard format or print the Score, the cast member number and contents of text cast members in the Cast window, all scripts or a range of scripts (movie, cast, Score, and sprite scripts), the comments in the Markers window, the Cast window artwork, or the entire Cast window. Jean wants to print a storyboard of the Stage and the Score, and compare it with the project plan.

Steps

QuickTip

You can also press [Ctrl][P] (Win) or [Command][P] (Mac) to open the Print dialog box.

1. Click **File** on the menu bar, then click **Print**
   The Print dialog box opens. Table B-2 describes some of the options in the Print dialog box.

2. Click the **Print list arrow**, then click **Stage**

3. Click the **Frames All option button**, click the **Include One in Every option button**, click the Frames text box, then type **5** in the Frames text box
   The options are set to print the Stage image one in every 5 frames for the entire movie, as shown in Figure B-18.

4. Click **Options**, click the **Scale 50% option button**, then click the **Storyboard Format check box** to select it
   The Print Options dialog box opens. The storyboard format is available only when you select 50% or 25% images to print, as shown in Figure B-19.

5. Click the **Custom Footer check box**, click in the text box, then type **your name**

Trouble?

If you have printing problems, you may need to adjust the graphics intensity and mode settings of your printer. Click File on the menu bar, click Page Setup, then click Properties.

6. Click **OK** to close the Print Options dialog box, click **Print**, then click **OK** (Win) or **Print** (Mac) to print the storyboard

7. Click **File** on the menu bar, then click **Page Setup**
   The Print Setup dialog box opens. You can specify paper size and source, and the orientation, either portrait (8½ inches × 11 inches) or landscape (11 inches × 8½ inches).

8. Click the **Landscape option button**, then click **OK**

QuickTip

The print settings stay in effect until you change them.

9. Click **File** on the menu bar, click **Print**, click the **Print list arrow**, click **Score**, click **Print**, then click **OK** (Win) or **Print** (Mac)
   Director prints the entire Score window with a landscape orientation.

10. Click **File** on the menu bar, click **Exit**, then if asked to save your work, click **No** (Win) or **Don't Save** (Mac)
    Director closes.

FIGURE B-18: Print dialog box

Click arrow to select what to print

Click button to select what frames to print

Click button to select the frame interval to print

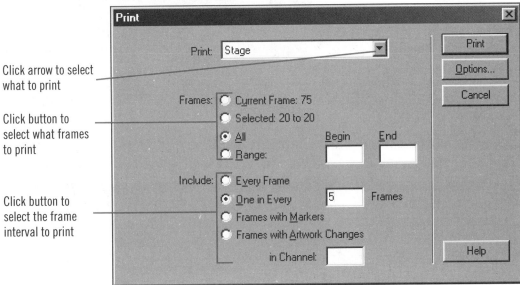

FIGURE B-19: Options dialog box

Your number of frames may be different

This option only appears when Scale is 50% or 25%

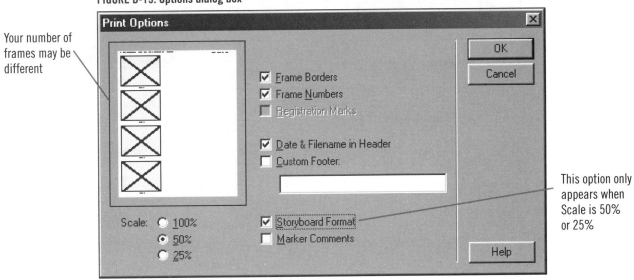

TABLE B-2: Options in the Print dialog box

print option	use to
Print	Specify what part of the movie to print; this includes the Stage, the Score, all scripts or a range of scripts, cast text, cast art, cast thumbnails, and marker comments
Frames	Specify which frames of your movie are printed
Include	Specify which frames in the defined range to print
Options	Determine the layout of the items to print; this includes scaling frames, frame borders, frame numbers, registration marks, date and filename in the header, a custom footer, and storyboards
Help	Display the Director 8 Help topic for printing movies

Practice

► Concepts Review

Label each of the elements of the screen shown in Figure B-20.

FIGURE B-20

Match each of the terms with the statement that describes its function.

6. Keyframe   a. The first frame in a sprite

7. End frame   b. An information point for a sprite

8. Keyframe indicator   c. An animation point in a sprite

9. Foreground Color box   d. The last frame in a sprite

10. Background Color box   e. The top color chip in the Tool palette

11. Sprite Overlay panel   f. The bottom color chip in the Tool palette

Select the best answer from the following list of choices.

12. **What do you need to determine first when planning a movie?**
    a. Purpose
    b. Audience
    c. Content and structure
    d. Computer system requirements

13. **What planning tool is good for developing the navigational structure of a movie?**
    a. Script
    b. Schematic flowchart
    c. Storyboard
    d. Director

14. **What planning tool is good for developing the text form of a movie?**
    a. Script
    b. Schematic flowchart
    c. Storyboard
    d. Director

15. **What can you load from a file in the Property Inspector?**
    a. Color palettes
    b. Font map settings
    c. All of the above
    d. None of the above

16. **The number of colors that a graphic or a computer system can display is called the:**
    a. Color number.
    b. Color set.
    c. Color display.
    d. Color depth.

17. **How many colors does the 8-bit setting display?**
    a. 4 colors
    b. 16 colors
    c. 256 colors
    d. 32,768 colors

18. **A small icon in the lower-right corner of each cast member identifies its:**
    a. Type.
    b. Size.
    c. Name.
    d. Control.

19. **The default span duration is:**
    a. 10 frames.
    b. 20 frames.
    c. 28 frames.
    d. 36 frames.

20. **The sprite overlay panel displays the sprite:**
    a. Properties.
    b. Keyframes.
    c. End frame.
    d. Keyframe indicators.

21. **The first frame of a sprite is the:**
    a. Keyframe indicator.
    b. Keyframe.
    c. End frame.
    d. Tween.

22. **Which is not a Print option in Director?**
    a. Cast Text
    b. Cast Art
    c. Cast Window
    d. Marker Comments

▶ Skills Review

1. **Plan a movie.**
   a. Write down the basic steps involved in planning a movie, without referring to the unit material.

2. **Set up a new movie.**
   a. Start Director.
   b. Click the Movie tab of the Property Inspector.
   c. Change the Movie Palette to Web 216, if necessary.
   d. Change the Stage Fill Color to black, if necessary.

3. **Import cast members.**
   a. Import all the media elements from the Media folder in the drive where your Project Files are located.
   b. Change the color depth to match the Stage setting and select a format for any images.

4. **Create and name cast members.**
   a. Open the file MD B-1.dir from the drive and folder where your Project Files are located and save it as *SpaceWorks Promotion2*. Don't save the previous movie.
   b. Change the foreground color to white and the background color to black.
   c. Open the Text window and resize it, if necessary.
   d. Drag the black bar to 3½" on the ruler, if necessary.
   e. Change the font attributes to the font Arial Black, size 24, and center alignment.
   f. Type **a new way to learn about ...**
   g. Name the cast member Learn About Text.
   h. Create a new text cast member.
   i. Type **your**, press the spacebar, change the font size to 36, then type **World**
   j. Name the cast member World Text.
   k. Close the Text window.

5. **Create sprites.**
   a. Position cast member 6 (Learn About Text) in the Score starting at frame 31 in channel 4, then drag the sprite to the center of the Stage, if necessary.
   b. Select frame 60 in the frame channel.
   c. Drag cast member 7 (World Text) from the Cast window to the top-center of the Stage.
   d. Drag cast member 1 (Blue Earth) from the Cast window to the Stage below the World text.
   e. Rewind and play the movie.

6. **Sequence and modify sprites.**
   a. Adjust the Learn About Text sprite in channel 4 to start at frame 31 and end at frame 50.
   b. Move the World Text sprite to channel 5, then adjust it to start at frame 51 and end at frame 75.
   c. Move the Blue Earth sprite to channel 6, then adjust it to start at frame 60 and end at frame 75.

7. **Create animation using keyframes.**
   a. Start the animation at frame 60.
   b. Move the Blue Earth image to the gray area directly to the right. (*Hint*: Do not grab the dots in the center of the earth.)
   c. End the animation at frame 70.
   d. Insert a keyframe.
   e. Move the Blue Earth image in a straight path from the gray area to the center of the Stage.
   f. Rewind and play the movie.
   g. Save the movie.

8. **Print a movie.**
   a. Create a custom footer with your name in it, then print the entire storyboard at 25% scale in portrait orientation. (*Hint*: If you have printing problems, you may need to adjust the graphics intensity and mode settings of your printer.)
   b. Print all the cast members as thumbnails in landscape orientation.
   c. Exit Director and don't save the movie.

Director 8

Independent Challenges

1. As the public relations manager for an international charity, you want to create a multimedia presentation that celebrates the 50th anniversary of the organization and promotes increased participation in charitable events. The charity wants to hire a multimedia development company to create the presentation. In order to get funds for the project, you need to create a project plan.

To complete this independent challenge:

a. Start WordPad (Win) or SimpleText (Mac) and create a project plan.

b. Save the document as Project Plan in the folder where your Project Files are located.

c. Determine the purpose.

d. Identify the audience.

e. Develop the content and organize the structure.

f. Develop the layout and design.

g. Identify the delivery computer system.

h. Type your name.

i. Print the project plan.

j. Exit WordPad (Win) or SimpleText (Mac).

2. As the lead designer for BannerAD Designs, you regularly use Director to create the designs. A new client recently approached you about creating a banner ad for a company called ABC123 Learning. You use the media creation tools in Director to create a banner ad with some animation.

To complete this independent challenge:

a. Start Director and save the new movie as *ABC123* in the location where your Project Files are stored.

b. Set up the Stage to be 468 x 60 with a blue background and Web 216 color palette.

c. Create a text sprite for the letters A, B, and C.

d. Create a text sprite for the numbers 1, 2, and 3.

e. Animate the letters and numbers.

f. Create a custom footer with your name in it.

g. Print all of the cast members and all of the Stage frames. (*Hint*: If you have printing problems, you may need to adjust the graphics intensity and mode settings of your printer.)

h. Save the movie and exit Director.

3. You're an independent multimedia producer. You just got a part time job teaching Director 8. The course materials use the tutorial included with the Director 8 package. In preparation for the first class, you want to open the completed tutorial, play the movie, and print the Stage, Score, and Cast. After reviewing the course materials, you want to print some handouts for class. The sample and instructional movies that are installed with the Director program are typically located in a subfolder inside the Director 8 folder.

To complete this independent challenge:

a. Display the Open dialog box.

b. Locate the Completed_Tutorials folder. For the typical Director 8 installation, the folder is located on the hard drive in the Programs Files folder, Macromedia folder, Director 8 folder, and Learning folder (Win) or Director 8 folder and Learning folder (Mac).

c. Open the fun.dir file.

d. Create a custom footer with your name in it.

e. Print the Stage every 20 frames, Score, and Cast.

f. Exit Director and don't save the movie.

4. You are an astronomy professor at a local college. You have been asked by a colleague to prepare a multimedia presentation on the topic of your choice for an upcoming space exploration convention. You use media elements from the NASA Web site and the media creation tools in Director to create a self-running slide presentation.

To complete this independent challenge:

a. Connect to the Internet and go to www.course.com. Navigate to the page for this book, click the link for the Student Online Companion. Use the link for Unit B to begin your search.

b. Find and download five media elements for your movie presentation.

c. Start Director and save the new movie as *Space Pres* in the drive and folder where your Project Files are located.

d. Set up the Stage to be 468 x 60 with a black background.

e. Import the media elements into the Cast.

f. Create sprites with the cast members to create a slide show.

g. Create text sprites for titles and animate the introduction title.

h. Create a custom footer with your name in it.

i. Print all the cast members and the Score.

j. Play and save the movie presentation.

k. Exit Director.

▶ Visual Workshop

Create the movie screen shown in Figure B-21. You can import the image Mwm Logo.tif from the location where your Project Files are stored. Save it as *MWM* in the drive and folder where your Project Files are located, create a custom footer with your name in it, then print frame 18 of the Stage.

FIGURE B-21

Creating
Graphic Cast Members

Objectives

- ► Understand vector shapes and bitmaps
- ► Draw a vector shape
- ► Add a gradient to a vector shape
- ► Edit a vector shape
- ► Use the Paint window
- ► Flip, rotate, and apply effects
- ► Apply Ink effects
- ► Apply Paint effects
- ► Add text to a bitmap

In Director, you can create new graphical media elements for the Cast or import ones that have already been developed. Director provides several tools for creating graphical cast members. This unit introduces you to basic Director skills for creating, editing, and enhancing graphical cast members. First, you'll learn how to draw and edit graphical elements. Then, you'll learn how to modify and enhance these elements. After creating a basic promotional movie for SpaceWorks Interactive, Jean wants to create a set of graphical cast members for use in an upcoming movie.

Understanding Vector Shapes and Bitmaps

With Director's graphical tools, you can create vector shapes or bitmaps. A vector shape is a mathematical description of a geometric form, which is composed of line thickness, line color, line slope, fill color, corner points, and so on, while a bitmap is a pixel-by-pixel representation of a graphic. A pixel is an individual point in a graphic with a distinct color. To understand the difference between a vector shape and a bitmap, imagine a simple line. You can draw a line pixel-by-pixel as a bitmap, as shown in Figure C-1, or you can draw a line from point A (the starting point) to point B (the ending point) as a vector shape, as shown in Figure C-2. The simple line looks the same on the screen using either method, but the vector shape is more versatile. If you need a simple shape with minimal detail, a vector shape is the best choice. If you need a more complex graphic that you can edit, a bitmap is the right choice. Jean is new to the process of creating graphics in Director, so she wants to learn the basic properties of vector shapes and bitmaps, as listed below.

Properties of a vector shape:

 A vector shape uses less drive storage and memory space than a bitmap and requires less download time from the Internet or other network.

 A vector shape can consist of only one distinct shape as a cast member. For example, a vector shape cannot contain a separate square and circle that do not connect.

 A vector shape can be resized without distortion, unlike a bitmap.

 A vector shape can be controlled with Lingo (a scripting language specific to Director) while a movie is playing.

 You can create a vector shape entirely with Lingo.

Properties of a bitmap:

 A bitmap requires more drive storage and memory space than a vector shape. The larger the bitmap, the greater the amount of storage and memory space required.

 A bitmap can consist of any arrangement of pixels, connected or disconnected.

 When you resize a bitmap, the image can become distorted. You can alleviate part of the problem by using the anti-aliasing feature. **Anti-Aliasing** blends the bitmap's colors with background colors around the edges to make the edge appear smooth instead of jagged.

 You can edit single pixels, groups of pixels, or the entire bitmap of pixels.

FIGURE C-1: A bitmap of a line

Bitmap

FIGURE C-2: A vector shape of a line

Point A
(starting point)

Point B
(ending point)

Vector shape

Understanding a PostScript graphic

Many graphic designers create graphics in a common format called **PostScript**, using programs such as Macromedia Illustrator or Adobe Illustrator. A PostScript graphic, known as an Encapsulated PostScript (EPS) file, is similar in nature to a vector shape; it is also described in mathematical terms, but is more complex. EPS files are commonly used to transfer graphics between applications and across platforms. EPS allows you to create a complex graphic with several shapes and still save storage and memory space. In Director, you cannot create or import a PostScript graphic. If you have an EPS file that you want to use in a movie, you will need another graphics program, such as Adobe Photoshop, to save it into a Picture (PICT) file, a graphic format that Director can import.

Director 8

Drawing a Vector Shape

A vector shape can be a line, a curve, or an open or closed shape that you can fill with a color or gradient. An **open shape** is one in which the starting point and the ending point do not connect. A **closed shape** is one in which the points do connect. A shape can be **regular**, such as an oval, rectangle, or rounded rectangle, or **irregular**, such as a free-form object. You can fill the inside of a closed vector shape with a solid color, two-color pattern, or **gradient** blend, which is shading from one color to another color. You create a vector shape in the Vector Shape window by plotting points to define a path and by controlling the curvature of the line between the points. When you create a vector shape, you create **vertices** (also called points), which are fixed points, and **control handles**, which determine the degree of curvature between the vertices. Every vector shape you create becomes a cast member. Jean draws a vector shape for use in an upcoming movie.

Steps

1. Start **Director**
Director opens, displaying the work area for a new movie.

2. Click **File** on the menu bar, click **Save As**, go to the drive and folder where your Project Files are located, type **SpaceWorks Graphics** in the File name text box (Win) or Saving Movie field (Mac), then click **Save**
The initial settings in Director will vary depending on the settings last used; you can change the Stage color for better viewing.

3. Click the **Stage window**, click the **Movie tab** in the Property Inspector, click and hold the **Stage Fill color box**, then click the **white color box** at the end of the second row of the color palette

4. Click the **Vector Shape Window button** on the toolbar
The Vector Shape window opens, displaying Vector Shape 1 on the title bar. Director will store this cast member in location number 1 in the Cast window.

QuickTip

To quickly create a vector shape, click a tool on the Tool palette, then click a blank area in the Vector Shape window.

5. Click the **Filled Ellipse tool** on the Tool palette in the Vector Shape window, then position ╋ in the drawing area
The Filled Ellipse tool is active and the pointer changes to ╋, as shown in Figure C-3.

6. Press and hold **[Shift]**, then drag ╋ in a right downward diagonal to create the shape shown in Figure C-4
As you drag, the vector shape draws an ellipse in perfect proportions to create a circle. When you drag the pointer, control handles appear on the vertices: round curve points for vertices with handles and square corner points for vertices without handles, as shown in Figure C-4.

QuickTip

To resize and keep the proportions of a vector shape, click the Arrow tool, press and hold [Ctrl], press [Alt] (Win), or press and hold [Command], press [Option] (Mac), point to a vertice, then drag to the size you desire.

7. Click the **Cast Member Name text box**, type **Jupiter**, then press **[Enter]** (Win) or **[Return]** (Mac)
The new name appears in the Vector Shape window title bar.

8. Click the **Close button** on the Vector Shape Window
The Vector Shape window closes. The new vector shape, Jupiter, appears in the Cast window as cast member 1.

FIGURE C-3: Vector Shape window

Drawing tools

Filled Ellipse button is active

Drawing pointer

FIGURE C-4: Vector shape of a circle

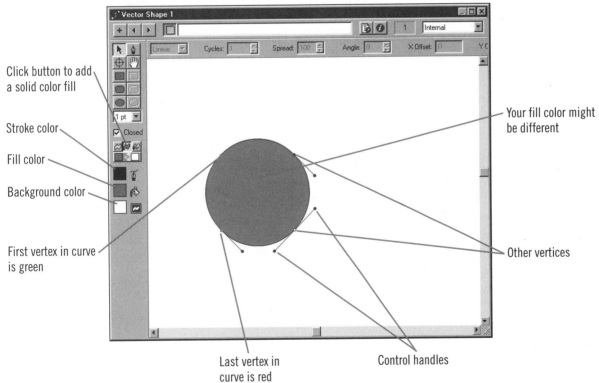

Click button to add a solid color fill

Stroke color

Fill color

Background color

First vertex in curve is green

Your fill color might be different

Other vertices

Last vertex in curve is red

Control handles

CLUES TO USE

Drawing on the Stage

With Director's Tool palette, you can create text, shapes, and buttons directly on the Stage. The shapes you create with the Tool palette are called **QuickDraw graphics**. These graphics are neither vector shapes nor bitmaps. You can resize and edit the QuickDraw shapes on the Stage, but you cannot edit them in the Paint window or in the Vector Shapes window. QuickDraw graphics use a lot less memory than bitmaps, print much better to laser printers, and animate more slowly than bitmaps or vector shapes.

Adding a Gradient to a Vector Shape

Once you create a vector shape, you can modify it by adding and changing the color, pattern, or gradient blend. A gradient can be **linear** (shading from one color on one side to another color on the other side) or it can be **radial** (shading from one color in the center to another color on the outside). Once you add a gradient, you can change how many times the gradient repeats, how it is distributed, at what angle it appears, and how offset from the vector shape's center the gradient appears. To modify a vector shape, you need to open the vector shape in the Vector Shape window. ✐ Jean modifies the vector shape to create a planet graphic.

Steps

Trouble?

To reselect control handles around a vector shape, click the Arrow tool ![arrow], position ⬚ in a blank area of the window, then drag ⬚ until the selection box surrounds any vertices on the shape.

1. **Double-click** the **Jupiter vector shape** cast member in the Cast window
   The Vector Shape window opens, displaying the selected vector shape. The vertices appear as colored round curve points, indicating that the vector shape is selected.

2. **Click and hold** the **starting Gradient Colors box**, click the **orange color box** at the beginning of the fifth row on the color palette, click and hold the **ending Gradient Colors box**, then click the **yellow color box** at the end of the third row on the color palette
   The starting Gradient Colors box changes to orange, and the ending Gradient Colors box changes to yellow.

QuickTip

To change the stroke color in a vector shape, click the Stroke Color box, then click a color. To change a fill color in a vector shape, click the Fill Color box, then click a color. To change the background color, click the Background Color box, then click a color.

3. Click the **Gradient tool** ![gradient] on the Tool palette
   A gradient of orange to yellow appears in the vector shape, as shown in Figure C-5.

4. Verify that the Gradient Type is Linear, then click the **Gradient Cycles up arrow** until it reaches **7**
   The **cycle value** determines how many times the gradient repeats from start color to end color within the vector shape.

5. Double-click the **Gradient Spread text box**, type **200**, then click a **blank area** of the Vector Shape window
   The **spread value** controls whether the gradient is weighted more towards the start color or end color. A value of 100 makes the gradient evenly distributed between starting and ending colors. Values greater than 100 weight the gradient toward the starting color, and values less than 100 weight it toward the ending color.

6. Double-click the **Gradient Angle text box**, type **75**, then click a **blank area** of the Vector Shape window
   For a linear gradient, the **angle value** controls the slope of the gradient.

QuickTip

To remove a gradient, select the shape, then click the No Fill tool ![nofill] on the Tool palette.

7. Click the **Stroke Width list arrow** ![arrow], then click **0 pt**
   The **stroke width** determines the thickness of lines and outlines. The outline of the vector shape is removed, as shown in Figure C-6.

8. Click the **Save button** ![save] on the toolbar
   The Vector Shape window remains open for the next lesson.

FIGURE C-5: Adding a gradient to a vector shape

Click button to add
a gradient

Starting gradient
color

Click area to display
the Gradient pop-up
menu

Ending gradient
color

FIGURE C-6: Modifying a gradient

Click list arrow to
select gradient type

Click list arrow to
change stroke width

Click arrows to
determine how
many times the
gradient repeats

Click arrows to
determine gradient
angle

Click arrows to
determine gradient
distribution

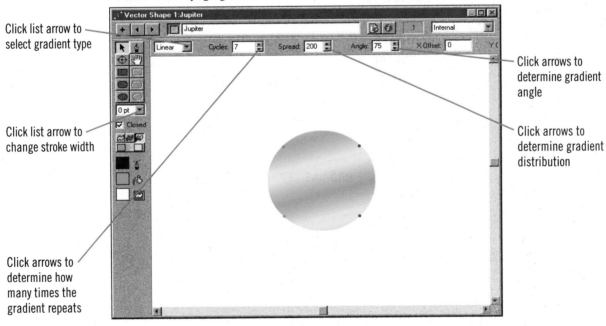

Adjusting the registration point

When you place a vector shape on the Stage, the shape is placed relative to its registration point. You use the registration point, which is initially set to the center of the shape, to accurately position the shape, bitmap, or cast member on the Stage. Director uses the registration point to determine the position when you animate a shape. To adjust the registration point for a vector shape, open the vector shape in the Vector Shape window, then click the Registration Point tool ⊕. The default registration point appears as cross hairs at the center of the vector shape. When you move the pointer in the drawing area, it changes to ┼. Click a new location in the window to set a new registration point. To reset the registration point to the center of the vector shape, you can double-click ⊕. To remove the cross hairs, click another button. You can change the registration point for a bitmapped cast member in the same way.

Editing a Vector Shape

In addition to inserting a gradient, you can edit a vector shape by moving, adding, or deleting control points and by changing the way the control points affect control curves. To edit a vector shape, you use the Pen tool, also known as the selection pointer tool, to select the point you want to edit. Once you select a point on a vector shape, you can press [Delete] or [Backspace] to remove it, or you can drag the point to a different location to change a curve. When you view a vector shape in the Vector Shape window, selected points are unfilled and unselected points are filled. For curves in a vector shape, the first point is green, the last point is red, and all other points are blue. ✒️ Jean decides to create a free-form vector shape and then edit it.

Steps

1. In the Vector Shape window, click the **New Cast Member button** ➕, click the **Stroke Width list arrow** ▾, then click **4 pt**
   A blank Vector Shape window entitled Vector Shape 2 appears. The Vector Shape window retains the formatting attributes from the previous Vector Shape window. The stroke width changes to 4 points so that you can create a thick line.

2. Click the **Pen tool** 🖋️ on the Tool palette, then position ┼ in the Vector Shape window
   The Pen tool is active, and the pointer changes to ┼. You can use this tool to create a straight line.

QuickTip

You can add a new point by clicking anywhere on the line.

3. Click in the **left side** of the Vector Shape window to start the first line segment, press and hold [Shift], then click in the **right side** to end the first line segment
   The line for the first segment appears, displaying two corner points: green on the left and red on the right. To constrain the control handle to vertical, horizontal, or a 45-degree angle, press and hold [Shift] as you drag the control handles.

Trouble?

If you release the mouse button before you drag the angle that you want, press [Delete] and redrag.

4. Click in the **bottom** of the Vector Shape window, approximately halfway down the window, even with the **end line segment**, then immediately drag to the left to create the **curve** shown in Figure C-7
   A curved segment appears. Notice that you can control the angle of the curve by pivoting a control handle. This type of curve is known as a **Bézier curve**.

QuickTip

If you want to close the path to create a shape that you can fill, click the Closed check box to select it.

5. Click the **Arrow tool** ⬆️ on the Tool palette, then position ⬚ over a point or a control handle
   When you position ⬚ over a point or a control handle, the pointer changes to ⬆️.

6. Drag the **green end point** to the top middle of the Vector Shape window
   The line segment adjusts to the new location when you release the mouse button, and the solid green point changes to an outline.

7. Click the **red end point**, then drag a **control handle** to adjust the curve, as shown in Figure C-8
   The wider you drag the control handle, the larger the curve; the closer you drag, the smaller the curve. If you drag a control handle out of the visible area, drag an edge of the Vector Shape window to resize it.

QuickTip

To change a corner point to a curve point, press and hold [Alt] (Win) or [Option] (Mac), then click a corner point and drag the control handle.

8. Click the **blue point** at the top of the curve, then press [**Backspace**] or [**Delete**]
   The point is removed and the vector shape is redrawn without the point.

9. Click the **Close button** on the Vector Shape Window, then press [**Backspace**] or [**Delete**]
   The Vector Shape window closes, and vector shape cast member 2 is deleted.

FIGURE C-7: Creating a free form vector shape

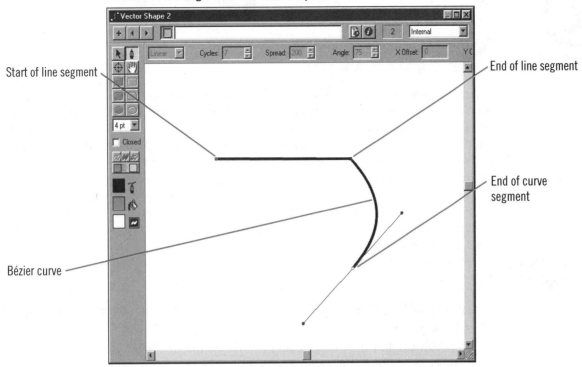

Start of line segment

End of line segment

End of curve segment

Bézier curve

FIGURE C-8: Adjusting the curvature of a vector shape

Drag point to adjust the position of a line

Drag control handle to adjust the curve

CLUES TO USE

Anti-aliasing a vector shape

When you create a vector shape with thick lines, the edges can look jagged around the curves. You can anti-alias a vector shape to blur the edges, which makes the jagged edges appear smooth. To anti-alias a vector shape, click the vector shape in the Cast window, click Modify on the menu bar, point to Cast Member, click Properties, click the Vector tab in the Property Inspector window, then click the Anti-Alias check box.

Unit C

Director 8

Using the Paint Window

Director includes a simple paint program that allows you to create and edit bitmapped cast members without having to open another program, such as Adobe Photoshop. You create and modify a bitmapped cast member by using the tools on the Tool palette. Table AP-3 describes the Paint tools available on the Paint Tool palette. A small arrow in the lower-right corner of a tool indicates that pop-up menu options are available for that tool. To display the pop-up menu, click a tool, then press and hold the mouse button. Before you can work on a bitmap, you need to select it. Director has two main tools that you use to select all or part of a bitmap: lasso and marquee. The **lasso** selects anything that you surround with the tool, while the **marquee** selects everything within its rectangular bounds. Once you select a bitmap, you can apply effects to it using the buttons on the toolbar at the top of the Paint window. Every bitmap you create in the Paint window becomes a cast member. Jean wants to create a space scene, using the Paint window.

Steps 1 2 3 4

1. Click the **Paint Window button** on the toolbar, then verify that the Ink setting is Normal

   The Paint window opens, displaying Paint 2 on the title bar. Director will store this cast member in location number 2 in the Cast window.

2. Click and hold the **Foreground Color box**, then click the **light gray color box** in the middle of the third row of the color palette

   The Foreground Color box changes to a medium shade of gray.

3. Click **File** on the menu bar, point to **Preferences**, then click **Paint**

   The Paint Preferences dialog box opens, as shown in Figure C-9. You can also double-click the Other Line Width button on the Tool palette to open the Paint Preferences dialog box.

4. Click the **"Other" Line Width right or left arrow** until it reaches **6**, then click **OK**

   The Other Line Width button on the Tool palette displays 6 pixels.

Trouble?

If the shape doesn't match Figure C-10, click the Eraser tool, drag ☐ over the shape to erase it, then repeat Step 5.

5. Click the **Ellipse tool** on the Tool palette, position + on the left side of the window, then drag an **elliptical shape**, as shown in Figure C-10

   An ellipse appears in the Paint window.

6. Click and hold the **Lasso tool** until the pop-up menu appears, then click **Lasso**

   The Lasso tool provides you with three selection options: No Shrink, Lasso, and See Thru Lasso. No Shrink selects everything that you encase with the selection marquee. Lasso makes the selection marquee tighten around the shape. See Thru Lasso is similar to Lasso, but it makes all white pixels in the selection transparent.

Trouble?

If you did not entirely enclose the selection, Director connects its starting and ending point when you release the mouse button.

7. Position 𝒫 **near the ellipse** in the Paint window, then drag an **outline** around the ellipse (try to end the selection at the point where you started it)

   The edges of the shape might appear to flash with the selection tight around the shape.

8. Click a **blank area** of the Paint window to deselect the shape

9. Click the **Cast Member Name text box**, type **Space Scene**, press **Enter** (Win) or **Return** (Mac), then click the **Close button** in the Paint window

   The Paint window closes and the new cast member is stored as cast member 2 in the Cast window.

FIGURE C-9: Paint Window Preferences dialog box

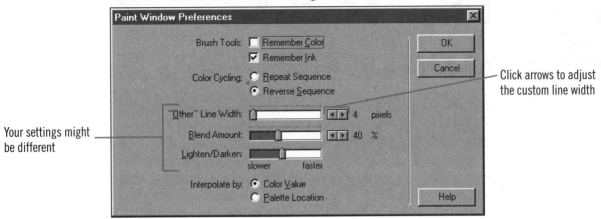

Your settings might be different

Click arrows to adjust the custom line width

FIGURE C-10: Drawing an elliptical shape

Start drag here

Foreground color

Other line width set to 6

Verify that the Ink setting is Normal

End drag here

CLUES TO USE

Selecting with the Lasso and Marquee tools

The Lasso tool and Marquee tool allow you to select a bitmap of any size and shape in the Paint window. You use the Lasso tool to select irregular areas or polygons and the Marquee tool to select a rectangular area. To select an irregular area with the Lasso tool, click the Lasso tool, then drag to enclose the area you want to select. To select a polygon area with the Lasso tool, press and hold [Alt] (Win) or [Option] (Mac) while you click to create anchor points to enclose the shape. The Lasso tool selects only those pixels that are of a different color than the ones you select when you first drag the selection. To select a rectangular area with the Marquee tool, drag

the tool to enclose the area you want to select. Once you select an area with the Marquee tool, you can press and hold [Ctrl] (Win) or [Command] (Mac), then drag a border of the selected area to resize the selection. To proportionately resize the selection, press and hold [Shift] at the same as you drag. To make a copy of the area that is selected with the Marquee tool, press and hold [Alt] (Win) or [Option] (Mac), then drag the selection. You can press and hold the Lasso tool to display a pop-up menu containing settings that control the way the selection occurs.

Director 8

Director 8

Flip, Rotate, and Apply Effects

The toolbar at the top of the Paint window contains buttons you can use to apply effects to bitmapped cast members. These effects allow you to flip, rotate, skew, and warp the contents of a selection. You can also create a perspective effect and an outline around the edges of a selected bitmap. The Paint window also includes tools for controlling the color and pattern of cast members. You can apply color effects to soften edges, reverse colors, increase or reduce brightness, fill solid or pattern, or switch colors. Table AP-4 describes the buttons on the Paint toolbar. Before you can apply an effect, you need to select all or part of the bitmap with the Lasso tool or Marquee tool. Effects that change the shape of the selection, such as flip, rotate, skew, warp, and perspective, work only when you make the selection with the Marquee tool. Effects that change colors within the selection work with both the Marquee and the Lasso tools. 🚀 Jean applies a few special effects to the space scene.

Steps

1. **Double-click the Space Scene cast member in the Cast window**
   The Paint window opens, displaying the Space Scene cast member.

QuickTip

To select the entire drawing, double-click the Marquee tool 🔲.

2. **Click and hold the Marquee tool 🔲, click No Shrink, then drag a selection rectangle around the ellipse**
   The rectangle selection marquee surrounds the ellipse.

3. **Click the Trace Edges button 🔲 on the Paint toolbar twice**
   Two sets of edges appear in place of the solid line, as shown in Figure C-11. To hide or display the Paint toolbar, click View on the menu bar, then click Paint Tools.

4. **Click the Free Rotate button 🔘 on the Paint toolbar**
   The pointer changes to +.

QuickTip

To add perspective to the shape, select a shape, click the Perspective button 🔲 on the Paint toolbar, then drag a corner handle.

5. **Position + on a corner rotate handle, drag to rotate the ellipse approximately 45 degrees, as shown in Figure C-12, then click a blank area of the window (outside the selection)**
   The shape is deselected.

6. **Click and hold 🔲, click Lasso, then drag a selection rectangle around the shape**
   The selected ellipse might flash.

QuickTip

To zoom in, click the Magnify Glass tool 🔍 on the Tool palette, then click the artwork. Click again to increase the magnification. Press [Shift] and click to zoom out. Notice that as you gain in magnification, a shape miniature appears in the corner of the Paint window.

7. **Drag the ellipse to the upper-left corner of the visible Paint window (don't scroll), then click a blank area of the window (outside the selection)**

8. **Click the Close button in the Paint window**
   The Paint window closes and the cast member is saved in the Cast window.

FIGURE C-11: A bitmap with trace edges

Arrow indicates a pop-up menu is available

No Shrink Marquee selection

Click button to trace edges

Trace edges

FIGURE C-12: Rotating a bitmap

Click buttons to rotate in 90-degree increments

Click button to rotate in 1-pixel increments

Drag any corner point to rotate a selection

CLUES TO USE

Using rulers in the Paint window

You can display vertical and horizontal rulers in the Paint window to help you align and size your bitmaps. To hide or show the rulers in the Paint window, click View on the menu bar, then click Rulers. The rulers can display measurement values in inches, centimeters, or pixels. The current unit of measurement displays in the upper-left corner. To change the display measurement value, click the upper-left corner where the unit of measurement is displayed. Instead of calculating odd measurements every time you want to align a bitmap, you can set an arbitrary zero point on the ruler to make measuring easier. To change the location of the zero point, click the ruler at the top or side of the window, then drag horizontally or vertically across the ruler until you reach the location where want the zero point to appear.

Director 8

Applying Ink Effects

Color is an important element of any bitmap. You can set three colors in the Paint window: foreground color, background color, and destination color. The **foreground color** is the default color that you use with the painting tools, the fill color for solid patterns, and the primary color in multicolored patterns. The **background color** is the secondary color in multicolored patterns. The **destination color** is the ending color of gradient blends that start with the foreground color. You can use Paint window inks to create color effects for bitmap cast members. You can select an ink effect from the Ink pop-up menu at the bottom of the Paint window. The result of the ink you choose depends on whether you are working in color or black and white. In addition, some inks work better when painting with patterns, and others work better when painting with solid colors. Table AP-5 describes the different ink effects. You apply Paint ink effects, which are permanent, in the Paint window. Jean creates a bitmap with an ink effect to add to the space scene.

Steps

1. Double-click the **Space Scene** cast member in the Cast window
   The Paint window opens, displaying the Space Scene cast member.

2. Click the **starting Gradient Colors box**, click the **orange color box** at the beginning of the fifth row on the color palette, click the **ending Gradient Colors box**, then click the **yellow color box** at the end of the third row on the color palette

3. Click the **middle Gradient Colors box**, then click **Sun Burst**
   A pop-up menu appears with a list of different gradients. Notice that when you click Sun Burst, a check mark appears next to it.

4. Verify that the Pattern tool ▨ is solid, click the **No Line tool** ▨ on the Tool palette, then click the **Filled Ellipse tool** ◉ on the Tool palette
   A filled shape tool must be active in order for the Gradient ink effect to appear as an Ink option.

5. Click the **Ink list arrow** ▼, then click **Gradient**
   When you draw a filled shape, the currently selected gradient settings appear.

6. Press and hold [Shift], position + beneath the ellipse, then drag a **circle**, as shown in Figure C-13
   A filled circle with the previously selected gradient settings appears.

7. Click and hold the **Marquee tool** ▨, click **Lasso**, then drag a **selection rectangle** around the circle
   A circular selection marquee might flash around the circle.

8. Click the **Ink list arrow** ▼, click **Darkest**, then drag the **circle** over the ellipse, as shown in Figure C-14
   The circle and ellipse overlap. Notice that the pointer changes to ⌇ when you position the pointer in a blank area of the Paint window.

9. Click a **blank area** of the window (outside the selection), then click the **Close button** in the Paint window
   The Paint window closes and the cast member is saved in the Cast window.

FIGURE C-13: **Applying a gradient ink effect**

Gradient end color

Click middle Gradient
Colors box to display
pop-up menu

Gradient start color

Pattern tool

No Line tool

Gradient ink effect

FIGURE C-14: **Moving artwork**

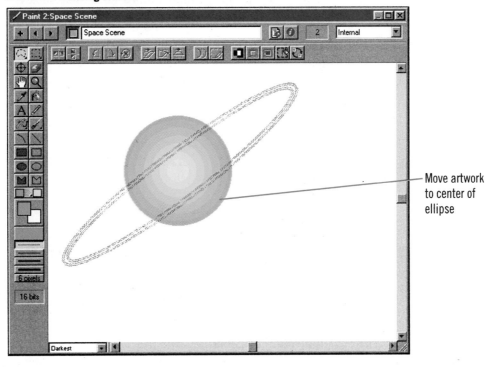

Move artwork
to center of
ellipse

Using patterns

Instead of using a solid fill color in a bitmap, you can use a pattern. A pattern consists of a small image that is repeated continuously to fill in a shape, such as a rectangle, ellipse, or polygon. The current foreground and background colors are the primary and secondary colors, respectively, in a multicolored pattern. To display a palette of patterns, click and hold the Pattern tool on the Tool palette. The pattern palette includes preset patterns, but you can also click Pattern Settings to add your own patterns. When you create your own pattern, the Pattern Settings dialog box displays an enlarged version of any pattern you select, then you can edit it.

Applying Painting Effects

The Paint window includes tools for applying painting effects to your artwork. The main painting tools are the Paint Bucket, Eyedropper, Brush, and Air Brush tools. You can use the Paint Bucket tool to fill all adjacent pixels of the same color with the foreground color. The Eyedropper tool is commonly used with the Paint Bucket tool; it selects a color from the artwork, which you can then use as the foreground, background, or destination color. You use the Brush tool to brush strokes with the current foreground color, ink, and fill pattern. The Brush tool displays a pop-up menu where you can define five different brush sizes and shapes. You use the Air Brush tool to spray the current foreground color, ink, and fill pattern. The longer you spray the Air Brush tool in one spot, the more it fills in the area. You define spray settings in the Air Brush pop-up menu, just as you do in the Brush tool pop-up menu. The spray settings include flow rate, spray area, dot size, and dot options. ✎ Jean applies some painting effects to the space scene.

Steps

1. **Double-click** the **Space Scene** cast member in the Cast window
   The Paint window opens, displaying the Space Scene cast member.

2. **Click and hold** the **Foreground Colors box**, then click the **black color box** at the beginning of the first row on the color palette

Trouble?

If the inside of the ring does not fill with black, click ✎ inside the ring in a blank area to fill the entire area black.

3. Click the **Paint Bucket tool** ✎ on the Tool palette, then click ✎ in a **blank area** of the Paint window
   When you click the mouse button, the Paint Bucket fills all adjacent pixels of the same color in the visible portion of the Paint window with the foreground color, black, as shown in Figure C-15. Since the ring bitmap is not white (the same color of the adjacent pixels), the inside of the ring remains the original background color until you click inside the ring.

4. **Click and hold** the **starting Gradient Colors box**, then click the **white color box** at the end of the second row on the color palette

5. **Click and hold** the **Brush button** ✎ on the Tool palette, then click **Brush 1**
   The Brush 1 settings are selected.

QuickTip

To quickly open the Brush Settings dialog box, double-click the Brush tool ✎.

6. **Click and hold** ✎ on the Tool palette, then click **Settings**
   The Brush Settings dialog box opens, as shown in Figure C-16.

7. Click the **smallest dot** in the lower-left corner, then click **OK**
   The new Brush 1 settings are saved.

8. Click **individual brush dots** in the Paint window, as shown in Figure C-17
   When you position the pointer in the Paint window, it changes to the shape and size of the brush. When you click in the Paint window, the brush shape paints with the foreground color.

9. Click the **Close button** in the Paint window

FIGURE C-15: Applying the Paint Bucket effect

Paint Bucket tool

Foreground color

Foreground color applied to background

FIGURE C-16: Brush Settings dialog box

Current brush size (yours might differ)

FIGURE C-17: Applying the Brush effect

Brush tool

Arrow indicates a pop-up menu is available

Brush tool used to create dots

Selecting colors with the Eyedropper tool

If you want to match the color of one or more pixels with another set of pixels, you can use the Eyedropper tool. This tool allows you to select a color currently in the Paint window as the foreground, background, or destination color. To select a color as the foreground, click on the Tool palette, position the bottom tip of over the color you want to select, then click in the Paint window. To use to select a background color, press [Shift], then click a color. To select a color as the destination color, press [Alt] (Win) or [Option] (Mac), then click a color. You can also press [D] to temporarily activate while using other paint tools. Once you select a color, you can use the Paint Bucket tool to fill an area of pixels to match colors.

Adding Text to a Bitmap

When the Paint window is open, you can add text to a bitmap. When you add text to a bitmap, the text becomes part of the bitmap and is difficult to edit. If you decide to change a word, font style, or text spacing, you must erase the original text and start over again. However, you can use effects in the Paint window to transform and change bitmapped text just as you would any other bitmap. You can flip, rotate, skew, and warp bitmapped text. Because bitmapped text is difficult to edit, carefully consider the text you want to include in your bitmaps. Jean adds copyright text to the space scene.

Steps 1234

1. **Double-click the Space Scene** cast member in the Cast window
   The Paint window opens, displaying the Space Scene cast member.

2. Click the **Text tool** A on the Tool palette in the Paint window

3. Click **Modify** on the menu bar, then click **Font**
   The Font dialog box opens, as shown in Figure C-18.

4. In the Font list, click **Arial** (scroll if necessary), click the **Size list arrow** ▼, click **10**, then click **OK**

> **QuickTip**
>
> You can also select a color by clicking the color box in the Font dialog box.

5. Click the **Foreground Color box**, click the **orange color box** at the beginning of the fifth row on the color palette

6. Click in the **lower-left corner** of the Paint window
   A small empty text box appears, displaying a blinking cursor. You can type and edit text in the text box in the same way as in a word-processing program.

> **QuickTip**
>
> To move the text box, drag any edge of the text box.

7. Type **Copyright, SpaceWorks Interactive**
   The text box expands as you type the text, as shown in Figure C-19. You can press [Enter] (Win) or [Return] (Mac) to start a new line. If you want to edit the text, you can press [Backspace] (Win) or [Delete] (Mac). Once you deselect the text box, you can no longer edit the text.

8. Click the **Marquee tool** ▦ to deselect the text box
   When you deselect the text box, the text becomes part of the bitmap.

9. Click the **Close button** in the Paint window, click the **Save button** 🖫, then click **File** on the menu bar, click **Exit** [Win] or **Quit** [Mac]
   The movie is saved and Director closes.

FIGURE C-18: Font dialog box

Font list

Your settings might be different

Current font style

Current font size

Current font color

Arial

FIGURE C-19: Adding text to a bitmap

Text tool

Current insertion point position

Text box

Creating a custom tile

A **tile** is a graphic that you can repeat in a pattern to create backgrounds, textures, or fillers. Custom tiles provide an effective way to create a background without using a lot of memory or increasing the download time for movies on the Web. A custom tile uses the same amount of memory no matter what size area it fills. You can create tiles from an existing cast member. To create a custom tile, display a bitmap cast member in the Paint window, click and hold the Pattern tool ▉, click Tile Settings, click an existing tile position to edit, click Cast Member, drag the dotted rectangle to the area of the cast member you want tiled, specify the size of the tile, then click OK. The new tile appears at the bottom of the Pattern palette. You can use the custom tile as a fill pattern. To select the custom tile as a fill pattern, click and hold ▉, then click the custom tile at the bottom of the Pattern palette. You can use one of the Filled drawing tools or the Paint Bucket tool ▉ to fill an area with the custom tile.

Practice

► Concepts Review

Label each of the elements of the screen shown in Figure C-20.

FIGURE C-20

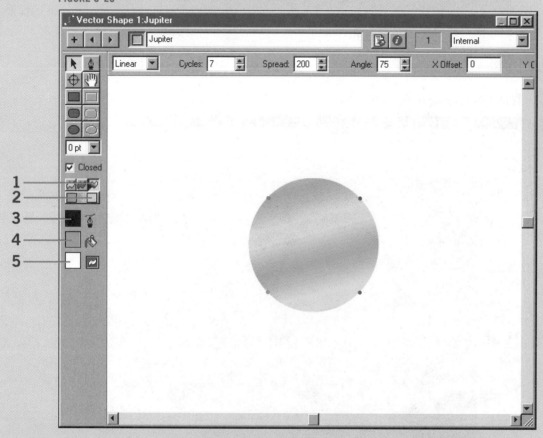

Match each of the terms with the statement that describes its function.

6. Vertices	**a.** The point used for animation
7. Handles	**b.** An individual point in a bitmap
8. Gradient	**c.** Determine the degree of curvature between points
9. Pixel	**d.** Fixed points on a vector shape
10. Registration Point	**e.** Shading from one color to another color
11. Anti-Aliasing	**f.** Blending the edges of a bitmap with background colors

Select the best answer from the following list of choices.

12. A graphic represented by pixels is called a:

    a. Bitmap.   **c.** QuickDraw shape.

    b. Vector shape.   **d.** PostScript shape.

13. A graphic represented by a mathematical description in Director is called a:

    a. Bitmap.   **c.** QuickDraw shape.

    b. Vector shape.   **d.** PostScript shape.

14. **Which is NOT a vector shape property?**
    a. Uses less memory
    b. Uses less storage space
    c. Requires less download time
    d. Resizes with distortion

15. **A shape in which the starting and ending points do not connect is called a(n):**
    a. Closed shape.
    b. Regular shape.
    c. Open shape.
    d. QuickDraw shape.

16. **Which value determines how many times a gradient repeats?**
    a. Spread
    b. Angle
    c. Cycle
    d. Range

17. **What color is the first point in a vector shape?**
    a. Red
    b. Green
    c. Blue
    d. None of the above

18. **Which selection tool allows you to change the shape of the selection?**
    a. Lasso only
    b. Marquee only
    c. Lasso and Marquee
    d. None of the above

▶ Skills Review

1. **Understand vector shapes and bitmaps.**
   a. Write down at least three properties of vector shapes and bitmaps, without referring to the unit material.

2. **Draw a vector shape.**
   a. Start Director, then open the file MD C-1 from the drive and folder where your Project Files are located, then save it as *SpaceWorks Graphics Final*.
   b. Open the Vector Shape window.
   c. Create a new cast member, if necessary.
   d. Draw a circle, then name the cast member *Sun*.
   e. Close the Vector Shape window.

3. **Add a gradient to a vector shape.**
   a. Open the Sun vector shape cast member, then add a gradient to the circle.
   b. Change the starting Gradient Colors box to a bright yellow.
   c. Change the ending Gradient Colors box to a bright red.
   d. Change the Gradient Type to Radial, then change the Gradient Cycle to 2.
   e. Change the Stroke Width to 0 pt.

4. **Edit a vector shape.**
   a. Create a new cast member.
   b. Change the Stroke Width to 4 pt.
   c. Draw a line and add a curve to it.
   d. Adjust a line to a longer length, then change the curvature of a line.
   e. Close the Vector Shape window.

5. **Use the Paint window.**
   a. Open the Paint window.
   b. Change the foreground color to brown.
   c. Change the Other Line Width to 4, then draw a long narrow ellipse.

   d. Select the ellipse shape and move it to the center of the window.

   e. Name the cast member *Planet Scene* and close the Paint window.

6. Flip, rotate, and apply effects.

   a. Open the Planet Scene in the Paint window.

   b. Change the perspective of the oval shape.

   c. Rotate the ellipse shape 45 degrees, then flip the ellipse shape horizontally.

   d. Move the ellipse shape to the lower-left corner of the window.

   e. Close the Paint window.

7. Apply ink effects.

   a. Open the Planet Scene in the Paint window, then change the line width to No Line.

   b. Change the ink effect to Blend.

   c. Draw a filled oval shape in a blank area of the window.

   d. Change the ink effect to Normal.

   e. Select the oval shape tightly, then move the oval shape inside the ellipse.

   f. Close the Paint window.

8. Apply painting effects.

   a. Open the Planet Scene in the Paint window, then change the foreground color to black.

   b. Fill the background of the Paint window with black.

   c. Change the brush setting to the second-smallest dot.

   d. Change the foreground color to white, then click individual dots in the window.

   e. Close the Paint window.

9. Add text to a bitmap.

   a. Open the Planet Scene in the Paint window, then select the Text tool.

   b. Verify that the font is Arial, that the font size is 10, and that the color is orange.

   c. Add your initials to the lower-right corner of the Paint window.

   d. Close the Paint window, then save the movie and close Director.

► Independent Challenges

1. You are the chief designer and owner of Unique Pools, a company that designs uniquely shaped swimming pools. The owner of Gourmet Jelly Beans asks you to design the corporate swimming pool in the form of a jelly bean. You use Director's Vector Shape tools to create the jelly bean shape and add a blue gradient to represent water.

   To complete this independent challenge:

   a. Start Director and save the movie as *Unique Pools* in the drive and folder where your Project Files are located.

   b. Open the Vector Shape window.

   c. Draw a large circle and change the curves to form a jelly bean.

   d. Add a blue gradient from left to right to represent water.

   e. Change the Stroke Width to 2 pt and the Stroke Color to dark blue.

   f. Name the cast member *Jelly Bean Pool*, and close the Vector Shape window.

   g. Create a text cast member with the text **Pool designed by Unique Pools**.

   h. Place both cast members on the Stage and add a color background.

   i. Print the Stage, save the movie, and exit Director.

2. You are a student at the State University. Your history professor gives you an assignment to create a multimedia presentation on your home state. You use Director's Vector Shape tools to create the shape of your state and add a gradient to represent the terrain.

To complete this independent challenge:

a. Start Director and save the movie as *US State* in the drive and folder where your Project Files are located.

b. Open the Vector Shape window.

c. Draw a free-form shape with lines and curves to represent any state in the U.S. (*Hint*: If you live in Colorado, Kansas, Nebraska, North Dakota, South Dakota, New Mexico, or Wyoming, try to pick another state.)

d. Modify the lines and curves to display the outline of the state.

e. Add a gradient that represents the terrain of the state.

f. Change the Stroke Width to 1 pt and the Stroke Color to black.

g. Name the cast member *US State*, and close the Vector Shape window.

h. Create a text cast member with the text **US State presentation by [Your Name]**.

i. Place both cast members on the Stage and add a color background.

j. Print the Stage, save the movie, and exit Director.

3. You are the chief designer at Borderlines, a company that designs signs and banners. The president of Garfield Graffiti Removal, Inc. asks you to design a company logo and a sign for the front of their company building. You use Director's Paint tools to create a sign with the company logo.

To complete this independent challenge:

a. Start Director and save the movie as *Borderlines* in the drive and folder where your Project Files are located.

b. Open the Paint window, then draw a large unfilled rectangle with a gray 2 pt border for the sign.

c. Add the text **Garfield Graffiti Removal, Inc.** to the sign, using the Text tool.

d. Add different color graffiti to the sign, using the Airbrush tool. (*Hint*: Do not cover the text with the Airbrush tool.)

e. Name the cast member *GGRI Logo*, and close the Paint window.

f. Create a text cast member with the text **GGRI Sign designed by Borderlines**.

g. Place both cast members on the Stage, then print the Stage, save the movie, and exit Director.

4. You are a graphics designer at Fifth Avenue Advertising & Design. The president of the New York City Olympic Committee asks you to create an Olympic logo for a multimedia presentation they are developing for the International Olympic Committee. You use Director's Paint tools to create the Olympic logo.

To complete this independent challenge:

a. Connect to the Internet and go to www.course.com. Navigate to the page for this book, click the link for the Student Online Companion, click the link for this Unit, then review past Olympic logos for ideas.

b. Start Director and save the movie as *NYC Olympics* in the drive and folder where your Project Files are located.

c. Open the Paint window, then draw the Olympic rings.

d. Add the text **New York** to the logo, using the Text tool.

e. Design the rest of the logo, using the Paint tools.

f. Name the cast member *NYCOC*, and close the Paint window.

g Create a text cast member with the text **New York Olympic Logo designed by Fifth Avenue Advertising & Design**.

h. Place both cast members on the Stage and add a color background.

i. Print the Stage, save the movie, and exit Director.

▶ Visual Workshop

Recreate the screen shown in Figure C-21. Print the screen. Save the file as *Letters* in the drive and folder where your Project Files are located. (For Windows, use the Windows Paint program. Press the Print Screen key to make a copy of the screen. Start the Paint program by clicking Start, pointing to Programs, pointing to Accessories, then clicking Paint. Click Edit on the menu bar, click Paste to paste the screen into Paint, then click Yes to paste the large image if necessary. Click File on the menu bar, click Print or OK in the dialog box, then exit Paint. For the Macintosh, use the SimpleText program. Hold and press the Command, Shift, and 3 keys to make a copy of the screen, double-click the document Picture 1 located on your hard drive, click File on the menu bar, click Print, then click Print in the dialog box. *Note*: When you create a new document with a copy of the screen, and a document Picture 1 already exists, the Macintosh names the new document Picture 2.)

FIGURE C-21

Managing
and Modifying Cast Members

Objectives

► **Create a Cast**
► **Use the Cast window**
► **Organize cast members**
► **Find cast members**
► **Change cast member properties**
► **Transform a paint cast member**
► **Add and edit a text cast member**
► **Modify a text cast member**
► **Save and unlink a Cast**

A complex Director movie can often require a large number of cast members. When you assemble a large number of cast members in a Cast window, it can sometimes be difficult to locate the one you want. You can use management and organization tools in Director to help alleviate the hassle of scrolling through a long list of cast members. This unit introduces you to basic skills for managing, organizing, and modifying cast members. First, you'll learn how to create a new Cast. Then you'll learn how to change Cast preferences, organize and find cast members, change cast member properties, and modify cast members. Finally, you'll learn how to save and unlink a Cast. ✐ After creating graphical cast members in Director, Jean wants to organize them with other imported cast members in an External Cast for use in an upcoming movie.

Creating a Cast

In Director, your movies literally can have a Cast of thousands—you can include up to 32,000 cast members in a Cast window. Before you create and assemble a large number of cast members for a movie, it is important to think about how you want to organize them. Director allows you to create and work with multiple Casts within a movie. If you notice that you use certain media elements repeatedly, you can organize them into separate Casts. Separating them saves the time and inconvenience of importing them individually for each movie. Each Cast has its own window. When you create a new Cast, you need to decide whether to create an **Internal Cast**, which is saved as part of the movie, or an **External Cast**, which is saved in a separate file outside of the movie. When you use cast members from an External Cast, it's easiest if you first link the Cast to the movie. However, even if you don't link an External Cast to the movie, you can still open the External Cast and add, remove, and modify cast members. If you plan to use cast members in one movie only, then use an Internal Cast. If you plan to share cast members in more than one movie, then use an External Cast. You can add as many Internal or External Casts as you want; each Cast is viewed in a separate Cast window. ✒ Jean creates an external cast so she can organize and reuse cast members for several upcoming movies.

Steps

1. Start **Director**, open the file **MD D-1** from the drive and folder where your Project Files are located, then save it as **SpaceWorks Game Promo**
   Director opens, displaying the movie. Initial settings in Director can vary, depending on previous usage.

2. Position ↖ on the lower-right corner of the **Stage window**, then drag the **border** diagonally to the right to expand the window to display the gray area around the Stage

3. Click the **Close button** in the Score window, click **Window** on the menu bar, then click **Cast**, if necessary, to display the Internal Cast window

4. Click and hold the **Choose Cast button** 🎞 in the Internal Cast window
   A pop-up menu appears, displaying a list of current Casts and the New Cast command.

QuickTip

You can also click File on the menu bar, point to New, then click Cast to open the New Cast dialog box.

5. On the pop-up menu, click **New Cast**
   The New Cast dialog box opens.

6. In the Name box, type **Space Graphics**

7. Click the **External option button**
   The Use in Current Movie option becomes available and is selected, as shown in Figure D-1. This option links the new External Cast to the current movie.

QuickTip

To open an unlinked External Cast to the current movie, click File on the menu bar, click Open, select an external cast file, then click Open.

8. Click **Create**
   The new blank Cast window opens. When you link an External Cast to the current movie, Director opens that Cast whenever you open the movie.

9. Drag the **title bar** of the Space Graphics Cast window to the blank area below the Stage
   The Space Graphics Cast window appears in the Director window, as shown in Figure D-2.

FIGURE D-1 **New Cast dialog box**

Name of new
External Cast

When selected, the
Cast is linked to
the current movie

FIGURE D-2 **New External Cast window**

Internal Cast
window

External Cast
window

CLUES TO USE

Techniques for organizing cast members

Organizing your cast members from the beginning will
ensure that both your movie-making process and your
movie will run smoothly. You can use several techniques
to organize and manage cast members: (1) name each
cast member with a unique identifier, (2) group similar
cast members together, and (3) create multiple Casts,
either Internal or External. It is important to name each
cast member. Lingo, Director's programming language,
identifies cast members in scripts by their name. The
naming convention should identify the media element's
function or purpose. Appropriate cast member names
could be Help button, Space background, Blue Earth

graphic, or Welcome text, instead of simply Button,
Graphic, Text, or no name at all. Another technique is to
group similar cast members together. You can move cast
members around to any location in the Cast window;
they are not required to be in consecutive order. You can
leave a few blank cast member windows in between each
group, to visually separate each section of the cast.
Finally, you can create multiple Cast windows that
contain cast members by type, such as buttons and
navigation, text, pictures, sounds, videos, transitions
and effects, and behaviors and scripts.

Using the Cast Window

The Cast window allows you to view and organize all of the media elements in a movie, move one cast member or groups of cast members around in a Cast, sort cast members by type, and use paint and text tools on cast members. In the Cast window, you can view the Cast in List view or Thumbnail view. You can use the Cast View Style button in the Cast window to easily toggle between List and Thumbnail views. You can use Cast window preferences to control the appearance of the current or all Cast windows. You can also open the Property Inspector to view and modify cast member properties. Jean changes the Cast window view and preferences to make it easier to organize the cast members.

Steps

1. Click the **title bar** of the Space Graphics Cast window, if necessary

The Space Graphics Cast window is active. When you import graphics, Director places them in the active Cast window.

2. Click the **Import button** 🔲 on the toolbar, go to the drive and folder where your Project Files are located, then double-click the **Media folder**

The Import Files dialog box opens, displaying a list of the files in the Media folder.

Trouble?

If the Image Options dialog box or Select Format dialog box appears, use the selected settings, click the Same Settings for Remaining Images check box (if available) to select it, then click OK as necessary.

3. Click **Add All**, click **Import**, then click **OK** to accept the selected graphic settings for each of the remaining images and files

All the files in the file list appear in the Space Graphics Cast window, identified by their location number, name, and type.

4. Click the **Cast View Style button** 📧 in the Cast window, if necessary, to display the Space Graphics Cast window in List view

The Space Graphics Cast window appears in List view. Table D-1 describes the display features of List view.

5. Position ↕ over the bottom-right corner of the Space Graphics Cast window, then drag ↖ to resize the window, as shown in Figure D-3

The Space Graphics Cast window is resized.

QuickTip

You can also open the Cast Window Preferences dialog box by right-clicking a cast member (Win), or pressing and holding [Option] and clicking a cast member (Mac), then clicking Cast Preferences.

6. Verify that the Space Graphics Cast window is active, click **File** on the menu bar, point to **Preferences**, then click **Cast**

The Cast Window Preferences for "Space Graphics" dialog box opens, as shown in Figure D-4. The title bar of the dialog box displays the names of the Cast window preferences that you can change.

7. Click the **Size check box** to select it, then click the **Apply to All Casts** check box to clear it, if necessary

The options you check in the List Columns area appear as new columns in List view.

8. Click the **Label list arrow** ▾, then click **Number:Name**

The number and name of the cast member appear below the thumbnail in Thumbnail view.

QuickTip

To make your preferences settings the default settings, click Save as Default. To apply your preferences to all Cast windows, click the Apply to All Casts check box to select it.

9. Click **OK**

The Space Graphics Cast window appears with the Size column added to the list. These settings are only set for the Space Graphics Cast window. The Internal Cast window remains the same.

FIGURE D-3: External Cast window in List view

Click button to switch Cast views

Cast member type

External Cast window in List view

Resize the window to here

FIGURE D-4: Cast Window Preferences dialog box

Click check box to change all Cast windows

Click button to set preferences as default

List view options

Thumbnail options

TABLE D-1: List view display features

column title	description	column title	description
Name	Name of the cast member and an icon describing its type	Comments	Comments field in the Member tab of the Property Inspector
#	Number assigned to the cast member	Size	Size in bytes, kilobytes, or megabytes
×	Cast member changes need to be saved	Created	Date and time the cast member was created
Script	Script type: *Member* means the cast member is a script; *Movie* means the cast member is a movie script; *Behavior* means the cast member is a behavior	Modified By	Name of the person who modified the cast member
Type	Cast member type	Filename	Full path to the cast member if it is a linked asset
Modified	Date and time the cast member was changed		

Director 8

Organizing Cast Members

Director allows you to move, copy, delete, and sort cast members. However, before you perform some of these organizational functions, you need to first select the cast members in the Cast window. You can easily move or copy a cast member in the same Cast window or to another one. You might want to create copies of a cast member with minor differences, such as color or position, to create an animation effect. Sometimes you will import or create cast members but not use them in the movie. You can delete them at any time. When you delete a cast member, it is removed from the movie, even if it is being used on the Stage and in the Score. You can use the Sort command to arrange cast members by their media type, name, size, or usage in the Score. You can also use the Sort command to remove empty locations in a Cast window. ✐ Jean organizes cast members in the external Space Graphics Cast window.

Steps

QuickTip

To resize the columns in List view, position ↔ over the column title border, then drag the column to the desired size.

1. In the Space Graphics Cast window, click the **Name column title** (Win)
   List view is sorted in descending order by the name of the cast members, as shown in Figure D-5. You can click the column titles in List view to easily toggle between ascending and descending sort order. When you click a column title, List view changes the display of the cast member information, but it doesn't change their physical location in the Cast.

2. Click the **Cast View Style button** 🗎 on the Space Graphics Cast window to display the Cast window in Thumbnail view, then click the **Cast View Style button** 🗎 on the Internal Cast window to display it in Thumbnail view, if necessary
   The cast members appear in Thumbnail view, displaying the cast member number, name, and type.

3. Click the **Jupiter cast member** in the Internal Cast window, press and hold [Shift], then click the **Space Scene cast member** to its right
   Both cast members are selected.

4. Click the **Copy button** 🖺 on the toolbar, click the empty **cast member 11** in the Space Graphics Cast window, then click the **Paste button** 🖺 on the toolbar
   The copied cast members appear in locations 11 and 12. Notice that the copied cast members retain the exact same name as the originals.

Trouble?

If you drag a cast member to a location that already contains a cast member, the selected cast member will move where you place it, and the existing one will move one location to the right.

5. Drag the **Space Background cast member** in the Space Graphics Cast window to empty **cast member 23**, then drag the **cast members** to the locations shown in Figure D-6
   When you drag a cast member in Thumbnail view, the pointer changes to 🖑, and a highlight bar appears in the new location. When you move a cast member to a new location, Director assigns it a new location number and updates all references to the cast member in the Score, but it does not update references to the cast member number in Lingo scripts.

QuickTip

Make sure the cast member Name box is not highlighted when you delete the cast member.

6. Click the **orange Jupiter cast member** in the Space Graphics Cast window, then press [Delete] or [Backspace]
   The cast member is deleted.

7. Click the **4 Planets cast member** in Space Graphics Cast window, press and hold [Shift], then click the **Uranus cast member** to select all of the cast members in the first row

8. Click **Modify** on the menu bar, then click **Sort**
   The Sort dialog box opens.

9. Click the **Name option button**, then click **Sort**
   The cast members in the first row of the Space Graphics Cast window are sorted by name, as shown in Figure D-7. Notice that when you sort the cast, any empty cast members are removed.

FIGURE D-5: **Sorting columns in List view**

Column titles ————

Click column title
to sort list

Drag border
to resize
columns

FIGURE D-6: **External Cast window in Thumbnail view**

Click button to
switch views

Thumbnail view
displays cast
member number,
name, and type

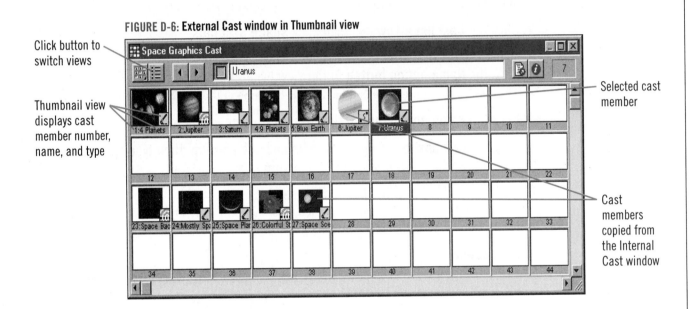

Selected cast
member

Cast
members
copied from
the Internal
Cast window

FIGURE D-7: **Sorting cast members**

Cast members
sorted by name

Finding Cast Members

Director 8

If your movie contains several cast members, it may be difficult to locate a particular one. You can use the Find feature to locate cast members by name, type, color palette, or usage in the Score, and then select them in the Cast window. When you name your cast members logically, you make it easy to find them. You can find multiple cast members with similar names. For example, cast members with the names Space Background and Space Scene share the common word "space". When you search, Director finds all the cast members with the common word at the beginning of the name. Once Director completes the word search, you can specify which cast members to select in the Cast window. ▟▬▬▬ Jean wants to find all the cast members that begin with the word "space".

Steps

1. Click **Edit** on the menu bar, point to **Find**, then click **Cast Member**
   The Find Cast Members dialog box opens, as shown in Figure D-8. The list of cast members at the bottom of the dialog box displays all the cast members in both Casts.

2. Click the **Cast list arrow** ▼, then click **Space Graphics**
   The search criteria are narrowed down to cast members in the Space Graphics Cast window.

3. Click the **Name option button** in the View by: area
   The cast members are sorted alphabetically by name in the list of cast members

QuickTip

You can also select the option button by clicking the text box and typing your criteria.

4. Click the **Name option button** that has an accompanying text box

5. Click the **text box** to the right of the Name option button, then type **space**
   All cast member names that start with the word "space" appear in the list of cast members.

6. Click **Space Planet** in the list of cast members
   The Space Planet cast member is selected, as shown in Figure D-9. You can specify whether to select one or all of the cast members in the Cast window.

7. Click **Select**
   The Find Cast Member dialog box closes, and the Space Planet cast member is selected in the Space Graphics Cast window.

FIGURE D-8: Find Cast Member dialog box

Click options to find cast members

Click list arrow to change Casts

FIGURE D-9: Finding and selecting cast members

Find criteria

Find results

Click button to select only the highlighted cast member in the list

Click button to select all the cast members in the list

Finding and deleting unused cast members

Sometimes you will import or create a cast member that you don't end up using in the movie. Director makes it easy to find and delete unused cast members. When you delete unused cast members, your movie's file size becomes smaller, faster to load, and more efficient in using computer memory. Before you close your finished movie, it's important to remove unused cast members. To delete unused cast members, click Edit on the menu bar, point to Find, then click Cast Member. In the Find Cast Member dialog box, click the Cast list arrow, click a Cast with unused cast members, click the Usage option button, click in the cast member list, then click Select All. Director finds and selects all cast members not used in the Score from the selected Cast. Before you complete the deletion, make sure that the selected cast members are not used in any Lingo scripts, which do not appear in the Score. To view a Lingo script for a selected cast member, click the Cast Member Script button 🖼 in the Cast window. To delete the selected cast members, click Select or Select All in the Find Cast Member dialog box, then press [Delete] or [Backspace], or click Edit on the menu bar, then click Clear Cast Members.

Director 8

Changing Cast Member Properties

You can view and change cast member properties for one or more cast members. If you select multiple cast members with different types, the information common to all of the selected cast members appears. When you view cast member properties, a tab labeled with the cast member's type appears in the Property Inspector. For example, if you click the Blue Earth cast member in the Cast window, the Bitmap tab in the Property Inspector appears. The property information available depends on the type of the selected cast member. You can also use cast member properties to manage memory usage in a movie. If Director determines that memory is running low while you play a movie, it unloads some cast members from memory so that other ones can be loaded. If you are about to perform a memory-intensive operation, you can use the Memory Inspector to monitor usage and purge all removable items from memory. ✎——— Jean views cast member properties for a bitmap and changes a memory-related setting.

Steps 1234

1. Verify that the Space Planet cast member is selected in the Space Graphics Cast window

2. Click the **Cast Member Properties button** 🔘 in the Space Graphics Cast window
   The Bitmap tab appears in the Property Inspector, as shown in Figure D-10. The Bitmap tab displays options for selecting a color palette, highlighting a bitmap, such as a button, when you click it, dithering a bitmap (color matching), trimming white space around a bitmap, setting bitmap quality, and selecting Alpha settings (the transparent area of a bitmap). The Bitmap tab also displays the dimension and color depth of the cast member.

3. Click the **Dither check box** to select it
   When a color is not available due to a color palette problem, the Dither option estimates the color by combining the pixel pattern.

4. Click the **Member tab** in the Property Inspector
   The Member tab appears in the Property Inspector. The Member tab displays text boxes for changing the cast member's name, adding a comment that appears in the Comments column of the Cast window in List view, and selecting an unload value. The **unload value** determines which cast members stay in memory and which ones are removed when the movie plays. The Member tab also displays the size of the cast member, the date when the cast member was created and modified, and the name of the person who modified it.

5. Click the **Cast tab** in the Property Inspector
   The Cast tab appears in the Property Inspector, as shown in Figure D-11. The Cast tab displays text boxes, including boxes that change the cast member's name and link to an External Cast window, and boxes that select a preload value. The **preload value** determines when cast members are loaded into memory as the movie plays.

6. Click the **Preload list arrow** 🔽, then click **After Frame One**
   The After Frame One setting loads the cast members for the first frame as quickly as possible and then loads other cast members in the order in which they are used in the Score, up to the limit of available memory. Table D-2 describes the preload values.

7. Click **Window** on the menu bar, point to **Inspectors**, then click **Memory**
   The Memory Inspector opens, as shown in Figure D-12. The Memory Inspector displays information about how much memory is available to Director for your movie and indicates how much memory different parts of the current movie use and the total disk space the movie occupies. Notice how much space is allocated in the Total Used area.

8. Click **Purge**, then click the **Close button** on the title bar
   The Memory Inspector purges all removable items from memory.

9. Click the **Bitmap tab** in the Property Inspector

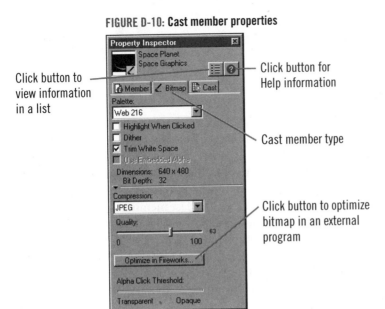

FIGURE D-10: Cast member properties

Click button to view information in a list

Click button for Help information

Cast member type

Click button to optimize bitmap in an external program

FIGURE D-11: Cast properties

Click list arrow to set memory loading order

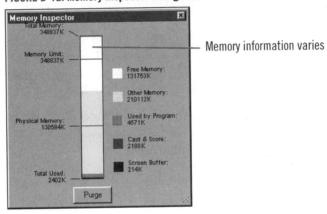

FIGURE D-12: Memory Inspector dialog box

Memory information varies

TABLE D-2: Preload values

preload value	description
When Needed	Loads each cast member into memory when it is needed by the movie
After Frame One	Loads all cast members, except those required for frame 1, when the movie exits frame 1
Before Frame One	Loads all cast members before the movie plays frame 1

CLUES TO USE

Setting cast member priorities in memory

Director loads and unloads cast members in order to keep the movie playing as smoothly as possible. When memory is limited on the playback computer, the priority setting for loading and unloading cast members becomes crucial to the movie's performance. You can set unload values to determine which cast members stay in memory and which ones are removed. To set a cast member's priority in memory, click a cast member in a Cast window, click Modify on the menu bar, point to Cast Member, click Properties, click the Member tab in the Property Inspector, click the Unload list arrow, then click an unload value. The unload value ranges from 0 to 3, where 0 means to never remove this cast member from memory, and 3 means to unload this cast member from memory first (before cast members that have a 2 or 1 value assigned to them). You should assign heavily used cast members, such as a background, a 0 value, moderately used cast members a 2 or 1 value, and sparingly used cast members a 3 value.

Director 8

Transforming a Paint Cast Member

Sometimes, after you import a bitmap into a Cast, you may need to resize it or change its color settings to match the movie. You can use the Transform Bitmap command to change the size, color depth, and palette of selected cast members. You cannot undo the changes you make to a cast member after using the Transform Bitmap command. Make sure you have a duplicate of the original cast member before making any changes. You can change the physical dimensions of a cast member by setting the Scale value as a percentage of the cast member's current size or by entering width and height values in pixels. The color depth option allows you to reset the number of colors used in the cast member, while the palette option allows you to assign a new color palette to the cast member. When you change to a new palette, you can choose the method with which to match current colors with the ones in the new palette. You can either remap or dither the colors. **Remapping** replaces the original colors in the bitmap with the most similar solid colors in the new palette. This is the preferred option in most cases. **Dithering** blends the colors in the new palette to approximate the original colors in the bitmap. ✒ Jean wants to resize a bitmap cast member to fit on the Stage. The Stage is set to 320 × 240 pixels.

1. Verify that the Space Planet cast member is selected in the Space Graphics Cast window

2. Click **Modify** on the menu bar, then click **Transform Bitmap**

Trouble?

If you click Launch External Editor, an imaging program, such as Fireworks opens, in which you can modify the bitmap.

3. If a dialog box opens, asking you to launch an external editor, click **Continue**
   The Transform Bitmap dialog box opens, as shown in Figure D-13. The original size of the bitmap is 640 × 480 pixels.

4. Click the **Maintain Proportions check box** to clear it
   When you clear this option, it allows you to enter specific measurements in the Width and Height boxes.

5. Double-click the **Width box**, type **320**, press [Tab], then type **240** in the Height box

6. Click **Transform**
   A confirmation dialog box opens, asking if you want to transform the bitmap. You cannot undo the change.

7. Click **OK**
   The dimensions of the bitmap change from 640 × 480 pixels to 320 × 240 pixels in the Bitmap tab of the Property Inspector.

8. Drag the **Space Planet cast member** on the Stage, click the **cast member** on the Stage, then press the **Arrows keys** to reposition the cast member in the center of the Stage
   When you drag a cast member to the Stage, the pointer changes to 🖑.

9. Click the **gray area** around the Stage to deselect the cast member, then click the **Space Planet cast member** in the Space Graphics Cast window
   The bitmapped cast member appears on the Stage, as shown in Figure D-14.

FIGURE D-13: Transform Bitmap dialog box

Sizing options

Your color options might be different

FIGURE D-14: Sizing a bitmapped cast member

Resized bitmapped cast member

Dimensions of the bitmapped cast member

Bitmapped cast member

Converting text to a bitmap

You can use the Convert to Bitmap command to change a text or field cast member to a bitmap. This command works only with text and field cast members; you cannot convert a shape to a bitmap. To convert text to a bitmap, select the text cast member, click Modify on the menu bar, then click Convert to Bitmap. The cast member type changes from text to bitmap. Once you convert a cast member to a bitmap, you cannot undo the change. Make sure you have a duplicate of the original cast member before making the change. You can modify the converted bitmap in the Paint window to create special effects, such as gradients, textures, and fills, and manipulate the bitmapped text with warp, flip, and rotate commands.

Adding and Editing a Text Cast Member

Director provides several ways to create text cast members. You can add and edit text directly on the Stage using the Text tool or the Field tool, and format it using the Text Inspector. If you prefer a separate window in which to work, you can also use the Text window or the Field window. The text you create using the Text tool or Text window is called **regular text**, while the text you create using the Field tool or Field window is called **field text**. Regular text looks good at large sizes because you can use anti-aliasing, which smoothes the jagged edges and curves of text. Field text works best for short passages of small-sized text. Field text allows you to save space and use less memory. The Text Inspector allows you to modify both regular text and field text. You can use the Text Inspector to change text formatting on the Stage without having to move to the Cast window and open the text in the Text or Field windows. ▰▰▰▰ Jean adds regular and field text directly on the Stage.

Steps 1 2 3 4

1. Click **cast member 3** in the Internal Cast window, click the **Text tool** ☒ on the Tool palette, position ＋ in the upper-left side of the Stage, then drag ＋ to the right side of the Stage

   As you drag ＋ to create a text box, a sprite overlay panel appears on the Stage. When you release the mouse button, a text box appears with an insertion point, and a slanted-line selection box surrounds the text box. You can edit the text in the text box.

Trouble?

To select the correct Foreground and Background colors, click the Foreground Color box on the Tool palette, click the white color box in the color palette, click the Background Color box on the Tool palette, then click the black color box on the color palette.

2. Verify that the Foreground Color box is white and that the Background Color box is black, then type **discover the universe beyond your world**

   Director might pause as it wraps the text to the next line. The text appears on the Stage, as shown in Figure D-15.

3. Click the **gray area** around the Stage to deselect the text box, position the pointer over **any word** in the text box, then click the text

   A selection text box with double borders appears. The double-border selection box indicates that the entire text box is selected. Any formatting changes are applied to all the text in the text box.

QuickTip

To edit text in a text box, double-click the text box. A slanted-line selection box appears around the text box.

4. Click **Window** on the menu bar, point to **Inspectors**, then click **Text**

   The Text Inspector opens, as shown in Figure D-16.

5. Click the **Align Center button** ☰ on the Text Inspector, click the **Font list arrow** ▾, click **Arial Black**, click the **Size list arrow** ▾, then click **18**, if necessary

6. Drag the right-middle sizing handle and **center** the text box to match Figure D-17

   When you position ↖ over a sizing handle, the pointer changes to black (Win) or white (Mac). The text box appears on the Stage.

7. Click the **Field tool** ☒ on the Tool palette, position ＋ in the lower-left side of the Stage, then drag ＋ to the right side of the Stage

   As you drag to create a field text box, a sprite overlay panel appears on the Stage. When you release the mouse button, a field text box appears with a slanted-line selection box surrounding the text box and an insertion point in the text box.

8. Click ☰ on the Text Inspector, click the **Font list arrow** ▾, click **Arial**, click the **Size list arrow** ▾, then click **12**, if necessary

9. Type **www.spaceworksgames.com**, drag the edge of the slanted-line selection box to center the text, then click the **gray area** around the Stage to deselect the field text box

   The field text appears on the Stage.

Your font attributes might be different

Text box

Slanted-line selection box

FIGURE D-16: Text Inspector

Formatting and spacing options

Enter Web address to create a hyperlink

FIGURE D-17: Formatting a text cast member on the Stage

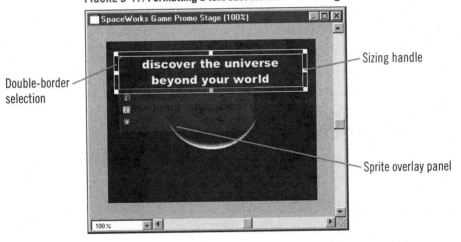

Sizing handle

Double-border selection

Sprite overlay panel

CLUES TO USE

Creating a hyperlink

You can turn any part of a text cast member into a hyperlink. Director adds standard hyperlink formatting to the selected text so that it initially appears underlined in blue and then becomes purple after a user clicks the hyperlink. To make the hyperlink actually connect to a Web site address or jump to a location, you need to write an *on hyperlinkClicked* event handler in Lingo. For more information about the Lingo event handler, see Director 8 Help. You cannot create a hyperlink bitmapped text and field text. To create a hyperlink, select the text you want to make into a link, click

Window on the menu bar, point to Inspectors, then click Text. In the hyperlink box, type the Web address or other text you want to send on the *on hyperlinkClicked* handler, then press [Enter] (Win) or [Return] (Mac). Director styles the text as a hyperlink. If the text is not styled as a hyperlink, click the Text tab on the Property Inspector, then click the Use Hypertext Style check box. This makes the hyperlink appear as it does in a Web browser, initially appearing with a blue underline, and then switching to red once the link has been visited.

Director 8

Modifying a Text Cast Member

In the Text window, you can change the alignment, indentation, tabs, and spacing for each paragraph in a text cast member. The ruler in the Text window contains controls for indentation and tabs. You can change the indentation from the right or left margins (or both), or you can indent just the first line of text and leave the remaining lines aligned with the left margin. **Indent markers** on the ruler show the indent settings for the paragraph that contains the insertion point in the Text window. Dragging the **Left Indent marker** indents the entire text, dragging the **First Line Indent marker** indents only the first line of the text, and dragging the **Right Indent marker** indents the text from the right margin. Since field text is limited, you can't change indentation and tabs in the Field window. Line spacing controls the vertical spacing between lines of text. **Kerning** is a specialized form of spacing between certain parts of characters. Kerning improves the appearance of text in large sizes but does very little to improve small text. You can change kerning for an entire text cast member or for individual text. When you kern individual text, you can refine letter spacing without affecting the kerning for an entire text cast member. ◀━━━ Jean modifies the spacing and alignment of a text cast member.

Steps

1. Double-click the **"discover the universe beyond your world"** text on the Stage, then select all the text in the text box (Mac)
   A slanted-line selection box surrounds the selected text.

2. Click the **Line Spacing up arrow** or **down arrow** on the Text Inspector until it reaches **28**
   The spacing between the lines increases. If you want to use kerning, you must use regular text; it doesn't work in field text or bitmapped text.

3. Click the **Kerning up arrow** or **down arrow** on the Text Inspector until it reaches **2**
   The spacing between the letters increases, as shown in Figure D-18. You can't change margins using the Text Inspector. You need to open the text cast member in the Text window to change the margins or text alignment.

4. Click the **Close button** in the Text Inspector

5. Double-click **cast member 3** in the Internal Cast window
   The Text window opens with the text.

6. Drag the **Left Indent marker** ▣ to **1"** on the ruler
   The left margin for the text starts at 1", as shown in Figure D-19. The size of the text box doesn't change.

7. Drag the **First Line Indent marker** ▽ to **0"** on the ruler
   The first-line left margin starts at 0", while the margin for the remaining lines starts at 1". This is called a **hanging indent**.

8. Drag the **Hanging Indent marker** △ to the position on the ruler to match Figure D-20

9. Click the **Cast Member Name text box**, type **Discover Universe Text**, then click the **Close button** in the Text window
   The Text window closes and the cast member is updated on the Stage and saved in the Cast window.

QuickTip

To control kerning for a text cast member, select a text cast member, click Modify on the menu bar, point to Cast Member, click Properties, click the Kerning list arrow, then select a kerning option.

Trouble?

If the text doesn't appear as shown in Figure D-20, adjust the Hanging Indent marker to match the figure.

FIGURE D-18: Changing line spacing and kerning

Click arrows to change line spacing

Click arrows to change kerning

FIGURE D-19: Dragging Left Indent marker

First Line Indent marker

Hanging Indent marker

Left Indent marker

Right Indent marker

FIGURE D-20: Dragging Hanging Indent marker

Drag the Hanging Indent marker here

Hanging indent

CLUES TO USE

Customizing text alignment using tabs

Numerical information is often easier to read when you align the text with tabs. A **tab** is used to position text at a specific location in the Text window. You can use tabs rather than the Spacebar to vertically align your text because tabs are more accurate, faster, and easier to change. When you press [Tab], the insertion point moves to the next tab stop. A **tab stop** is a predefined position in the text to which you can align tabbed text. By default, tab stops are located every ½"

from the left margin, but you can also create and modify tab stops. You can click the tab indicator on the left side of the ruler to select the type of tab you want. The tab indicator ⌐ aligns text to the left, ⌐ aligns text to the right, ⌐ aligns text to the center, and ⌐ aligns numbers to the decimal point. After you select the type of tab you want, click the position on the ruler where you want to place the tab.

Unit D

Director 8

Saving and Unlinking a Cast

You can use the Save button on the toolbar to save a movie, save an External Cast, or save both. When you select the Stage window before you save, Director saves the movie and all linked Cast windows; when you select an unlinked External Cast window, Director saves just the External Cast. Before you can use external cast members in a movie, you need to link the External Cast to the movie. After you link an External Cast to the current movie, Director opens that Cast whenever you open the movie. When you unlink an External Cast from a movie, the Cast is not available the next time you open the movie unless you open the Cast and relink it. When you make changes to an External Cast that is not linked to your movie, you need to save the External Cast. Director doesn't save changes to an External Cast when you save the movie, because the External Cast is not recognized as being part of the movie file. When you want to save an unlinked External Cast, you can select the External Cast window and use the Save button on the toolbar. Once you save an unlinked External Cast, you can use the Save All button on the toolbar to save the unlinked External Cast and the current movie. Remember to include the External Cast file when you distribute and package a movie. ✈ Jean saves the External Cast and the movie.

Steps 1 2 3 4

QuickTip

To save an External Cast with a new name, click the Cast window, click File on the menu bar, then click Save As.

1. Click the **title bar** in the Space Graphics Cast window, then click the **Save button** 🖫 on the toolbar
   The Save Cast "Space Graphics" dialog box opens.

2. Navigate to the drive and folder where your Project Files are located, then click **Save**
   The Space Graphics cast and the SpaceWorks Game Promo are saved. The External Cast file is saved with a .cst extension (Win).

3. Click **Modify** on the menu bar, point to **Movie**, then click **Casts**
   The Movie Casts dialog box opens, as shown in Figure D-21.

4. Click **Space Graphics** in the text box, then click **Remove**

QuickTip

To link an External Cast to the current movie, click Modify on the menu bar, point to Movie, click Casts, click Link, double-click the External Cast file, then click OK.

5. Click **OK**
   Since a cast member in the Space Graphics cast is used in the movie, a warning dialog box opens, asking if you want to remove the Cast and remove the cast member from the movie.

6. Click **Cancel**
   The Space Graphics Cast remains linked to the movie. Figure D-22 shows the Director window. The next time you open this movie, Director looks in the specified path in Cast Properties and opens the Cast.

QuickTip

To open a linked Cast, click Window on the menu bar, point to Cast, then click a Cast name.

7. Click the **Close button** in the Space Graphics Cast window
   The Space Graphics Cast window closes. The Cast window is still linked to the movie—it's just not open.

8. Click the **Score Window button** 🖿 on the toolbar
   The Score window opens.

9. Click **File** on the Menu bar, click **Exit** (Win) or **Quit** (Mac) then if asked to save your work, click **Yes** (Win) or **Save** (Mac)
   Director closes.

FIGURE D-21: Movie Casts dialog box

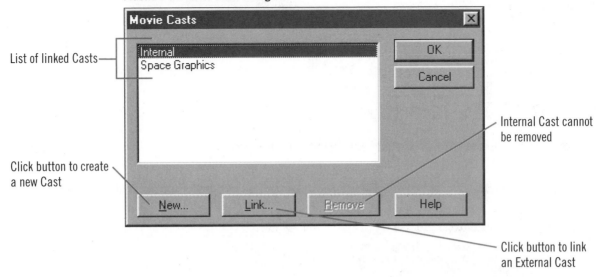

List of linked Casts

Internal Cast cannot be removed

Click button to create a new Cast

Click button to link an External Cast

FIGURE D-22: Director window with linked External Cast

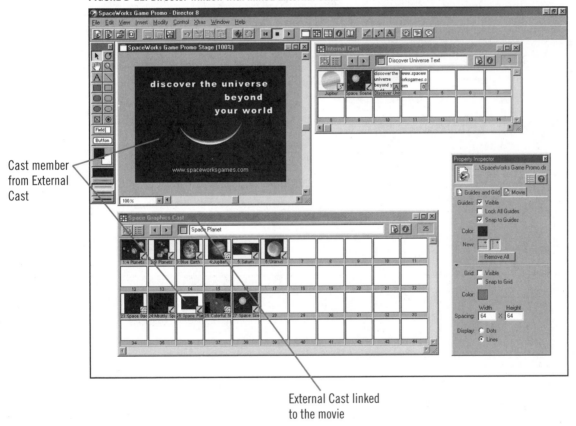

Cast member from External Cast

External Cast linked to the movie

Creating a cast library

If you save an unlinked External Cast in the Libs folder in the Director folder, you create a cast library. A **cast library** is a special type of unlinked external cast. When you drag a cast member from an External Cast library to the Stage or Score, Director copies the cast member to one of the movie's Internal Casts. Libraries are useful for storing any type of commonly used cast members, especially behaviors. Unlike an External Cast, a library cannot be linked to a movie.

Director 8

► Concepts Review

Label each of the elements of the screen shown in Figure D-23.

FIGURE D-23

Match each of the terms with the statement that describes its function.

6. **Regular**

7. **Unload**

8. **Dither**

9. **Preload**

10. **Field**

11. **Remap**

a. Determines which cast members stay in memory

b. A type of text that uses less memory

c. Replaces original color with similar colors in another palette

d. Determines when cast members are loaded into memory

e. Blends colors in a palette to approximate the original colors

f. A type of text that uses anti-aliasing

Select the best answer from the following list of choices.

12. **How many Casts can be added to a movie?**
    a. 32,000
    b. 1,000
    c. 5,000
    d. Unlimited

13. **An External Cast is:**
    a. Saved as part of the movie.
    b. Saved as a separate file.
    c. Always linked to a movie.
    d. None of the above

14. **An Internal Cast is:**
    a. Saved as part of the movie.
    b. Saved as a separate file.
    c. Always unlinked to a movie.
    d. None of the above

15. **Regular text allows you to:**
    a. Create attractive, large text.
    b. Save disk space.
    c. Use less memory.
    d. Edit it in the Field window.

16. **Field text allows you to:**
    a. Create attractive large text.
    b. Edit it in the Text window.
    c. Create a hyperlink.
    d. Save disk space.

17. **Which feature allows you to change the spacing between characters?**
    a. Line spacing
    b. Kerning
    c. Indent markers
    d. Tabs

18. **A cast library is a(n):**
    a. Unlinked External Cast.
    b. Linked External Cast.
    c. Unlinked Internal Cast.
    d. Linked Internal Cast.

▶ Skills Review

1. **Create a cast.**
   a. Start Director.
   b. Save the new movie as *SpaceWorks Star* in the drive and folder where your Project Files are located.
   c. Close the Score window, if necessary.
   d. Create a linked External Cast as **Space Backgrounds**.
   e. Move the Cast window to a blank area in the Director window.

2. **Use the Cast window.**
   a. Import all the files in the Media folder where your Project Files are located into the Space Backgrounds Cast window (select format as Bitmap Image when requested).
   b. Change the Cast view to a list.
   c. Change the Cast preferences to display number, type, and size, if necessary.

3. **Organize cast members.**
   a. Sort the list in descending order by size (Win).
   b. Change the Space Backgrounds Cast window view to Thumbnail.
   c. Move the cast members into two rows by planets and backgrounds.
   d. Sort each row by name.
   e. Select the Colorful Star and Mostly Space cast members in the Space Backgrounds Cast window.
   f. Copy and paste the cast members in the Internal Cast window (locations 1 and 2).

4. **Find cast members.**
   a. Find all cast members in the Internal Cast.
   b. Select the Colorful Star cast member in the Internal Cast window.

5. View and change cast member properties.

   a. Select the Colorful Star cast member in the Internal Cast window, if necessary.

   b. Change the unload value to last and change the preload value to Before Frame One.

   c. Purge all removable items from memory.

6. Transform a paint cast member.

   a. Select the Colorful Star cast member in the Internal Cast window.

   b. Change the dimensions of the cast member to 320 × 240.

   c. Drag the Colorful Star cast member in the Internal Cast window on the Stage.

   d. Use the Arrow keys to reposition the cast member in the center of the Stage.

7. Add and edit a text cast member.

   a. Select cast member 3 in the Internal Cast window.

   b. Use the Text tool to create a text box in the upper-right corner in the black area.

   c. Change the Foreground color to white and the Background color to black.

   d. Type **You can be a STAR!**

   e. Open the Text Inspector and change the text to align right.

   f. Change the text to a spacey-looking font and a large font size.

   g. Close the Text Inspector.

8. Modify a text cast member.

   a. Open cast member 3 in the Internal Cast window.

   b. Create a hanging indent so that **You can** appears on the top line, **be a** appears on the next line, and **Star!** appears two lines down.

   c. Change the line spacing and kerning to fill in the black area in the upper-right corner.

   d. Name the cast member **Shining Star** and close the Text window.

9. Save and unlink a cast.

   a. Save the cast as *Space Backgrounds* in the drive and folder where your Project Files are located.

   b. Unlink the Space Backgrounds cast from the movie.

   c. Open the Score window, save the movie, and then exit Director.

▶ Independent Challenges

1. You are an estate planner at Langford Financial Services, an insurance and estate planning company. After years of using the same brochure, you decide it's time to create a customizable presentation about company products and services for clients. You use Director's Text and Paint tools to create media elements and an External Cast to organize them.
  To complete this independent challenge:

   a. Start Director and save the movie as *Langford Financial* in the drive and folder where your Project Files are located.

   b. Create a linked External Cast and save it as *Financial Symbols* in the drive and folder where your Project Files are located.

   c. Using the Text tool, create and name cast members in the Financial Symbols Cast window with numbers and financial symbols.

   d. Copy cast members in the Financial Symbols Cast window and convert the text to bitmaps.

   e. Create a text cast member with the text **Langford Financial Services**.

   f. Organize the cast members by type (text and bitmap) in the Financial Symbols Cast window.

   g. Resize a bitmap to 320 × 240 and create a background.

   h. Place the background and the cast members on the Stage.

   i. Print thumbnails of the Financial Symbols Cast window and the Stage.

   j. Save the movie and the External Cast, then exit Director.

2. You are a software developer at the Keenen Group, a Web design and development company that was recently selected by your local Professional Web Designers Group as an industry model in Web development. You've been asked to create a multimedia demo of their development process. You use Director's Paint, Vector Shape, and Text tools to create flow-charting shapes and instructions, and an External Cast in which to organize them.

To complete this independent challenge:

a. Start Director and save the movie as *Keenen Group* in the drive and folder where your Project Files are located.

b. Create a linked External Cast and save it as *Flowchart Symbols* in the drive and folder where your Project Files are located.

c. Using the Paint and Vector Shape tools, create and name cast members in the Flowchart Symbols Cast window with flow-charting shapes and connecting lines. (*Hint:* See Figure B-2 for an example of a flowchart.)

d. Organize the cast members by type (shapes and lines) in the Flowchart Symbols Cast window.

e. Create a text cast member with the text **Keenen Group**.

f. Resize a bitmap to 320 × 240 and create a background.

g. Place the background and the cast members on the Stage.

h. Print thumbnails of the Flowchart Symbols Cast window and the Stage.

i. Save the movie and the External Cast, then exit Director.

3. You are the chief designer at Designer Flags, a custom flag company. The manager of Victory Homes asks you to design a flag for the front of their model home developments. You use Director's Paint and Text tools to create a flag with a house and the company name, and an External Cast in which to organize them.

To complete this independent challenge:

a. Start Director and save the movie as *Designer Flags* in the drive and folder where your Project Files are located.

b. Create a linked External Cast and save it as *Victory Flags* in the drive and folder where your Project Files are located.

c. Using the Paint and Text tools, create and name cast members in the Victory Flags Cast window with several different flag designs and the company name.

d. Organize the cast members by type (shapes and text) in the Victory Flags Cast window.

e. Create a text cast member with the text **Victory flag designs by Designer Flags**.

f. Place the cast members on the Stage and add a color background.

g. Print thumbnails of the Victory Flags Cast window and the Stage.

h. Save the movie and the External Cast, then exit Director.

4. You are the owner and chief baker at Only Desserts, a catering and specialty dessert company. To help promote the company, you want to create a kiosk with photos and prices of your delicious desserts. You use Director's importing feature to assemble photos, and an External Cast to organize them.

To complete this independent challenge:

a. Connect to the Internet and go to *www.course.com*. Navigate to the page for this book, click the link for the Student Online Companion, then click the link for this unit.

b. Browse the Food & Dining section for photos.

c. Download six dessert photos in the drive and folder where your Project Files are located.

d. Start Director and save the movie as *Only Desserts* in the drive and folder where your Project Files are located.

e. Create a linked External Cast and save it as *Dessert Photos* in the drive and folder where your Project Files are located.

f. Import the photos in the Dessert Photos Cast window.

g. Organize the cast members by type (photos and text) in the Dessert Photos Cast window.

h. Create text titles and prices, using the Text tool.

i. Create a text cast member with the text **Only Desserts**.

J. Place the cast members on the Stage and add a color background.

k. Print thumbnails of the Dessert Photos Cast window and the Stage.

l. Save the movie and the External Cast, then exit Director.

▶ Visual Workshop

Recreate the screen shown in Figure D-24. Print the screen. Save the file as *Planets* in the drive and folder where your Project Files are located. (For Windows, use the Windows Paint program. Press the Print Screen key to make a copy of the screen, start the Paint program by clicking Start, pointing to Programs, pointing to Accessories, then clicking Paint, click Edit on the menu bar, click Paste to paste the screen into Paint, then click Yes to paste the large image if necessary. Click File on the menu bar, click Print or OK in the dialog box, then exit Paint. For the Macintosh, use the SimpleText program. Hold and press the Command, Shift, and 3 keys to make a copy of the screen, double-click the document Picture 1 located on your hard drive, click File on the menu bar, click Print, then click Print. (*Note*: When you create a new document with a copy of the screen, and a document Picture 1 already exists, the Macintosh names the new document Picture 2.)

FIGURE D-24

Creating
and Modifying Sprites

Objectives

► Create and select sprites
► View sprite properties
► Layer sprites
► Apply sprite inks
► Change the sprite display
► Change sprite properties
► Position and align sprites
► Extend, join, and split sprites
► Set text for end users to change

A sprite is an object that consists of a cast member and a set of properties and behaviors. The properties and behaviors control how, where, and when cast members appear in a movie. You use the Stage to control where a sprite appears, and you use the Score to control when it appears. This unit introduces you to basic skills for creating, selecting, moving, and modifying sprites. First, you'll learn how to create, select, and move sprites. Then you'll learn how to apply sprite inks, change the sprite display in the Score, change sprite properties, align sprites on the Stage, and modify sprite spans. Finally, you'll learn how to set text for users to change during a movie. ✎ Jean wants to create and modify sprites for a matching game about planets.

Director 8

Creating and Selecting Sprites

You can create sprites by placing cast members either on the Stage or in the Score; regardless of where you create the sprite, it will appear in both locations. Before you can edit, copy, or move a sprite, you need to select it first. You can select sprites either on the Stage or in the Score. To select a sprite, you use the Arrow tool on the Tool palette. You can select sprites in different channels, all the sprites in a single channel, or frames within sprites. If you need to select a frame within a sprite (not the keyframes, the start frame and the end frame), you can use the Edit Sprite Frames command on the Edit menu. If the option is not set, the entire sprite is selected. ✎ Jean takes some time to familiarize herself with the techniques for selecting and deselecting sprites in an existing movie and for creating a new one.

1. Start **Director**, open the file **MD E-1** from the drive and folder where your Project Files are located, then save it as **Planet Game**

   Director opens, displaying the movie. Your initial settings in Director might vary, depending on previous usage.

QuickTip

To change Stage view size, click the Zoom list arrow ▼ at the bottom-left of the Stage, then click a view percentage.

2. Position ⬉ on the lower-right corner of the **Stage window**, then drag the **border** diagonally to the right to expand the window until the gray area around the Stage is displayed

3. Click the **Play button** ▶ on the toolbar

   The movie plays on the Stage, and the playback head moves frame to frame through the Score until it reaches the end. You can see the initial development of the Planet game.

4. Click the **Stop button** ■ on the toolbar, then click **number 31** on the frame channel in the Score window

   The playback head moves to frame 31.

5. Click the **Sun cast member** on the Stage

   The selected sprite appears on the Stage with a double border, as shown in Figure E-1. Attached to the bottom of the sprite selection rectangle is the Sprite Overlay panel. The selected sprite appears in the Score with a solid thick line in the sprite bar.

6. Press and hold [Shift], click a **black area** on the Stage to select both sprites (Sun and Planets Start), then click the **gray area around the Stage** to deselect the sprites

   When the background takes up the entire Stage area, the easiest way to deselect all the sprites is to click the gray area around the Stage.

QuickTip

To select a range of frames, press and hold [Shift][Alt] (Win) or [Shift][Option] (Mac), then click an end frame.

7. Click **frame 31 in channel 7**

   When you select a sprite's keyframe or its first or last frame, the sprite appears on the Stage with a single border. Selecting a frame is useful for modifying keyframes and for creating animation.

8. Click **channel number 5** at the left side of the Score

   All of the sprites in channel 5 are selected.

9. Drag the **Earth cast member** from the Cast window to **frame 31, channel 6** in the Score, as shown in Figure E-2

   The Earth sprite appears in the center of the Stage behind the Sun sprite. When you drag a cast member in the Score, an outline of the sprite appears, indicating the current location of the sprite when you release the mouse. When you place a cast member in the Score, the sprite appears in the center of the Stage surrounded by a double border.

FIGURE E-1: Selecting a sprite

Selected sprite on the Stage

Selected sprite in the Score

FIGURE E-2: Creating a sprite

Earth cast member

Earth sprite on the Stage

Frame 31, channel 6 in the Score

Earth sprite in the score

Editing sprite frames

At times, you might want to change how Director selects a sprite and how Director creates a keyframe. You can use the Edit Sprite Frames option for animated sprites that you need to adjust frequently. It is especially useful for an animated cell where each frame contains a different cast member in a different position. When you set the Edit Sprite Frames option for a certain sprite, clicking the sprite selects a single frame (surrounded by a single border) instead of the entire sprite (surrounded by a double border). Any change you make to an animation property defines a new keyframe. To use the Edit Sprite Frames option, select the sprite, click Edit on the menu bar, then click Edit Sprite Frames. To return sprites to their normal state, select the sprite, click Edit on the menu bar, then click Edit Entire Sprite.

Viewing Sprite Properties

Director 8

Each sprite includes a set of properties that describe how the sprite looks and behaves in a movie. These properties include a sprite's location on the Stage, its size, blend percentage, ink effect, start frame and end frame, and rotation and skew angles. You can also set sprite properties to add basic user interaction and simple animation. You can change some sprite properties, such as size and Stage location, by directly moving or resizing a sprite on the Stage. For other sprite properties, you need to use the Sprite tab in the Property Inspector, as shown in Figure E-3. To view sprite properties, you select a sprite in the Score, click Window on the menu bar, point to Inspector, then click Property. The information in the Sprite tab of the Property Inspector is also visible at the top of the Score Window, as shown in Figure E-4. To display and hide the Sprite toolbar, you click the Score window, click View on the menu bar, then click Sprite Toolbar. You can access some sprite properties using the keyboard shortcuts. Table AP-6 provides a list of the common sprite shortcuts. Jean takes some time to familiarize herself with the elements of the Sprite tab in the Property Inspector. Refer to your screen and Figure E-3 as you locate the elements described below.

 Sprite tab main features

- Set a sprite's **start frame** and **end frame** by entering new values to adjust how long the sprite plays.

- Set a sprite's locking property by using the **Lock button** 🔒. The **locking property** allows you to lock a sprite on the Stage to prevent you from making any changes to the sprite. Locking sprites is not supported during playback.

- Set a text sprite's editable property by using the **Editable button** . The **editable property** allows users to enter text on the Stage while the movie is playing.

- Set a sprite's moveable property by using the **Moveable button** . The **moveable property** allows users to drag a sprite on the Stage while the movie is playing.

- Set a sprite's trail property by using the **Trails button** . The **trail property** leaves a trail of images on the Stage.

- **Flip** a sprite horizontally or vertically by using the **Flip Horizontal button** or **Flip Vertical button** .

- Set an **Ink effect** for a sprite by using the **Ink list arrow** to select an ink effect. Ink effects change the display of a sprite's colors.

- Change a sprite's **Foreground** or **Background colors** by using the **Foreground** or **Background Color box** to select a color from the palette.

- Set the **Blend**, or transparency level, of a sprite by using the **Blend list arrow** to select a percentage. A 100% blend makes a sprite completely opaque, while a 0% blend makes it transparent.

 Sprite tab expander arrow features

- Change the **registration point** by entering a horizontal (X) and vertical (Y) value measured from the top-left corner of the Stage.

- **Rotate** a sprite by entering a number of degrees; a positive number rotates the sprite clockwise in degrees, and a negative number rotates it counterclockwise.

- **Restore** the height and width of the cast member by using the Restore All button.

- **Resize** a sprite by dragging a resize handle on the Stage or by entering width (W:) and height (H:) dimensions in the Sprite tab of the Property Inspector. You can also use the **Scale button** to proportionately resize a sprite.

- **Skew**, or tilt, a sprite by entering a positive value, which skews the sprite to the right, or a negative value, which skews it to the left.

FIGURE E-3: Sprite tab in the Property Inspector

Editable

Start frame

Lock

Ink

Foreground color and background color

Registration point horizontal and vertical

Rotation angle

End frame

Moveable

Trails

Flip horizontal and flip vertical

Blend

Width and height

Skew angle

FIGURE E-4: Sprite toolbar in the Score

Sprite toolbar

Organizing sprites using color

When you create a sprite, it appears in the Score window in the default purple color. After you create several sprites, sometimes it is hard to distinguish them without looking intently at each sprite label. You can organize sprites in the Score window using color. For example, to help you distinguish sprites in the Score window you can set all text sprites to one color and all graphic sprites to another color. You can use the color boxes █████ in the bottom-left corner of the Score window to change the color of a sprite label. The color boxes only change the appearance of the sprite label in the Score window; they do not affect the sprite on the Stage or in the Cast. To change the color of a sprite in the Score window, select the sprite in the Score window, then click a color box.

Layering Sprites

A sprite is displayed on the Stage layered according to its channel in the Score. Sprites in higher-numbered channels appear in front of sprites in lower-numbered channels. For example, the Sun sprite appears in channel 7, and the Earth sprite appears in channel 6, which means that the Sun sprite appears in front of the Earth sprite. When you position the sprite that contains the background for your movie, it is important to place that sprite in a lower-numbered channel, generally channel 1, so that the background always appears on the back layer. There are several ways to change sprite layering. If there is an empty area in a higher-numbered channel, you can drag the sprite in the Score from one channel to another. If no space is available in a channel, you can use the Arrange command on the Modify menu to switch sprites in channels. When you are working with layers, it is sometimes difficult to work with sprites. You can hide the contents of any channel on the Stage. To hide or show the contents of a channel, you use the button to the left of the channel number in the Score. Jean changes the layering of a sprite to uncover it from behind another sprite.

Steps

1. **Verify that the Earth sprite is selected on the Stage and in the Score**
   The selected sprite appears on the Stage with a double border and in the Score with a solid thick line or is highlighted in the sprite bar.

2. **Click Modify on the menu bar, point to Arrange, then click Move Forward**
   The sprites' positions are switched on the Stage and in the Score. The Earth sprite appears in front of the Sun sprite. Notice that the Earth sprite appears in channel 7 and that the Sun sprite appears in channel 6. The Move Forward command moves the sprite up one to the next highest channel.

3. **Position the Arrow pointer over the Earth sprite (not on the colored circle in the middle or on the sizing handles on the edge) on the Stage, then drag the Earth sprite to the left between the Sun sprite and the Mercury sprite, as shown in Figure E-5**
   The Earth sprite is layered between the Sun sprite and the Mercury sprite.

4. **Click Modify on the menu bar, point to Arrange, then click Bring to Front**
   The Earth sprite moves to the top layer.

5. **Click the title bar in the Score, then click the scroll down arrow to display channel 15 in the Score**
   The Earth sprite is in channel 15, the highest-numbered sprite in the movie, as shown in Figure E-6.

6. **Click the gray button ▣ in the first column of the Score window to the left of channel 15**
   A dark gray button indicates that the channel is hidden, as shown in Figure E-7. The Earth sprite is no longer visible on the Stage, but it is still visible in the Score. When you hide a channel, the hide option does not affect the movie as a projector movie or Shockwave movie.

7. **Click the dark gray button ▣ in the first column of the Score window to the left of channel 15**
   The Earth sprite is visible on the Stage.

8. **Position the Arrow pointer over the Earth sprite (not on the colored circle in the middle or the sizing handles on the edge) on the Stage, then drag the Earth sprite over the white dot on the lower-right side of the Sun sprite**

FIGURE E-5: Layering sprites

Sprite in middle layer

Sprite in higher level

Sprite in lower level

FIGURE E-6: Switching channels

Earth sprite in the highest-numbered sprite

FIGURE E-7: Hiding sprites on the Stage

Gray button

Dark gray button

Earth sprite is no longer visible on the Stage

Earth sprite remains visible in the Score

Applying Sprite Inks

Sprite inks change the display of a sprite's colors. Inks are most useful to hide white backgrounds, but they can also create useful and dramatic color effects. Inks can reverse and alter colors, make sprites change colors depending on the background, and create masks that obscure or reveal portions of a background. Unlike Paint ink effects, which are applied in the Paint window and are permanent, sprite ink effects are applied in the Score and can be changed at any time. Table AP-7 describes the different sprite ink effects. For many of the ink effects, you can set a blend value. The **blend value** makes a sprite more or less transparent. A blend value of 100% makes a sprite completely opaque, and a blend value of 0% makes a sprite completely transparent. You can set the end points of a sprite to different blend values, and Director will blend together the points in between. This creates a fading in or fading out effect. ✐ Jean experiments with different sprite ink effects.

Steps

1. **Verify that the Earth sprite is selected on the Stage and in the Score**
   The selected sprite appears on the Stage with a double border and in the Score with a solid thick line or is highlighted in the sprite bar.

2. **Click Window on the menu bar, point to Inspectors, then click Property, if not checked**
   The Property Inspector appears with the Sprite tab in front. The current sprite properties for the Earth sprite appear in the Property Inspector.

3. **Click the Ink list arrow ▼, then click Ghost**
   The Earth sprite appears on the Stage with the ghost effect (washed-out color).

4. **Click the Ink list arrow ▼, then click Mask**
   The Earth sprite appears on the Stage with a mask of the Saturn cast member, which is the cast member that follows the Earth cast member in the Cast. You can use blending to make sprites transparent.

   > **QuickTip**
   >
   > The Blend percentage value affects only Copy, Background Transparent, Matte, Mask, and Blend inks.

5. **Click the Blend list arrow ▼, then click 50%**
   The mask ink effect for the Earth sprite is more transparent.

6. **Click the Blend list arrow ▼, then click 100%**
   The Earth sprite blend is restored to 100%.

7. **Click the Ink list arrow ▼, then click Background Transparent (scroll up, if necessary)**
   The Earth sprite appears on the Stage with a transparent background, as shown in Figure E-8.

Earth sprite with the
Background Transparent
ink effect

Applying the mask ink effect

You can apply the mask ink to a sprite to create transparent effects. The mask ink allows you to define which parts of a sprite are transparent and which are opaque. To use the mask ink, you first create the cast member that will be masked. You can use any color depth when you create the cast member. Then, in the Cast window position immediately following the cast member to be masked, create the mask cast member with a color depth of 32 bits. The black areas of the mask cast member make the sprite completely opaque, and white areas make it completely transparent. Colors between black and white are more or less transparent. However, darker colors are more

opaque than the lighter colors. The mask ink effect is a memory-intensive feature, so use it sparingly for movies on playback machines that have limited memory. To create a mask effect, select the cast member you want to mask, copy and paste it in the next position in the same Cast, edit the mask cast member in the Paint window using black, white, or any colors in between, transform the bitmap of the mask cast member to 32 bits (if necessary), drag the cast member to the Stage or Score to create a sprite, display the Sprite tab in the Property Inspector, click the Ink list arrow, then click Mask. The parts of the sprite revealed by the mask appear on the Stage.

Director 8

Director 8

Changing the Sprite Display

The text that identifies the sprite in the Score window is called a **sprite label**. To make it easier to work with sprites, you can change the display for sprite labels in the Score to show different information about the sprite, such as member name and number or ink effect. When you select a sprite on the Stage or in the Score, the sprite overlay panel appears on the Stage at the bottom of the sprite. You can determine when the sprite overlay panel appears; the panel can appear when you move the mouse over, or roll over, a sprite, when you select a sprite, or all the time. If the text in the sprite overlay is difficult to read, you can change the panel text display color or the shading of the panel. Jean changes the sprite display to view the ink effects currently used in the movie.

Steps

QuickTip

To change the Extended display in the Score, click File on the menu bar, point to Preferences, click Score, then click the Extended Display check boxes in the Score Window Preferences dialog box to select them.

1. Click the **title bar** in the Score window, click the **Display list arrow** ▼ on the left side of the Score window, then click **Extended**

   The Score window displays extended information for the display options selected in the Score Window Preferences dialog box. Extended settings include cast member number (depending on your Director settings) and name, ink blend, and location. Figure E-9 displays the Score window under the Extended setting. Table E-1 describes the display options for sprite labels.

2. Drag the **vertical scroll box** in the scroll bar of the Score window to the top, click the **Display list arrow** ▼ on the left side of the Score window, then click **Ink**

   The Score window displays the sprite labels with ink effects.

QuickTip

To show or hide keyframes in the Score, click View on the menu bar, then click Keyframes.

3. Click the **Display list arrow** ▼ on the left side of the Score window, then click **Member**

   The Score window displays the sprite labels with member names.

4. Click the **Earth sprite** on the Stage, if necessary

   The selected sprite appears on the Stage with a double border and a sprite overlay with information about the sprite.

5. Click **View** on the menu bar, point to **Sprite Overlay**, then click **Settings**

   The Sprite Overlay Settings dialog box opens. You can select sprite overlay color and display options.

6. Press and hold the **Text Color box**, then click the **white color box** at the end of the second row on the color palette

QuickTip

To open the Bitmap, Sprite, or Behavior tabs in the Property Inspector, you can click the corresponding icon in the Sprite Overlay panel.

7. Click **OK**, then click the **Planets Start sprite** (the black background)

   The sprite overlay text changes from black to white, which makes it easier to see against the black background.

8. Drag down the **slider** that appears on the right edge of the Sprite Overlay panel, as shown in Figure E-10, to change the shading of the panel

9. Click **View** on the menu bar, point to **Sprite Overlay**, then click **Show Info** to deselect

   The sprite overlay is removed from the selected sprite on the Stage.

FIGURE E-9: Score window with extended sprite display

Click list arrow to change the sprite display options

Sprite display options

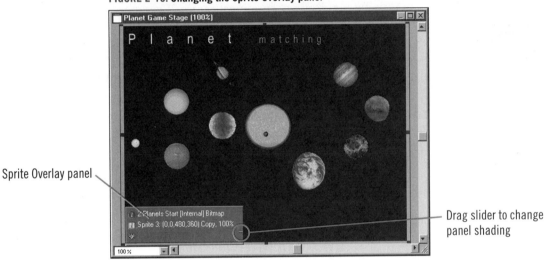

Extended sprite display

FIGURE E-10: Changing the Sprite Overlay panel

Sprite Overlay panel

Drag slider to change panel shading

TABLE E-1: Score Window display options

format	description
Member	Identifies the number and name of the cast member (depending on your Director settings)
Behavior	Tells you which (if any) behaviors have been assigned to the sprite by number or name
Ink	Displays the ink effect that is applied to the sprite
Blend	Indicates the percentage of the sprite's blend setting
Location	Describes the sprite's registration point relative to the top-left corner of the Stage
Extended	Displays Member, Behavior, Ink, Blend, and Location information

Viewing multiple Score windows

You can display different views of the Score window to make it easier to display information or to move a sprite to a different part of the Score without scrolling. If you have a large Score window and want to move a sprite a long distance, you can open the same Score window, scroll to a different portion, then drag the sprite between the two windows. To open a copy of the Score window, click the title bar in the Score window, click Window on the menu bar, then click New Window. You can change the Score display settings for sprite labels in the new window. When you change the Score display options in one Score window, the other Score window retains its original settings, but if you alter a sprite in either window, both Score windows update the change.

Director 8

Director 8

Changing Sprite Properties

While you develop a movie, you can lock sprites to avoid making unintentional changes to them. For example, if you are working with a background sprite and do not want to move it as you make changes to other sprites, you can use the Lock button in the Sprite tab of the Property Inspector to make sure the background sprite cannot move or change. When you lock a sprite, you can no longer change its settings. A locked sprite appears with a lock icon in front of its name in the Score and in the upper-right corner of a sprite on the Stage. When you use the Moveable button, you can allow end users to move sprites around while your movie is playing. This option is useful for creating educational games. If you need to resize a sprite, you can use the Scale button to set a specific height and width or a percentage. ✐ Jean locks the background sprite, resizes a sprite, and sets a group of sprites for movement in the Planet game.

Steps

1. Verify that the **Planets Start sprite** is selected on the Stage, press and hold **[Shift]**, then click the **Sun sprite** on the Stage
   The selected sprites appear on the Stage with a double border and in the Score with a solid thick line or is highlighted in each sprite bar.

QuickTip

To unlock a sprite, select the sprite, then click the Lock button 🔒 in the Sprite tab of the Property Inspector. To select a locked sprite on the Stage, press and hold [L], then click a sprite.

2. Click the **Lock button** 🔒 in the Property Inspector
   A lock icon appears on the sprite border on the Stage and in the sprite bar in the Score, as shown in Figure E-11.

3. Click the **Earth sprite** on the Stage
   The selected sprite appears on the Stage with a double border and in the Score with a solid thick line or is highlighted in the sprite bar.

4. Click **Scale** in the Property Inspector
   The Scale dialog box opens.

5. Double-click the **Scale box** (if necessary), type **75**, then click **OK**
   The Earth sprite is scaled to 75%.

QuickTip

You can skew sprites with the Rotate and Skew tool on the Tool palette. To skew the sprite, click the Rotation and Skew tool 🔄, click a sprite on the Stage, then drag a border until you achieve the desired effect.

6. Click the **title bar** in the Score, click the **scroll up arrow** to display channel 6, press and hold **[Shift]**, then click the **Sun Sprite** in channel 6 to select all the planet sprites
   The planet sprites from channel 15 to channel 6 are selected on the Stage and in the Score.

7. Click the **Copy button** 🗐 on the toolbar, click **frame 59** in **channel 6**, then click the **Paste button** 🗐 on the toolbar
   A copied set of planet sprites is pasted in frame 59 and selected in the Score.

8. Press and hold **[Ctrl]** (Win) or **[Command]** (Mac), click the **Sun Sprite** in frame 59 of channel 6, then click the **Moveable button** 🖱 in the Property Inspector
   The Moveable property is set for the planet sprites. When you play the movie, you can move the planets.

9. Click the **Center Current Frame button** ⚡ in the bottom row of the Score window
   The frames in the Score are centered to the playback head, as shown in Figure E-12. You can view both sets of planet sprites in the Score.

FIGURE E-11: Locking sprites

Lock icon on the Stage

Planets Start sprite selected on the Stage and in the Score

Lock icon in the Score

Click button to lock sprite

FIGURE E-12: Setting sprites to move during playback

Click button to center current frame in the Score

Click button to move sprites during playback

CLUES TO USE

Creating a trail effect

You can set sprites to leave a trail of images as they move on the Stage. When you click the Trails button in the Property Inspector, the Stage doesn't erase previous versions of the sprite as the playback head moves through the Score. The result is an impression of a continuous string of sprites, as shown in Figure E-13. This option is useful for fine-tuning animations. When you select a sprite with an animation and set the Trails option, you can determine where motion in an animation needs to slow down, speed up, or smooth out. You cannot select or move any of the trailed images, but you can change the animation points, or keyframes, in the Score. You can also use the trail effect with the Moveable option. When you

select the Moveable option and the Trails option for a cast member, the end user can drag the cast member on the Stage during playback to create a trail effect.

FIGURE E-13: Sprite with trails

Director 8

Positioning and Aligning Sprites

Director 8

Sometimes you need to change the position of a sprite or align a group of sprites on the Stage. You can drag a sprite, use the arrow keys, or set coordinates in the Sprite tab of the Property Inspector to position sprites on the Stage. You can align sprites on the Stage using the grid, the guides, or the Align window. The **grid** is a set of rows and columns of a specified height and width that you can use to help place sprites on the Stage. When you select the Snap to Grid option, sprites snap to the grid points, whether the grid is visible or not. The **guides** are horizontal or vertical lines you can either drag around the Stage or lock in place to help you align sprites in a straight line. When you select the Snap to Guides option, sprites snap to the guide line. When you are not using the grid or guides, you can hide them. The **Align window** moves sprites not to a specific location on the Stage, but to positions relative to one another. Jean positions and aligns the planet sprites at the bottom of the Stage, as part of the Planet game.

Steps

1. Click the **Planets Start sprite** (the black background), then click the **Guides and Grid tab** in the Property Inspector, if necessary
   Your initial settings for the Guides and Grid tab might be different. The Visible check box and the Snap to Guides check box in the Guides: area are selected, and the Snap to Grid check box in the Grid: area is selected.

2. Click the **Visible check box** in the Grid: area to select it, then click the **Snap to Grid check box** in the Grid: area to select it, if necessary
   A grid appears on the Stage. You can change the grid lines to dots by clicking the Dot option button in the Guides and Grid tab of the Property Inspector.

3. Position the Arrow pointer over the bottom part of the Earth sprite, drag the pointer down to the bottom horizontal grid, as shown in Figure E-14, then click the **Planets Start sprite**
   When you drag the sprite, a green plus sign appears, indicating where the sprite will snap to the grid. The position where you drag the sprite determines where the green plus sign appears in the sprite. For example, when you drag the left side of the Earth sprite, the green plus sign appears to the left of a grid line.

4. Click the **Visible check box** in the Grid: area on the Guides and Grid tab of the Property Inspector to clear it, click the **Visible check box** in the Guides: area to select it, if necessary, then click **Remove All**
   Any guides on the Stage are removed.

5. Press and hold 🖑 over the **New Horizontal guide** ⬛ in the Guides and Grid tab of the Property Inspector, then drag the **guide** to the bottom of the Stage, as shown in Figure E-15

6. Drag the bottom part of each **planet** (don't forget Pluto on the far left) to the horizontal guide in any order, position ⬍ over the **horizontal guide** on the Stage, then drag the **horizontal guide** down off the Stage to remove it

7. Click a **planet sprite** on the Stage, press and hold [Shift], then click each of the other **planet sprites** to select all the planet sprites

8. Click **Modify** on the menu bar, then click **Align**
   The Align window opens, as shown in Figure E-16.

9. Click the **Horizontal Alignment list arrow** ▼, click **Distribute Widths**, click **Align**, then click the **Close button** in the Align window
   The sprites are evenly aligned horizontally across the bottom of the Stage.

QuickTip
To change the height and width of the rows and columns in the grid, enter a value in the Spacing: Height or Width box in the Guides and Grid tab of the Property Inspector, then press [Enter] (Win) or [Return] (Mac).

QuickTip
You can add as many horizontal and vertical guide lines as you want.

FIGURE E-14: Positioning a sprite on the Stage using a grid

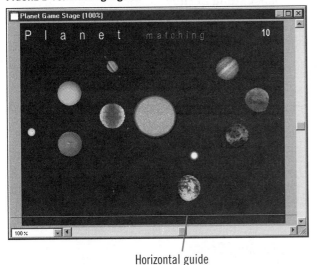

Grid

Use green plus sign for positioning a sprite

Drag to create horizontal or vertical guides

Grid display settings

FIGURE E-15: Creating a guide

Horizontal guide

FIGURE E-16: Aligning sprites

Alignment settings preview

Vertical alignment

Horizontal alignment

CLUES TO USE

Tweaking the placement of a sprite

Sometimes you need to make only minor adjustments to the placement of a sprite. You can drag the sprite with the mouse, use the arrow keys, or use the Sprite tab in the Property Inspector to enter specific coordinates, but these techniques can sometimes be time-consuming or inefficient in achieving the exact placement you want. The Tweak window allows you to make an adjustment with the mouse and know the exact distances involved. To open the Tweak window, click Modify on the menu bar, then click Tweak. You can drag the alignment in the Tweak window to a line to set a specific movement and then use the horizontal and vertical arrows to make any final adjustments to the sprite's location. When you finish making adjustments, you select one or more sprites and click Tweak to apply the movement. You can apply the Tweak settings to as many sprites as you want. The Tweak settings stay in effect until you change them or close the Tweak window.

Director 8

CREATING AND MODIFYING SPRITES   DIRECTOR E-15 ◀

Director 8

Extending, Joining, and Splitting Sprites

You can change the duration of a sprite on the Stage by adjusting the length of the sprite. The longer the length of the sprite, the longer the sprite appears in the movie. You can drag the end frame of a sprite to change the length or use the Extend command on the Modify menu. The Extend command is an easy way to fill up channels with blocks of sprites. You can also use the Extend command to shorten a sprite. Sometimes you might need to split an existing sprite into two separate sprites, or join separate sprites. For example, if you create a text sprite with a long duration and need to separate it into two sprites to make changes in one of them, you can use the Split Sprite command. Similarly, if you create a complex animation as separate sprites and need to consolidate them into a single sprite, you can use the Join Sprite command. ✍ Jean extends a group of sprites, joins all the sprites in a channel, and splits a sprite in two.

Steps

1. Click the **title bar** in the Score, then verify that the copied set of 9 planets is selected (channels 7 through 15 starting at frame 59)

2. Drag the **horizontal scroll box** to frame 365, then click **365** in the timeline
   The playback head appears in frame 365.

3. Click **Modify** on the menu bar, then click **Extend Sprite**
   The selected sprites are extended to frame 365, as shown in Figure E-17.

4. Click **341** in the timeline, then click the **Center Current Frame button** 🔲 on the bottom row of the Score window
   The playback head is centered in the middle of the Score window at frame 341.

5. Click **Sprite channel 5** on the left side of the Score to select all the sprites in the channel

QuickTip

Drag the horizontal scroll box to confirm that the sprites are joined.

6. Click **Modify** on the menu bar, then click **Join Sprites**
   All the sprites in channel 5 are joined together to create one sprite, as shown in Figure E-18.

7. Click **341** in the timeline (if necessary), then click the **Planet Matching Text sprite** in channel 4

8. Click **Modify** on the menu bar, then click **Split Sprite**
   The Planet Matching Text sprite is split into two sprites at frame 341, as shown in Figure E-19. You can select the new text sprite that starts at frame 341 and modify it without affecting the Planet Matching Text sprite that ends at frame 340.

FIGURE E-17: Extending sprites

Selected sprites extended to playback head

FIGURE E-18: Joining sprites

Click sprite channel
to select all sprites

Selected sprites joined
together

FIGURE E-19: Splitting sprites

One sprite split
into two at the
playback head

Setting Text for Users to Change

You can set regular text and field text cast members so that end users can edit the text as the movie plays. For example, if your movie calls for end users to enter their names, include an editable text or field sprite where the users can click and type. During a movie, users can click the text box to place a blinking cursor there and modify the contents of the text box. You can use the Editable button in the Sprite tab or the Editable check box in the Text tab and Field tab of the Property Inspector to make text and field sprites editable. You can also use the Editable button to make a field sprite editable in only a certain range of frames in the Score. If you choose the Edit Sprite Frames command on the Edit menu, you can select individual frames and make a text box editable in one frame but not in another. Keep in mind that any edits you make to a text or field sprite will also affect the original text or field cast member, as well as all succeeding sprites that you create. Jean changes a text sprite setting so that end users can change text as the Planet game plays.

Steps

1. Scroll to frame 365 and channel 17 in the Score, then click the **Score Box sprite**

QuickTip

You can also click the Editable check box in the Text or Field tab of the Property Inspector to edit text for an entire sprite while the movie plays.

2. Click the **Editable button** in the Property Inspector

The Editable text property is set for the Score box sprite, as shown in Figure E-20. When you play the movie, you can add text in the text box.

3. Click the **Rewind button** on the toolbar, then click the **Play button** on the toolbar

The movie plays on the Stage, and the playback head moves frame to frame through the Score until it reaches the end. You can test the Planet match game.

Trouble?

If you need to restart the movie, click the Rewind button , then click the Play button.

4. When the timer in the upper-right corner starts, drag the **planets** to their original positions around the sun

5. When the timer reaches 0, count how many planets you placed in the correct position on the screen

Trouble?

If the movie plays again, click the Stop button on the toolbar. To turn off the playback loop, click Window on the menu bar, click Control Panel, then click Loop Playback.

6. Double-click the **score box** in the lower-right corner, type **your score** on the screen, as shown in Figure E-21, then click a **blank area** of the screen

7. Click **View** on the menu bar, point to **Sprite Overlay**, click **Settings**, press and hold the **Text Color box**, click the **black color box** at the beginning of the first row on the color palette, then click **OK**

8. Click **View** on the menu bar, point to **Sprite Overlay**, click **Show Info**, click any sprite on the Stage, then drag the **slider** to the middle of the Sprite Overlay panel

9. Click the **Save button** on the toolbar, click **File** on the menu bar, then click **Exit** (Win) or **Quit** (Mac)

Director closes.

Text sprite set for editing during playback

Click button to edit text during playback

FIGURE E-21: Editing text during playback

Play the movie

Select and edit text during playback

Changing text and field properties

You can use the Text or Field tab in the Property Inspector to view and change settings for selected text sprites. You can select a framing option to determine how Director places text within the boundaries of a text box. The Framing options include Adjust to Fit, Scrolling, Fixed, and Limit to Field Size. The Adjust to Fit option expands the text box vertically when text that is entered extends beyond the current size of the box. The Scrolling option attaches a scroll bar to the right side of the text box, which is useful when there is a large amount of text. The Fixed option retains the original size of the text box. If you enter text that

extends beyond the limits of the box, the text is stored but not displayed. The Limit to Field Size option for field text accepts only the amount of text that fits within the limits of the box. You can also set editing and display options in the Text or Field tab of the Property Inspector. The Editable option makes the cast member editable while the movie plays. The Wrap option increases the vertical size of the text box or field on the Stage so that all text is visible. The Tab to Next Editable Item option advances the text insertion point to the next editable sprite on the Stage when the end user presses Tab.

Director 8

Practice

► Concepts Review

Label each of the elements of the screen shown in Figure E-22.

FIGURE E-22

Match each of the terms with the statement that describes its function.

6. Blend
7. Trail
8. Grid
9. Ink effect
10. Label
11. Guide

a. Change the display of a sprite's colors
b. A transparency level
c. A string of continuous sprite images on the screen
d. Text that identifies a sprite
e. A set of rows and columns that you use the place sprites
f. A horizontal or vertical line that you use the place sprites

Select the best answer from the following list of choices.

12. Which tool do you use to select a sprite?
    a. Hand tool
    b. Magnifying Glass tool
    c. Arrow tool
    d. none of the above

13. Which is NOT a sprite property?
    a. Location
    b. Blend
    c. Keyframe
    d. End frame

14. **What is the base point of reference for the horizontal (X) and vertical (Y) value for the registration point?**
    a. Top-left corner
    b. Top-right corner
    c. Bottom-left corner
    d. Bottom-right corner

15. **A 100% blend makes a sprite:**
    a. Completely opaque.
    b. Partially opaque.
    c. Completely transparent.
    d. Partially transparent.

16. **A sprite will appear in front in channel:**
    a. 1.
    b. 5.
    c. 10.
    d. 15.

17. **Which is NOT an ink effect?**
    a. Copy
    b. Transparent
    c. Contrast
    d. Reverse

18. **Which ink effect removes the white bounding box around a sprite?**
    a. Transparent
    b. Ghost
    c. Mask
    d. Matte

19. **Which ink effect defines the transparent or opaque parts of a sprite?**
    a. Blend
    b. Mask
    c. Matte
    d. Copy

▶ Skills Review

1. **Create and select sprites.**
   a. Start Director, open the file **MD E-2** from the drive and folder where your Project Files are located.
   b. Save the file as *States Game* in the drive and folder where your Project Files are located.
   c. Resize the Stage to display the gray area around the Stage.
   d. Select the Title cast member on the Stage with a double border and then with a single border.

2. **View sprite properties.**
   a. View the sprite properties for the Title sprite.
   b. Write down the sprite feature name and properties in the Sprite tab for the Title sprite.

3. **Layer sprites.**
   a. Select the Name Title sprite in the Score, then move the sprite forward one channel.
   b. Drag the Name Title sprite on the Stage above the Name sprite.
   c. Drag the Name sprite on the Stage below and aligned with the Name Title sprite.
   d. Hide channel 1 to display the background, then show channel 1 to restore it.

4. **Apply sprite inks.**
   a. Select the USA Map Blank sprite.
   b. Open the Property Inspector.
   c. Change the ink to Background Transparent.
   d. Select the Title sprite, then change the ink to Matte.

5. **Change the sprite display.**
   a. Change the display in the Score window to Extended, Ink, and then Member.
   b. Open the Sprite Overlay Settings dialog box, then change the color to blue.
   c. Change the shading of the Sprite Overlay panel, then hide the Sprite Overlay panel.

6. **Change sprite properties.**
   a. Select and lock the USA Map Blank sprite.
   b. Select all the state text sprites and set them to Moveable.

7. Position and align sprites.

a. Display the Guides and Grid tab in the Property Inspector.

b. Drag a horizontal guide on the Stage.

c. Align the state text sprites in four rows at the top of the Stage.

d. Remove the guide.

e. Select each row of state text sprites individually and change the horizontal alignment to Distribute Widths.

8. Extend, split, and join sprites.

a. Select all the state text sprites.

b. Extend the state text sprites to frame 1250. (*Hint*: Depending on the speed of your computer, you might need to wait a few moments for Director to perform this task.)

c. Click 1000 in the timeline, select the Title sprite in channel 2, then split the sprite.

9. Set text for users to change.

a. Select the Name sprite and set it to Editable.

b. Rewind the movie, then play it.

c. Select the text *Your Name* (if necessary), type **Your Name**, then deselect the text box.

d. Drag the state names for the purple states in the map until the answers appear.

e. When the movie stops, show the Sprite Overlay panel.

f. Open the Sprite Overlay Settings dialog box and change the color to black.

g. Change the shading of the panel to the middle.

h. Save the movie and exit Director.

▶ Independent Challenges

1. You are a student at Benson Art College. The multimedia department is having a graphic design contest. First prize is $500.00. Recently, you have been experimenting with the ink effects in Director and want to use your newly acquired skills for the contest. You use Director's Paint tool to create two cast members and apply the Mask ink effect.

To complete this independent challenge:

a. Start Director and save the movie as *Design Contest* in the drive and folder where your Project Files are located.

b. Open the Paint window, then open the Pattern pop-up menu on the Tool palette and select a tile at the bottom.

c. Create a filled rectangle with the pattern, then close the Paint window.

d. Copy the cast member.

e. Paste the cast member in the next location to the right.

f. Open the duplicate cast member and change the tile color and pattern to black, then use the Paint tools to fill the rectangle with black.

g. Use the Airbrush tool to create white brush strokes in the black area, then close the Paint window.

h. Transform the duplicate cast member bitmap to 32 bits. (*Hint*: Use the Transform Bitmap command on the Modify menu.)

i. Drag the original cast member on the Stage, then change the ink effect for the cast member to the mask effect.

j. Create a text cast member with the text **Designs by [Your Name]**.

k. Print the Stage and the cast members, then save the movie and exit Director.

2. You are a game designer at Freeware Games, a software company that develops memory games for kids. Your boss asks you to create a simple shape matching game for ages three to four. You use Director's Paint tool to create circle, square, and triangle cast members and a background cast member with the outline of the shapes.

To complete this independent challenge:

a. Start Director and save the movie as *Shape Matching* in the drive and folder where your Project Files are located.

b. Create and name a background cast member with the outline of a circle, square, and triangle.

c. Create and name filled cast members with the circle, square, and triangle shapes.

d. Drag the background on the Stage and lock it.

e. Drag the shapes on the Stage and set them to be moveable.

f. Create a text cast member with the text **Shape Matching Game**.

g. Change the duration and modify the shape sprites to create a matching game.

h. Print the Stage and the cast members, then save the movie and exit Director.

3. You are a customer service specialist at 24-7 Answers, an online technical support company. You've been tasked with creating a data structure with the information you need from your customers, including different types of information, such as name, e-mail address, and problem. You use Director's Text tool to create text labels and empty text boxes where users can enter text.

To complete this independent challenge:

a. Start Director and save the movie as *Answers Prototype* in the drive and folder where your Project Files are located.

b. Write down on paper a list of the different types of information you might need from a person to provide online technical support.

c. Create and name text label cast members, using the Text tool.

d. Create and name empty text cast members, using the Text tool, and set them to be editable.

e. Extend the sprites in the Score for enough time to enter information in the editable text cast members.

f. Create a text cast member with the text **24-7 Answers**.

g. Place and arrange the cast members on the Stage and add a color background.

h. Play the movie and enter text in the editable text cast members.

i. Print the Stage, then save the movie and exit Director.

4. You run the Fun and Games truck, a mobile teaching unit that delivers books and software games to kids in rural areas. You want to create a new animal matching game for four to five year olds. You use Director's import capabilities to create a cast of animals, and the Paint tool to create a background for matching the animal with its name.

To complete this independent challenge:

a. Connect to the Internet and go to www.course.com. Navigate to the page for this book, click the link for the Student Online Companion, then click the link for this unit.

b. Browse the Animals section for clip art.

c. Download six different animals in the drive and folder where your Project Files are located.

d. Start Director and save the movie as *Animal Matching* in the drive and folder where your Project Files are located.

e. Create and name a background cast member with an unfilled rectangle and a text label with the name of each animal.

f. Drag the background on the Stage and lock it.

g. Drag the animal cast members on the Stage and set them to be moveable.

h. Create a text cast member with the text **Animal Matching Game**.

i. Change the duration and modify the animal sprites to create a matching game.

j. Print the Stage and the cast members, then save the movie and exit Director.

Director 8

Visual Workshop

Re-create the screen shown in Figure E-23. Print the screen. (For Windows, use the Windows Paint program. Press the Print Screen key to make a copy of the screen, start the Paint program by clicking Start, pointing to Programs, pointing to Accessories, then clicking Paint, click Edit on the menu bar, click Paste to paste the screen into Paint, then click Yes to paste the large image if necessary. Click File on the menu bar, click Print, click Print or OK in the dialog box, then exit Paint. For the Macintosh, use the SimpleText program. Hold and press the Command, Shift, and 3 keys to make a copy of the screen, double-click the document Picture 1 located on your hard drive, click File on the menu bar, click Print, then click Print in the dialog box. (*Note*: When you create a new document with a copy of the screen and a document Picture 1 already exists, the Macintosh names the new document Picture 2.)

FIGURE E-23

Adding
Navigation and User Interaction

Objectives

► **Understand navigation and user interaction**
► **Change the tempo**
► **Compare tempo performance**
► **Add a wait time**
► **Create navigation with behaviors**
► **Add and name markers**
► **Create navigation with markers**
► **Add rollover effects**
► **Add a transition**

Adding navigation and user interaction to your movies lets you involve your audience in the movie. You can use these features to jump to different parts of movies during authoring or in the completed movie, or to allow end users to perform functions such as clicking buttons and downloading files from the Internet. In the previous unit, you learned how to move objects and enter text on the Stage while the movie is playing. This unit introduces you to basic skills for changing the tempo, or speed, of a movie, adding a wait time, creating navigation controls and markers, and adding transitions between movie scenes. ✐▬ Jean wants to add navigation and user interaction for an informational multimedia movie about space exploration.

Unit F

Director 8

Understanding Navigation and User Interaction

As you discovered in the planning process, the script and schematic flowchart are important planning tools for the multimedia developer. While the script tells the story of your movie production in text form, as shown in Figure F-1, the schematic flowchart sketches out the navigational structure of a movie to ensure that each of the sections is properly connected, as shown in Figure F-2. Once you have the script and schematic flowchart mapped out on paper, you can see the correlation between what you have developed and what you will begin to set up in Director. Jean develops an initial script and schematic flowchart for the Space Journey project. First, Jean takes some time to familiarize herself with some of the navigational and interactive elements available in Director.

Types of navigation and user interaction

 Moveable sprites

The moveable property allows users to drag a sprite on the Stage while the movie is playing. You can set a sprite's moveable property by clicking the Moveable button in the Sprite tab of the Property Inspector.

 Editable sprites

The editable property allows end users to enter text (in a field or text sprite) on the Stage while the movie is playing. You can set a sprite's editable property by clicking the Editable button in the Sprite tab of the Property Inspector.

 Tempo settings

The tempo settings allow you to set the speed of the movie and to pause the movie at a specific frame, such as when the end user clicks a mouse or presses a key, or when a specific cue point occurs in a sound or video. You can change tempo settings by double-clicking a frame in the Tempo channel, and then selecting the tempo options you want to change. You can use the Control Panel to compare the current tempo settings with actual tempo results.

 Library behaviors

The Library behaviors allow you to add navigation controls and interaction to a movie using a built-in behavior from the Library palette with a prewritten Lingo script. You can attach a behavior to a sprite or frame by opening the Library Palette window, selecting a behavior category, and then dragging a behavior to a frame or sprite.

 Lingo scripts

The Lingo scripts allow you to create simple scripts that you can attach to sprites or frames to navigate to a specific location in a movie. You can create a script by double-clicking a frame in the Behavior channel, and then typing one or more Lingo instructions, such as *go to frame "Menu"*.

 Transition settings

The transition settings allow you to select a transition effect that you can use to move smoothly from one scene to another, and to set the duration and smoothness of a transition. You can select a transition effect and set other related settings by double-clicking a frame in the Transition channel, and then selecting a transition and setting other options you want to apply to the frame.

FIGURE F-1: Project planning script

Script

Project: Space Journey

Scene	Text	Graphics	Audio	Video	Animation	Navigation	Transition
1	SpaceWorks	SpaceWorks Background					
1	presents						
2	a journey through space	Rocket graphic	TBD		Fly from bottom left to center		
2	click to continue					Pause: wait for click	
3		Title graphic					
3	Videos			TBD		Scene 5	
3	Sounds		TBD			Scene 6	
3	Pictures	TBD				Scene 7	
3		Credits button				Scene 4	
3		Exit button				Quit	
4		Credits graphic					Zoom Close
4	Credits list				Fly from bottom center	Pause 4 seconds, then Scene 3	

FIGURE F-2: Project planning schematic flowchart

Unit F

Director 8

Changing the Tempo

Director plays a movie at a particular **tempo**, or speed. You can set the tempo rate to control the maximum speed at which the movie plays from frame to frame. The tempo rate is measured in frames per second (fps). The higher the tempo rate, the faster Director plays back animation. You can make animated sprites fly across the Stage to create a high-speed effect, or crawl across the Stage to create a slow-motion effect. You can set the tempo for the entire movie or selected frames. You use the Tempo channel in the Score window to set the tempo rate. It's a good idea to set the tempo rate for a movie in the first frame. Otherwise, the playback speed will be determined by the frame-by-frame settings in the Control Panel, which can be inconsistent. When you set the tempo rate in the Tempo channel, Director uses the tempo rate from the selected frame until it reaches the next different tempo setting. You can set the tempo rate from 1 to 999 frames per second. The tempo rate doesn't affect the playback rate of sounds and video or the duration of transitions. ✎ Jean sets the tempo rate at the beginning of a new space movie and then changes the tempo rate towards the end to slow down an animation.

Steps 1 2 3 4

1. Start **Director**, open the file **MD F-1** from the drive and folder where your Project Files are located, then save it as **Journey**

   Director opens, displaying the movie. Your initial settings in Director can vary, depending on previous usage.

2. Position ↖ (Win) or ⬉ (Mac) on the lower-right corner of the **Stage window**, then drag the **border** diagonally to the right to expand the window until the gray area around the Stage is displayed

   The window is now resized on each side. You can also resize a window's height or width by dragging any border.

Trouble?

If the movie loops, click Window on the menu bar, click Control Panel, click the Loop Playback button to deselect it, then click the Close button on the Control Panel.

3. Click the **Play button** ▶ on the toolbar

   The movie plays on the Stage, and the playback head moves frame to frame through the Score until it reaches the end. You can see the initial development of the multimedia project. Now, you will change the movie tempo and add navigation and user interaction to complete the project.

4. Click the **Hide/Show Effects Channels button** ⊞ in the Score window to display the effects channels, then click **frame 1** in the **Tempo channel** 🕑 in the Score window

   The effects channels appear in the Score window with frame 1 selected in the Tempo channel, as shown in Figure F-3.

5. Click **Modify** on the menu bar, point to **Frame**, then click **Tempo**

   The Frame Properties: Tempo dialog box opens, as shown in Figure F-4.

QuickTip

To zoom the Score window, click the Zoom Menu button ⊞ at the right edge of the Sprite channel, then click a percentage.

6. Click the **Tempo option button**, click the **Tempo arrow buttons** until the setting reaches 25 fps (or as close as possible), then click **OK**

   The tempo for the movie is set to 25 frames per second. The tempo rate appears in frame 1 of the Tempo channel. If you can't read the number, you might need to zoom the Score window.

7. Drag the horizontal scroll box to the right in the Score window to display frame 78, then double-click **frame 78** in 🕑

   The Frames Properties: Tempo dialog box opens.

QuickTip

To pause the movie until a sound or video cue point passes, in the Frame Properties: Tempo dialog box, click the Wait for Cue Point option button, choose a channel and cue point, then click OK.

8. Click the **Tempo option button**, click the **Tempo arrow buttons** until the setting reaches 15 fps (or as close as possible), then click **OK**

   The tempo for the movie changes from 25 frames per second to 15 frames per second at frame 78.

9. Click the **Rewind button** ◀ on the toolbar, then click ▶ on the toolbar

   The movie plays on the Stage, and the playback head moves frame to frame through the Score at 25 frames per second for frames 1 to 77 then changes to 15 frames per second until it reaches the end.

FIGURE F-3: Effects channels in the Score window

Color channel · Transition channel · Behavior channel · Sound channels · Tempo channel · Click button to hide and show the Effects channels

FIGURE F-4: Frame Properties: Tempo dialog box

Click arrow buttons or drag the slider to set tempo

CLUES TO USE

Understanding tempo rate on different computers

Director always attempts to play a movie at the specified tempo rate, but the computer running the movie might not be fast enough to play it at the desired tempo rate. If you want your movie to play on a variety of computer systems, you need to set a tempo rate that allows low-end computers (low CPU speed and small amount of RAM; see Director Help for system requirements) to play the movie at the desired tempo rate. If you have complex animations and transitions or large cast members in the movie that might cause slower playback, you might need to redesign parts of the movie to play at slower tempo rates. Otherwise, low-end computer users might be disappointed with the playback performance.

Comparing Tempo Performance

Director tries to play the movie at the tempo rate you set in the Tempo channel. However, the actual playback speed might be different. Computer systems run at different speeds and include different hardware, which can slow down the performance of a movie on the playback computer. You can alleviate this performance problem by testing your movie on a computer similar to the ones your target audience will use. The Control Panel includes the tempo rate you set in the Tempo channel and the actual speed of the movie. While you play the movie, you can compare the tempo rate, also known as the target tempo, with the actual tempo rate. You can change tempo settings in the Tempo channel or use the Tempo up and down arrows in the Control Panel to adjust the tempo rate for specific frames. ✐ Jean compares the target tempo rate with the actual tempo rate for the Journey movie.

Steps

QuickTip

The tempo you set in the Tempo channel overrides any value you set in the Tempo box in the Control Panel.

1. Click **Window** on the menu bar, then click **Control Panel** (if necessary), then click **frame 75** in the **Frame channel**

The Control Panel appears, displaying the target and actual tempo settings for frame 75, as shown in Figure F-5.

2. Click the **Step Forward button** ▮▶ on the Control Panel until you reach the end of the movie, frame 95, and compare the tempo and actual tempo settings on the Control Panel

Notice that the target and actual tempo settings change over the course of the movie. The target tempo value is how fast you want the computer to play back the given frame, while the actual tempo value is how fast the computer did play back the given frame.

QuickTip

If you leave Actual Tempo set to Estimated Total, the movie might play back at a reduced speed due to its more intensive calculations.

3. Click the **Actual Tempo Mode button** fps on the Control Panel, then click **Running Total**

The Actual Tempo Mode button changes to tot, as shown in Figure F-6. Running Total indicates the total elapsed time in seconds from the start of the movie to the current frame, which in this case is the end of the movie. You can also choose Seconds Per Frame, also known as SPF, or Estimated Total; it is similar to Running Total, but is more accurate because it includes palette changes and transitions in its calculations of the frame's length.

4. Click the **Actual Tempo Mode button** tot on the Control Panel, then click **Frames Per Second**

The Actual Tempo Mode button changes to fps.

QuickTip

If the movie jumps to other parts, make sure you play through all of these parts to record the actual speed at which to store these values in the Actual Tempo box.

5. Click the **Rewind button** ◀▮ on the Control Panel, then click the **Play button** ▶ on the Control Panel

When you play back the movie from beginning to end, Director records the actual speed at which it plays each frame, and stores these values in the Actual Tempo box in the Control Panel.

6. Click **Modify** on the menu bar, point to **Movie**, then click **Playback**

The Movie Playback Properties dialog box opens, as shown in Figure F-7.

7. Click the **Lock Frame Durations check box** to select it, then click **OK**

Each frame is locked to play at the actual speed recorded when the movie is played back.

8. Click ◀▮ on the Control Panel, click ▶ on the Control Panel, then click the **Close button** on the Control Panel

The movie plays with each frame locked to play at the actual speed recorded.

9. Click **Modify** on the menu bar, point to **Movie**, click **Playback**, click the **Lock Frame Durations check box** to clear it, then click **OK**

The movie's playback speed is unlocked.

FIGURE F-5: Control Panel with tempo settings

Tempo setting for frame 75

Actual tempo value for frame 75

FIGURE F-6: Control Panel with total running time

Click button to change the actual tempo display

Total running elapsed time in seconds from the start to the end of movie, slide 95; your total might be different

FIGURE F-7: Movie Playback Properties dialog box

Click check box to lock the movie playback speed

Unit F

Director 8

Adding a Wait Time

You can use the Tempo channel to add a wait time in the playback of a movie. You can set a movie to wait at a frame for a specified number of seconds until a specific event occurs, such as a mouse click, key press, or a specific cue point in a sound or video. A **cue point** is a marker in a sound or video that you can use to trigger an event in Director. For example, you can use cue points to synchronize an animation with narration. A common use for cue points is to wait for the end of a sound or video to occur before Director starts the next frame in a movie. Jean adds two wait times to the Journey movie.

Steps

1. Click **frame 55** in the **Tempo channel** ⏱ in the Score window
   The selected sprite appears in the Tempo channel, as shown in Figure F-8.

2. Click **Modify** on the menu bar, point to **Frame**, then click **Tempo**
   The Frame Properties: Tempo dialog box opens, as shown in Figure F-9.

QuickTip

To quickly open the Frame Properties: Tempo dialog box, double-click a frame in the Tempo channel.

3. Click the **Wait for Mouse Click or Key Press option button**, then click **OK**
   The Wait for Mouse Click or Key Press option is applied to frame 55. Director waits until the end user clicks the mouse button or presses a key before it continues.

4. Double-click **frame 95** in ⏱
   The Frame Properties: Tempo dialog opens.

5. Click the **Wait option button**, then drag the **Wait slider** or click the **Wait arrow buttons** until the number reaches 4 seconds (or as close as possible)

QuickTip

To delete a tempo, select the frame with the tempo setting, then press [Delete].

6. Click **OK**
   A four-second wait period is applied to frame 95.

7. Click the **Rewind button** ⏮ on the toolbar, then click the **Play button** ▶ on the toolbar
   The movie plays on the Stage and stops at frame 55.

8. When the movie stops at frame 55, position ✧ on the Stage, then click anywhere on the **Stage** to continue playing the movie
   The movie plays on the Stage, and the playback head moves frame to frame through the Score until it reaches the end.

FIGURE F-8: Frame selected in the Tempo channel

Frame 55 in the
Tempo channel

FIGURE F-9: Frame Properties: Tempo dialog box

Click button to set the
frame to wait for a
specified number of
seconds

Click button to set the frame to
wait for mouse click or key press

Inserting cue points in sound and video files

To use the Wait for Cue Point option in the Frame Properties: Tempo dialog box to pause the playback head at certain points in a sound or video, you need to place cue points in the sound or video file that correspond to the times when you want to trigger an event, such as displaying text or starting an animation in Director. In Windows, use Sound Forge 4.0 or later, or Cool Edit 96 or later to insert cue points (called markers or regions within these programs). Cue points are not supported in AVI video. On the Macintosh, use Sound Edit 16 2.07 or later, or Peak LE 2 or later, to insert cue points in AIFF and Shockwave Audio sounds, and in QuickTime video. If you insert cue points into QuickTime files on the Macintosh, you can also use the QuickTime files in Director on the Macintosh and in Windows.

Creating Navigation with Behaviors

You can add navigation controls and interaction to a movie without having to understand and write Lingo, Director's scripting language. You can use a behavior with a prewritten Lingo script to add interactivity to a movie. Director provides a Library palette of useful built-in behaviors that you can drag-and-drop onto sprites and frames in the Score and on the Stage. The Library palette of ready-to-use behaviors is grouped by category, such as animation, controls, text, navigation, and Internet, and comes with a tooltip description of each built-in behavior that makes it easier for you to find and use in a movie. You can attach the same built-in behavior to multiple sprites and frames. You can attach multiple behaviors to an individual sprite, but only one to a frame. If you want a behavior to affect the entire movie, such as Hold on Current Frame, you attach the behavior to a frame. When you attach a behavior to a sprite or frame, a Parameters dialog box might appear, asking you for specific settings. Director copies the behavior from the Library palette to the cast member in the Cast window. Jean adds a navigation control from the Library palette to the Journey movie.

1. Click **Window** on the menu bar, then click **Library Palette**
   The Library Palette window opens, displaying the previous Library List selection.

QuickTip
To hide/show the names of the behaviors in the Library Palette window, click the Library List button, then click Show Names.

2. Click the **Library List button**, then click **Navigation**
   The Library Palette window displays navigational controls, as shown in Figure F-10.

3. Click the **down arrow** at the bottom of the Library Palette window until the **Hold on Current Frame behavior icon** appears, as shown in Figure F-11

4. Position ✋ on the Hold on Current Frame behavior icon in the Library Palette window
   A brief description of the behavior appears. The Hold on Current Frame behavior prevents you from accidentally changing the original behavior.

QuickTip
To attach the same behavior to several sprites at once using the Library Palette window, select the sprites on the Stage or in the Score, then drag a behavior to any one of them. You cannot apply every behavior to every sprite.

5. Drag the **Hold on Current Frame behavior icon** in the Library Palette window to **frame 63** in the Behavior channel
   The behavior is attached to frame 63, and the behavior is copied as cast member 14 in the Cast window, as shown in Figure F-12. If you attach a behavior to a frame that already has a behavior, the new behavior replaces the old one.

6. Click the **Close button** in the Library Palette window
   The Library Palette window closes.

7. Click the **Rewind button** on the toolbar, then click the **Play button** on the toolbar
   The movie plays on the Stage and stops at frame 55.

8. When the movie stops at frame 55, position ✷ on the Stage, then click the **Stage** to continue playing the movie
   The movie plays on the Stage and stops at frame 63.

9. Click the **Stop button** on the toolbar
   The movie stops playing.

FIGURE F-10: **Library palette window with built-in behaviors**

Click button to display Library list categories

Current Library list category

Library

Navigation

Go Loop

Go Next Button

Built-in behaviors

Go Previous Button

Click arrow to display remaining behaviors

FIGURE F-11: **Library palette window**

Library

Navigation

Move mouse pointer here to display a brief description

Go to URL

Hold on Current Frame

Loop for X Seconds

Drag icon to frame or sprite

Drag corner to resize window

FIGURE F-12: **New behavior in the Cast window**

New behavior appears in the Cast window

Frame 63 in the Behaviors channel

Drag icon to frame 63

![CLUES TO USE icon]

Getting information about behaviors

Behaviors included in the Library palette come with brief tooltip descriptions that appear when you position 🖑 over a behavior icon. Some behaviors have long descriptions and instructions, which you cannot read using the tooltip description in the Library palette. To read a complete description and a set of instructions provided by the behavior's author for a behavior already attached to a sprite or frame, you can use the Behavior Inspector. To display more information about a behavior in the Behavior Inspector, attach a behavior to a sprite or frame, click Window on the menu bar, point to Inspector, then click Behavior. The behavior information appears in a scrolling pane at the bottom of the Behavior Inspector.

Adding and Naming Markers

Director 8

While writing a movie, you often might want to move to a specific scene. Markers make it easy to identify and navigate to specific locations in a movie. You can use the Markers channel at the top of the Score window to add and name markers. After you add and name a marker, you can use the marker name in behaviors or scripts to move the playback head to any marker frame in the Score window. Marker names are more reliable to use during authoring than frame numbers. Frame numbers can change if you insert or delete frames in the Score, whereas, unless you move them, markers are static. You can use the Markers window to write comments for individual markers and to move the playback head to a particular marker in the Score. Jean adds and names markers in the Journey movie.

1. **Click the Markers channel above frame 40**
   A marker appears in the Markers channel with the title highlighted, as shown in Figure F-13.

2. **Type Menu, then press [Enter] (Win) or [Return] (Mac)**
   The marker appears in the Markers channel with the name Menu.

   QuickTip

   To delete a marker, drag the marker up or down out of the Markers channel.

3. **Position 🖑 over the Menu marker ▽, then drag the marker to frame 63**
   The marker appears in frame 63, as shown in Figure F-14.

4. **Click the Markers channel above frame 78, type Credits, then press [Enter] (Win) or [Return] (Mac)**
   The Credits marker appears in frame 78.

5. **Click the Rewind button ⏮ on the toolbar, then click the Next Marker button ▶** on the left side of the Markers channel
   The playback head moves to the Menu marker at frame 63.

6. **Click the Next Marker button ▶ on the left side of the Markers channel**
   The playback head moves to the Credits marker at frame 78.

   QuickTip

   To jump to a specific marker, click the Markers Menu button, then click a marker name in the list.

7. **Click the Markers Menu button ▽ to the left of the Next Marker and Previous Marker buttons, then click Markers**
   The Markers window opens, displaying all the markers in the movie, as shown in Figure F-15. The current marker is selected in the left box, its comment is selected in the right box, and its current location appears above the boxes.

8. **Click Menu in the left box, then type Main Menu, then click [Enter] (Win)**
   The marker is renamed and appears in both boxes.

9. **Click the Close button in the Markers window**
   The Markers window closes and the renamed marker, Main Menu, appears in the Markers channel.

FIGURE F-13: Creating a new marker

Markers channel

New marker

Marker title

FIGURE F-14: Naming and moving a marker

Click button to dis-
play Markers Menu

Click button to move
to previous marker

Click button to move
to next marker

Marker with new title

FIGURE F-15: Marker window

Click button to
move to next
marker in the
Score

Markers

Marker name

Creating Navigation with Markers

Once you have added a marker to a frame, you can use the marker name in Lingo scripts and behaviors to navigate to a specific location in a movie. Sometimes it is easier to create a simple Lingo script in a movie than it is to find and use a built-in behavior in the Library palette. You can write a Lingo script to create simple navigation with markers. A Lingo script is a set of instructions that tells Director how to respond to specific events in a movie. A Lingo script is composed of one or more **handlers**, which respond to messages triggered by a specific event during the movie's playback. A handler starts in the Behavior Script window with the word *on* followed by the name of a trigger message, such as *mouseDown*. The handler waits for the specific movie event to occur (such as the end user pressing the mouse button), and then carries out the next Lingo instruction in the script. Table F-1 shows a partial list of movie events and Lingo trigger messages. You don't have to remember all of the Lingo instructions; Director provides a list of instructions by category in a pop-up menu. If the event associated with a handler doesn't occur in the duration of a sprite or frame, Director continues to play the movie. A handler stops when it comes to the word *end* in the script. ◢▬▬▬ Jean creates navigation between different points in the Journey movie, using markers and scripts.

Steps

1. Click **frame 95** in the **Behavior channel** 📃 in the Score window
   The selected frame appears in the Behavior channel.

2. Click **Modify** on the menu bar, point to **Frame**, then click **Script**
   The Behavior Script window opens, displaying the handler associated with a frame, as shown in Figure F-16. The script is color-coded to make it easier to identify different script elements.

3. Click the **Categorized Lingo button** 📑 on the toolbar, point to **Navigation**, then click **go to frame**
   The Lingo instruction *go to frame whichFrame* appears in the script with the text *whichFrame* selected.

4. Type **"Main Menu"**
   The Lingo instruction *go to frame "Main Menu"* appears in the script, as shown in Figure F-17. Lingo is not case-sensitive, but it does make the script easier to read when you use capital letters.

5. Click the **Close button** in the Behavior Script window
   The Behavior Script window closes, and the behavior is saved in the Cast window.

6. Click the **Credits button cast member** in the Cast window, then click the **Cast Member Script button** 📘 in the Cast window
   The Behavior Script window opens, displaying the handler, *on mouseUp*, associated with a sprite.

7. Type **go to frame "Credits"**, then click the **Close button** in the Behavior Script window
   The Cast Member Script icon appears in the Credits button cast member, as shown in Figure F-18. The cast member script is attached directly to the cast member. The cast member script is independent of the Score window, which means that the script is always available whenever the cast member is assigned to a sprite.

8. Click the **Exit button cast member** in the Cast window, click the **Cast Member Script button** 📘 in the Cast window, type **quit**, then click the **Close button** in the Behavior Script window
   The Cast Member Script icon appears in the Exit button cast member.

9. Click the **Rewind button** 📕 on the toolbar, click the **Play button** ▶ on the toolbar, click the **Stage** when the movie stops at frame 55, then click the **Credits button** on the Stage when the movie stops at frame 63
   The playback head jumps to frame 78, plays the movie until it reaches frame 95, jumps quickly back to frame 63, then stops.

FIGURE F-16: Behavior Script window with a handler

Starts the handler

Ends the handler

Trigger message

Begin typing new script

FIGURE F-17: Behavior Script window with Lingo instruction

Click button to display Lingo instructions by category

Lingo instruction

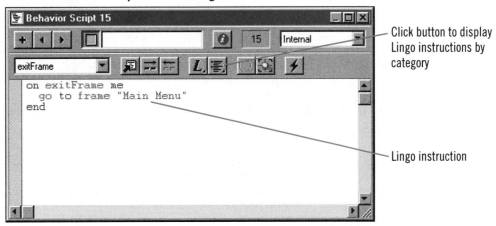

FIGURE F-18: Cast members with a script

Cast member script

Frame script

TABLE F-1: Movie events and Lingo messages

event	message	event	message
A window is closed	closeWindow	Playback head enters current frame	enterFrame
No event occurred	idle	A key is pressed	KeyUp
Mouse button released	mouseUp	Pointer enters sprite's region	mouseEnter
Movie starts playing	startMovie	A window is maximized or minimized	zoomWindow

Adding Rollover Effects

Director 8

Rollover effects allow you to change the appearance of sprites when the mouse pointer passes over them, even if the end user has not clicked the mouse. Rollover effects make it possible for you to give instructional help and feedback to the end user. For example, you can add a rollover effect to a graphical button that changes the appearance of the mouse pointer when it passes over the button. At this point, the end user can receive a cue where to click a button. The Library palette comes with two built-in behaviors to create rollover effects: Rollover Cursor Change and Rollover Member Change. The Rollover Cursor Change behavior allows you to modify a cursor when the mouse pointer rolls over a sprite. The Rollover Member Change behavior allows you to swap a sprite's cast member when the mouse pointer rolls over it.　　　Jean attaches the cursor change rollover effect to a graphical button.

Steps

1. Click **Window** on the menu bar, then click **Library Palette**
   The Library Palette window opens, displaying the previous Library List selection.

2. Click the **Library List button** ▦, point to **Animation**, then click **Interactive**
   The Library Palette window displays interactive animation controls.

3. Click the **down arrow** at the bottom of the Library Palette window until the Rollover Cursor Change behavior appears, shown in Figure F-19

4. Position 🖑 on the Rollover Cursor Change behavior icon in the Library Palette window
   A brief description of the behavior appears.

> **QuickTip**
>
> To attach the same behavior to several sprites at once using the Library Palette window, select the sprites on the Stage or in the Score, then drag a behavior to any one of them.

5. Drag the **Rollover Cursor Change icon** in the Library Palette window to the **Credits button** on the **Stage**
   When you drag the behavior icon on a sprite on the Stage, a gray rectangle appears around the object, indicating where the behavior will be attached. The Parameters for "Rollover Cursor Change" dialog box opens, asking which cursor you want to use. The default cursor for this behavior is the Finger.

6. Click **OK**, then click the **Close button** in the Library Palette window
   The behavior is saved in the Cast window, as shown in Figure F-20, and the Library Palette window closes.

> **QuickTip**
>
> To delete a behavior in the Cast window, select the behavior in the Cast window, then press [Delete].

7. Drag the **Rollover Cursor Change** cast member in the Cast window to the **Exit button** on the Stage, then click **OK**
   The Rollover Cursor Change behavior with the Finger cursor is attached to the Exit button.

8. Click the **Rewind button** ◄ on the toolbar, click the **Play button** ▶ on the toolbar, then click the **Stage** when the movie stops at frame 55

9. When the movie stops at frame 63, position 🖑 on the **Credits button** on the Stage, click the **Stop button** ■ on the toolbar, then click a **gray area** of the Stage
   The cursor changes to 🖑 when it moves over the Credits button.

FIGURE F-19: Library palette with rollover behaviors

Credits button

Drag icon to Credits button on the Stage

Rollover behaviors

FIGURE F-20: Rollover effect in Cast window

Rollover effect in Cast window

Removing and modifying a behavior

Once you attach a behavior to a sprite or frame, you can remove it or modify parameters at any time. Before you can remove or modify a behavior, you need to select the sprite or frame to which the behavior is attached, click the Behavior tab in the Property Inspector, and select the behavior you want to remove or modify, as shown in Figure F-21. To remove a behavior, click the Clear button ⊟ in the Behavior tab, then click Remove Behavior. To change parameters for a behavior attached to a sprite or frame, use the pop-up menus or text fields in the Behavior tab to change any parameters. The Behavior tab includes the same fields for the behavior as those included in the Parameters dialog box.

FIGURE F-21: Behavior tab in the Property Inspector

Behavior tab

Click button to remove behavior

Behavior

Behavior parameters

Director 8

Adding a Transition

Director provides special effects called transitions that you can use to move smoothly from one scene to another. You use the Transition channel in the Score window to add a transition to a frame. To create a transition between two scenes, you set the transition at the first frame of the second scene, not the last frame of the first scene. The transition begins between the frame you select and the frame that precedes it. In the Frames Properties: Transition dialog box, you can select a transition effect and adjust sliders to change the duration and smoothness of the transition as the movie plays. In addition, you can also select whether the transition will affect the entire Stage or just the area that changes in the switch between scenes. ✏️ Jean adds a transition to the Journey movie.

QuickTip

To play a sound while a transition occurs, place the sound in the frame immediately before the transition.

QuickTip

To quickly open the Frame Properties: Transition dialog box, double-click a frame in the Transitions channel.

QuickTip

To delete a transition, select the frame with the transition effect, then press [Delete].

1. Click **frame 78** in the **Transition channel** ▶◀ in the Score window

The selected frame appears in the Transition channel, as shown in Figure F-22.

2. Click **Modify** on the menu bar, point to **Frame**, then click **Transition**

The Frame Properties: Transition dialog box opens.

3. In the Categories box, click **Other**

A list of transitions for the Other category appears in the Transition box.

4. In the Transitions box, click **Zoom Close**

The Zoom Close transition is selected, as shown in Figure F-23.

5. Drag the **Duration slider** or click the **Duration arrow buttons** until the number reaches 2.30 (or as close as possible), then click **OK**

The Zoom Close transition with a duration of 2.3 seconds is applied to frame 78.

6. Click the **Save button** 🖫 on the toolbar.

Director saves the program.

7. Click the **Rewind button** ◀ on the toolbar, click the **Play button** ▶ on the toolbar, then click the **Stage** when the movie stops at frame 55

8. When the movie stops at frame 63, click the **Credits button** on the Stage

The Zoom Close transition is displayed, the playback head jumps to frame 78, and the movie continues to play until it reaches frame 95, waits 5 seconds, and then jumps back to frame 63 and stops.

9. Click the **Exit button** on the Stage

Director closes.

FIGURE F-22: **Frame selected in the Transition channel**

Frame 78 in the Transition channel

FIGURE F-23: **Frame Properties: Transition dialog box**

Click item to select a transition catogory

Drag the sliders to set transition duration and smoothness

Click item to select a transition

Adding Xtra transitions to Director

If you don't find exactly the transitions you want within Director, you can add new transitions by installing them as Xtras. An **Xtra** is a software module you can add to Director, which extends the capabilities of Director. To add Xtra transitions to Director, install a transition by copying the Xtra transition file into the Xtra folder within the Director program folder, exit and start Director, double-click a frame in the Transition channel for the transition, select the Xtra transition, then click OK. To see which Xtras are installed, click Modify on the menu bar, point to Movie, then click Xtras.

Director 8

► Concepts Review

Label each of the elements of the screen shown in Figure F-24.

FIGURE F-24

Match each of the terms with the statement that describes its function.

8. Behavior	**a.** Navigation points in a movie
9. Tempo	**b.** A marker in a sound or video
10. Transition	**c.** A software module that extends the capabilities of Director
11. Cue point	**d.** The speed of a movie
12. Markers	**e.** An effect that moves from one scene to another
13. Handler	**f.** A script that responds to messages triggered by events
14. Xtra	**g.** A ready-to-use script

Select the best answer from the following list of choices.

15. Which is NOT an Actual Tempo Mode display option?
  a. Seconds Per Frame
  b. Frames Per Minute
  c. Estimated Total
  d. Running Total

16. **Which is NOT a Tempo option?**
    a. Wait for Frame
    b. Wait for Cue Point
    c. Tempo
    d. Wait

17. **The Library palette contains:**
    a. Transitions.
    b. Markers.
    c. Behaviors.
    d. Cue points.

18. **How many behaviors can be attached to a frame?**
    a. 0
    b. 1
    c. 2
    d. Up to 999

19. **A handler starts with the word:**
    a. on.
    b. in.
    c. begin.
    d. at.

20. **In the Lingo script *go to frame "Credits"*, Credits refers to a:**
    a. Behavior.
    b. Marker.
    c. Script.
    d. Frame.

21. **A rollover effect is a:**
    a. Transition.
    b. Script.
    c. Behavior.
    d. Handler.

▶ Skills Review

1. **Understand navigation and user interaction.**
   a. Write down the basic types of navigation and user interaction in Director, with a description of each.
   b. Start Director, open the file **MD F-2** from the drive and folder where your Project Files are located.
   c. Save the file as *Nature's Gold* in the drive and folder where your Project Files are located.
   d. Resize the Stage to display the gray area around the Stage.

2. **Change the tempo.**
   a. Play the movie and show the Effects channel, if necessary.
   b. Change the tempo to 15 fps in frame 1.
   c. Change the tempo to 25 fps in frame 46.

3. **Compare tempo performance.**
   a. Open the Control Panel, if necessary.
   b. Rewind and play the movie.
   c. Compare the actual tempo to the tempo settings, and write down the results.
   d. Close the Control Panel.

4. Add a wait time.

  a. Add a wait until mouse click in frame 26.

  b. Add a 2-second wait time in frame 45.

5. Create navigation with behaviors.

  a. Attach the Hold on Current Frame behavior to frames 47, 66, 86, and 106.

6. Add and name markers.

  a. Add and name a marker "Main menu" at frame 46.

  b. Add and name a marker "Fruits" at frame 65.

  c. Add and name a marker "Vegetables" at frame 85.

  d. Add and name a marker "Treats" at frame 105.

7. Create navigation with markers.

  a. Attach a navigation script to *go to frame "Fruits"* to the text cast member Fruits text.

  b. Attach a navigation script to *go to frame "Vegetables"* to the text cast member Vegetables text.

  c. Attach a navigation script to *go to frame "Treats"* to the text cast member Treats text.

  d. Attach a navigation script to *quit* to the cast member Exit button.

  e. Attach a navigation script to *go to frame "Main menu"* to the cast member Menu button.

8. Add rollover effects.

  a. Add a rollover cursor change with the Finger cursor to the cast members Exit button, Menu button, Fruits text, Vegetables text, and Treats text.

9. Add a transition.

  a. Add the transition effect Dissolve, Pixels Fast with the Changing Area Only option to frame 46.

  b. Add the transition effect Wipe Right to frames 65, 85, and 105.

  c. Play the movie, then save the movie and exit Director.

▶ Independent Challenges

1. You are a multimedia Web designer at *Astronomy* magazine. In next month's issue, the feature article is about the increasing number of shooting stars. The magazine's editor asks you to create a shooting star animation for the magazine's Web site. You use Director's Paint tool to create a star and animation to move the star across a nighttime scene. You also change the tempo of the animation and compare it to the actual speed.

  To complete this independent challenge:

  a. Start Director and save the movie as *Shooting Star* in the drive and folder where your Project Files are located.

  b. Open the Paint window, then create a bright orange star.

  c. Change the background of the Stage to black.

  d. Create a text cast member with the text **Shooting Star**, and drag it to the top of the Stage.

  e. Animate the star across the Stage in frames 1 to 30.

  f. Set the tempo to 10 frames per second (fps) in the first frame.

  g. Change the tempo to 20 fps in frame 10, then change the tempo to 30 fps in frame 20.

  h. Play the entire movie to record the tempo settings.

  i. Play the movie again, compare the tempo settings to the actual speed, then write down your observations.

  j. Print the screen (see Visual Workshop for instructions), save the movie, and exit Director.

2. You work as a multimedia designer at Adventures in Reading. The company is coming out with a new line of books called *Follow the Bouncing Ball*. Your boss asks you to create a bouncing animation to promote the new series on the company's Web site. You use Director's Paint tool to create a ball, the Cast window to make copies and modify colors, and animation tools to bounce the ball three times with different colors and waiting times.

  To complete this independent challenge:

  a. Start Director and save the movie as *Bouncing Ball* in the drive and folder where your Project Files are located.

b. Create and name a Paint cast member of a ball with a filled color.

c. Make three copies of the ball cast member and change the fill color.

d. Create a text cast member with the text **Follow the Bouncing Ball**, and drag it to the top of the Stage.

e. Animate the first ball to bounce bottom-to-top on the Stage in frames 1 to 15. (*Hint:* Create a straight line angled animation from the bottom to the top.)

f. Animate the second ball to bounce bottom-to-top on the Stage in frames 15 to 30.

g. Pause the ball in frame 15 at the top of the bounce for 3 seconds.

h. Animate the third ball to bounce bottom-to-top on the Stage in frames 30 to 45.

i. Animate the fourth ball to bounce top-to-bottom on the Stage in frames 45 to 60.

j. Pause the ball in frame 45 at the top of the bounce until a mouse click.

k. Play the movie, print the screen (see Visual Workshop), save the movie, then exit Director.

3. You are a teacher at Happiness Hill Preschool. As part of a teaching lesson, you want to create an animated smiley face for the kids. You use Director's Paint tool to create a smiley face and behaviors to animate the eyes with a built-in behavior. To complete this independent challenge:

a. Start Director and save the movie as *Smiley Face* in the drive and folder where your Project Files are located.

b. Create and name a Paint cast member of a yellow circle and a black smiling mouth.

c. Create and name a Paint cast member of a small circle with a black dot on the right side for the eye.

d. Drag the yellow circle on the Stage and the small circle in the yellow circle twice, to create two eyes.

e. Create a text cast member with the text **Smiley Face**, and drag it to the top of the Stage.

f. Open the Library palette and display the Interactive list of behaviors.

g. Drag the Turn Towards Mouse behavior onto the small circles (eyes of the smiley face) on the Stage, then set the behavior to always turn.

h. Play the movie and move the mouse around to move the eyes.

i. Print the screen (see Visual Workshop for instructions), save the movie, then exit Director.

4. You are the owner of Last Chance Nursery, a small family-operated business. You want to add a small catalog of products to your Web site. You use Director's navigation and user interaction capabilities to create a main menu with plant categories and behaviors to branch to the different plant areas.

To complete this independent challenge:

a. Connect to the Internet and go to www.course.com. Navigate to the page for this book, click the link for the Student Online Companion, then click the link for this unit.

b. Browse the Plants section for photographs.

c. Download three different flower photographs and three different food photographs in the drive and folder where your Project Files are located.

d. Start Director and save the movie as *Last Chance* in the drive and folder where your Project Files are located.

e. Change the background of the Stage to green.

f. Create a text cast member with the text **Last Chance Nursery**, and drag it to the top of the Stage.

g. Create and name separate text cast members with the text **Main menu**, **Flowers**, and **Food**, and drag them on the Stage to create a Main menu similar to the unit.

h. Set the Hold on Current Frame behavior for this frame, known as the Main menu.

i. Create separate areas for Flowers, and drag the Flowers text cast member and flower photographs on the Stage.

j. Create separate areas for Food, and drag the Food text cast member and food photographs on the Stage.

k. Set markers for Main menu, Flowers, and Food in associated areas of the Score window.

l. Set the Flowers and Food text cast members on the Main menu to a rollover cursor effect, and add scripts so that the text cast members jump to their associated markers, and return to the Main menu.

m. Play the movie and jump to the Flowers and Food areas.

n. Print the screen (see Visual Workshop for instructions), save the movie, then exit Director.

► Visual Workshop

Recreate the screen shown in Figure F-25. Print the screen. (For Windows, use the Windows Paint program. Press the Print Screen key to make a copy of the screen, start the Paint program by clicking Start, pointing to Programs, pointing to Accessories, then clicking Paint, click Edit on the menu bar, click Paste to paste the screen into Paint, then click Yes to paste the large image if necessary. Click File on the menu bar, click Print, click Print or OK in the dialog box, then exit Paint. For the Macintosh, use the SimpleText program. Hold and press the Command, Shift, and 3 keys to make a copy of the screen, double-click the document Picture 1 located on your hard drive, click File on the menu bar, click Print, then click Print in the dialog box. (*Note*: When you create a new document with a copy of the screen, and a document Picture 1 already exists, the Macintosh names the new document Picture 2.)

FIGURE F-25

Unit G

Adding
Audio, Video, and Other Media

Objectives

▶ **Import audio and video media**
▶ **Control audio in the Score**
▶ **Stream Shockwave Audio**
▶ **Control video in the Score**
▶ **Play video direct to the Stage**
▶ **Crop and scale a video**
▶ **Synchronize media**
▶ **Import a Microsoft PowerPoint presentation**
▶ **Export a movie to video**

Director allows you to import audio, video, and other media into a movie and combine the cast members with text, animation, and other effects to create multimedia movies. This unit introduces you to basic skills for importing, controlling, playing, modifying, synchronizing, and exporting audio, video, and other media in Director movies. First, you'll learn how to import and play several types of media files in Director, using different options and techniques. Then, you'll learn how to control and synchronize the media to make sure everything works together smoothly. Finally, you'll learn how to import a Microsoft PowerPoint presentation into Director and export it to video. ✐ Jean wants to add audio, video, and other media to a new movie.

Director 8

Importing Audio and Video Media

If you already have created digital audio or video in other programs, you can import these media elements into the active Cast window. You can import a variety of sound formats, including AIFF (Audio Interchange File Format), WAV (either compressed or uncompressed), Shockwave Audio, AU (Sun audio), MP3, and Macintosh sounds. To create or alter a sound, you need to use another program, such as Macromedia's SoundEdit 16. You can import a sound into Director as an internal cast member, which is ideal for short sounds, or as an externally linked cast member, which is good for longer sounds, such as a voice narration. You can import QuickTime movies (Macintosh and Windows) and AVI movies as video cast members. You can also import other video formats, such as MPEG, but you need to install an Xtra to perform the function. When Director imports video, it creates and maintains a link to the external video file. If you change the video in Director or in the external video file, the corresponding external video file or video in Director changes to match. If you move the Director movie to another location on your hard disk or computer, you need to move the external sound and video files. Otherwise, the sound and video do not play. ▰▰▰ Jean imports sound and video media into the Journey II movie.

Steps

1. Start **Director**, open the file **MD G-1** from the drive and folder where your Project Files are located, then save it as **Journey II**
   Director opens, displaying the movie. Your initial settings in Director can vary.

2. Click the down scroll arrow in the Cast window to display cast member 31, then click **cast member 31** (blank)
   The blank cast member is selected. The media files will be imported into the current cast member location (if blank) or the next available location in the Cast window.

3. Click the **Import button** 🔲 on the toolbar
   The Import Files into "Internal" dialog box opens.

4. Click the **Look in list arrow** ▼, click the drive and folder where your Project Files are located, then double-click the **Media folder**
   A list of files for the Media folder appears.

5. Click the **Files of type list arrow** ▼, then click **Sound**
   All the sound files in the Media folder appear in the Look in file list, as shown in Figure G-1. You can select files in the list individually or together and import them into the active Cast window.

6. Click the **Blastoff.wav file**, click **Add**, click the **Meteor.wav file**, click **Add**, then click **Import**
   The sound files appear in the file list and as new cast members in the Cast window.

7. Click the **Import button** 🔲 on the toolbar, verify that the Media folder is selected, click the **Files of Type list arrow** ▼, then click **All Files** (scroll as necessary)
   The Import Files into "Internal" dialog box opens, and all file types appear in the Look in list.

8. Click the **Blastoff.mov file**, click **Add**, click the **Earthvenus.avi file**, click **Add**, then click **Import**
   The Select Format dialog box opens (Win), indicating that Director can import the Earthvenus AVI video using multiple formats.

9. Click **AVI**, then click **OK**
   The video files appear as cast members in the Cast window, as shown in Figure G-2.

QuickTip

To record a simple sound in Director (Mac), attach a microphone to your computer, click Insert on the menu bar, click Media Element, click Sound, click Record to begin, then click Stop to end. When you finish, click Save, then name the sound to store it in the Cast window.

QuickTip

To link an external sound file to a movie, click the Import button 🔲 on the toolbar, click the Media list arrow ▼, then click Link To External File.

QuickTip

The Macintosh converts AVI files to QuickTime files. The Select Format dialog box doesn't appear (Mac).

FIGURE G-1: Import Files into "Internal" dialog box

Your sound icon might vary, depending on your default sound program

Sounds in Media folder

Click arrow to select Sound files

Click arrow to link to an external file

FIGURE G-2: Cast window with audio and video cast members

QuickTime video

Internal WAV sounds

AVI video (Win) or QuickTime video (Mac)

Understanding sound cast members

When you import a sound as an internal cast member, the sound is stored in the movie or in an External Cast window, which increases the size of the movie or Cast file. When you play a movie, Director loads all internal sounds into RAM first. This allows Director to play the movie at any time without any delays. Short sounds, such as beeps or clicks, work best as internal sound cast members. An externally linked sound cast member is stored outside of the movie or an External Cast window, which reduces the size of the movie or cast file. When the playback head reaches an externally linked sound, Director must load the sound into RAM and then start to play the sound, which can cause an initial delay. To reduce the delay, Director streams externally linked sounds. Streaming allows Director to load a small portion of the sound and then play the sound while it continuously loads the rest of the sound. Long sounds, such as a narration or instruction, work best as externally linked cast members.

Controlling Audio in the Score

Once you import sounds into a Cast window, you can place them in either of the two Sound channels in the Score window. A sound plays in Director at the rate and duration in which it was recorded; Director's tempo settings do not affect the sound's playback speed. Audio and video files are time-based media, which means that files play according to a timeline with a start time and an end time. Director, on the other hand, is a frame-based medium, which means that movies play according to a set number of frames. When you place an audio or video in the Score, you need to assign it a sufficient number of frames so that the file plays completely. Otherwise, the audio or video file will cut off abruptly when you play the movie. You can quickly ensure that the sound has enough frames to play completely. Simply drag the sound in the Sound channel into more frames than the sound can possibly require, then play the movie. Watch the Score to determine at which frame the sound stops, then remove the extra frames. Instead of using frames, you can also set a wait time in the Tempo channel for the length of the sound, to make sure the sound plays completely. If a sound stops prematurely, you can set the sound to loop, or repeat. If you want to match a sound with an animation, you need to place the sound in the Score to match the frame with the action. Jean places sound cast members in the Score and modifies the number of frames to control the sound's length.

QuickTip

Although you can't set a volume for a specific sound, you can set the volume in the Control Panel for the entire movie.

1. Click the **Play button** ▶ on the toolbar, click navigation buttons to continue playing the movie, then click the **Rewind button** ◄ on the toolbar
   The movie plays on the Stage, and the playback head moves frame to frame through the Score until it reaches the Main menu (Let the Journey Begin). The Main menu contains the elements of the multimedia project. If you click the Exit button on the Stage, save any changes, then start the Journey II movie again. Now, you will add sound and video to complete the project.

2. Click the **Hide/Show Effects Channels button** in the Score window to display the Effects channels, if necessary
   The Effects channels appear in the Score window.

3. Click the **Blastoff sound cast member** in the Cast window, then click the **Sound tab** in the Property Inspector
   The Sound tab in the Property Inspector opens, displaying information about the sound, as shown in Figure G-3. The sound information includes the sampling rate, bit depth, and channels type.

QuickTip

To repeat the sound, click the Loop check box in the Sound tab of the Property Inspector to select it, then click the Play button.

4. Click the **Play button** ▶ in the Sound tab of the Property Inspector
   The sound plays once.

5. Drag the **Blastoff sound cast member** to **frame 35** in Sound channel 1, then drag the **end of the sprite** to **frame 60**
   The Blastoff sound cast member appears in frame 35 to frame 60, as shown in Figure G-4.

6. Click ◄ on the toolbar, click ▶ on the toolbar, then click the **Stop button** ■ on the toolbar after the playback head stops at frame 63
   The movie plays the sound from frame 35 to frame 60.

QuickTip

To play a sound in the Score, double-click a sound, select a sound in the Frame Properties: Sound dialog box, then click Play.

7. Scroll in the Score to display frame 115, drag the **Meteor sound cast member** to **frame 115** in Sound channel 2, then drag the **end of the sprite** to **frame 127**
   The Meteor sound cast member appears in frame 115 to frame 127.

8. Click ◄ on the toolbar, then click ▶ on the toolbar
   The movie plays the animation and sound and stops at the Main menu.

9. Click **Sounds** on the Stage, then click ■ on the toolbar when the playback head stops at frame 127
   The movie plays the sound until it reaches the hold on current frame behavior in frame 127.

FIGURE G-3: Sound tab in the Property Inspector

Click check box
to loop sound

Sound information

Click button to
play sound

FIGURE G-4: The Score window with a sound

Blastoff sound in
a Sound channel

Understanding sound

When you record or modify a sound, you should consider four factors that affect the performance and quality of a sound file. The first factor is the sampling rate of the sound. The **sampling rate** (measured in kilohertz, or kHz) is the frequency with which samples are taken per second. For example, a sound sampled at 22.050 kHz saves the audio value 22,050 times per second. The higher the sampling rate, the higher the sound quality. Common sampling rates include 5.5125 kHz (standard telephone call), 11.025 kHz (broadcast television audio), 22.050 kHz (FM radio), 44.100 kHz (compact disc), and 48.000 kHz (digital audio tape). The second factor is the bit depth at which the sound is recorded. The **bit depth** is a measure of how much data space is available to store

a given moment of sound. The sounds you import into a movie can have different bit depths. The two most common are 8 bits and 16 bits. The higher the bit depth, the higher the sound quality. The third factor is the channels type, **stereo** or **mono encoding**, which are two types of sound quality. Stereo encoding produces high-quality sound, but the file size associated with a stereo file is twice the size of a mono sound. The final factor is the compression rate of the sound file. **Compression** reduces the size of a file. There are different compression standards and different compression ratios, which can produce a wide range of sound quality. The higher the compression ratio, the smaller the file size. However, the reduction in size might result in lower quality or speed.

Streaming Shockwave Audio

Shockwave Audio is a technology that reduces the size of sound files and plays them faster from disk or from the Internet. You can use Shockwave Audio to compress the size of sounds by a ratio as high as 176 to 1. Compression reduces the size of a file. Director streams Shockwave Audio and MP3 sound files to reduce the delay time in playing a sound. When Director streams a sound, it doesn't have to load the entire sound file into RAM before it begins to play the sound. Director loads and plays the beginning of the sound as the rest of the sound continues to load. Before you can stream a Shockwave Audio cast member, you need to create a Shockwave Audio or MP3 sound file. You can use Peak LE 2 on the Macintosh or the Convert WAV to SWA command on Windows to convert a sound to the Shockwave Audio format. When you insert a Shockwave Audio or MP3 file, either from a local hard disk, network drive, or a URL or Web address, the sound is imported as an externally linked cast member. ✐ Jean creates a Shockwave Audio file and streams it in the Journey II movie.

Steps 1 2 3 4

1. Click **Xtras** on the menu bar, click **Convert WAV to SWA** (Win), or skip to **Step 4** (Mac)
   The Convert .WAV Files To .SWA files dialog box opens, as shown in Figure G-5. The default **bit rate**, or degree of compression, is set to 16 kbps (kilobytes per second). The higher the bit rate, the faster a sound streams, but the quality of the sound can suffer. If you are creating movies for Internet delivery, you should use 16 kbps for the best results.

2. Click **Add Files**, click the drive and folder where your Project Files are located, double-click the **Media folder**, then double-click the **Blastoff.wav** file
   The Blastoff sound file appears in the Files to Convert file list.

3. Click **Select New Folder**, click the drive and folder where your Project Files are located, click **Select Folder**, click **Convert**, then click **Close**
   The Blastoff WAV sound file is converted to an SWA sound file. The SWA sound file size is considerably smaller than the WAV sound file. To verify, you can use Windows Explorer (Win) or Mac Operating System to compare the two file sizes.

4. Click the **Blastoff sound** in Sound channel 1, then press **[Delete]**
   The Blastoff WAV sound is deleted from the Score.

5. Click **Insert** on the menu bar, point to **Media Element**, then click **Shockwave Audio**
   The SWA Cast Member Properties dialog box opens with a default URL, as shown in Figure G-6.

6. Click **Browse**, click the drive and folder where your Project Files are located, then double-click the **Blastoff.swa file** (Win), or the **Blastoffm.swa file** (Mac)
   The SWA Cast Member Properties dialog box appears with the full path to the SWA Blastoff sound file on your hard disk or network drive.

7. Drag the **Volume Slider** to the ¾ mark on the scale, click **Play**, then click **OK**
   The volume level is adjusted, and the Blastoff sound file plays. The SWA sound cast member is stored in the Cast window with no title, a blank thumbnail, and the 🔊 icon.

8. Drag the **SWA cast member** with the Blastoff sound to **frame 35** in Sprite channel 7, then drag the **end of the sprite** to **frame 60**
   The SWA cast member appears in the Score from frame 35 to frame 60.

9. Click the **Rewind button** ◄ on the toolbar, click the **Play button** ► on the toolbar, then click the **Stop button** ■ on the toolbar when the playback head stops at frame 63

FIGURE G-5: Convert .WAV Files To .SWA Files dialog box

Click arrow to specify bit rate

Click button to select a destination for the SWA files

Click button to select the WAV files

FIGURE G-6: SWA Cast Member Properties dialog box

Default location for SWA file

Click button to play sound and display sound information

Click button to select a file on your computer

CLUES TO USE

Compressing internal sounds with Shockwave Audio

You can store and compress a sound internally in Director, using Shockwave Audio. Compressing sounds decreases the size of the movie file, shortens the download time from the Internet, and reduces the preload time required to play a sound without a delay. You can use Shockwave Audio settings to compress internal sound cast members, but the compression takes place only when you compress the Director movie with the Create Projector, Save as Shockwave Movie, or Update Movies commands. To set the Shockwave Audio compression options for all internal sound cast members, click File on the menu bar, click Publish Settings, click the Compression tab, click the Compression Enabled check box to select it, select a bit rate setting from the kBits/seconds list (lower values produce smaller and faster files with lower quality), click the Convert Stereo to Mono check box to select it, if necessary, then click OK. You should try several different bit rates to see how the sounds change.

x

Director 8

ADDING AUDIO, VIDEO, AND OTHER MEDIA   DIRECTOR G-7

Controlling Video in the Score

Once you import digital videos into a Cast window, you can place them into any Frame channel in the Score window, just as you would any other sprite. Digital videos begin to play when the playback head reaches the sprite containing the video sprite. A digital video, like a sound, plays for the duration of the sprite. If you do not assign enough frames to play the video completely, it will cut off abruptly when you play the video. You can extend the video to occupy enough frames in the Score to play completely. You can use the QuickTime or AVI tab in the Property Inspector to make the video loop or pause. Director 8 supports Apple's QuickTime 4 or earlier for Macintosh and Windows. If you want to play or author Director movies that use QuickTime cast members, you must have QuickTime installed on your computer. You can download the latest version of QuickTime from the Apple Computer Web site at *www.apple.com*. In Windows, you can play AVI movies with no additional software requirements. ✒ Jean places a QuickTime and an AVI video on the Stage, adds a loop option to one of them, and plays them.

Steps

1. Click **frame 100** in **Sprite channel 8**
   The playback head appears in frame 100, and the Stage displays the Videos scene.

2. Drag the **Blastoff video cast member** to the Stage above the Menu and Exit buttons, then drag the **end of the sprite** to **frame 112** in the Score
   The Blastoff video appears on the Stage.

3. Click **frame 100** in **Sprite channel 9**, drag the **Earthvenus video cast member** to the **left side** of the Stage, then drag the **end of the sprite** to **frame 112** in the Score
   The Earthvenus video appears on the Stage along with the Blastoff video, as shown in Figure G-7.

4. Double-click the **Blastoff video sprite** on the Stage
   The QuickTime 33:Blastoff window opens, as shown in Figure G-8.

Trouble?

Macintosh users end lesson after Step 5.

5. Click the **Play button** at the bottom of the QuickTime window, then click the **Close button**
   The video plays once. Mac users stop here.

QuickTip

If the Direct to Stage check box in the QuickTime or AVI tab of the Property Inspector is not selected, you can apply ink effects to video sprites.

6. Click the **Earthvenus video sprite** in the Score, click the **AVI tab** ⬛ (Win) or the **QuickTime tab** ⬛ (Mac) in the Property Inspector, then click the **Loop check box** to select it, if necessary
   The AVI tab (Win) or the QuickTime tab (Mac) in the Property Inspector appears, and the Earthvenus video is set to continuously loop.

7. Double-click the **Earthvenus video sprite** on the Stage
   The AVI video window opens.

QuickTip

If you play an AVI video on a Macintosh, Director converts the video to QuickTime.

8. Double-click the **image** in the AVI Video window to play the video or click the **Play button** at the bottom of the QuickTime window
   The video begins to play.

9. After the video loops, click the **image** in the AVI video window to stop it, then click the **Close button**

FIGURE G-7: The Stage with digital video

QuickTime video

AVI video (Win)
or QuickTime
video (Mac)

FIGURE G-8: QuickTime cast member window

Click button to
play video

Click buttons to step
through video

Click button to
mute sound

Controlling an animated GIF

Many Web sites include animated GIF (Graphics Interchange Format) files that you can use in a Director movie. You can import an animated GIF in the same way you import a video. Director supports the GIF89a and GIF87 formats with a global color table. Once you import an animated GIF, you can set options to change the link to a file on your hard disk or a URL, play the GIF directly on the Stage at the fastest possible playback rate, or change the tempo to play the GIF at a rate consistent with the movie. To preview the GIF animation, double-click the GIF cast member in the Cast window, then click Play.

Playing Video Direct to Stage

The performance of a video can vary when it plays in Director. The Direct to Stage option provides the best performance for playing QuickTime or AVI videos in a Director movie. When you select the Direct to Stage option in the QuickTime or AVI tab of the Property Inspector, Director allows QuickTime or AVI software installed on your computer to completely control the video playback. The Direct to Stage option provides optimal performance in video playback, but it also limits where you can locate the video on the Stage in relation to other sprites, and it prohibits applying ink effects to a video. When Director plays the video, it always appears in front of all other sprites on the Stage, no matter which channel contains the video sprite. When you select the Direct to Stage option, you can also choose a playback option to play the video in synchronization with a soundtrack, play every frame of the video at a normal, maximum, or fixed speed without the soundtrack, or display the controller bar to start, stop, and step through a QuickTime video on the Stage. ◢◤◤ Jean experiments with the Direct to Stage and related options to achieve the best results for the Journey II movie.

Trouble?
If the Direct to Stage check box is not selected, click the Direct to Stage check box to select it.

1. Click the **Blastoff video sprite** on the Stage, click the **QuickTime tab** 🔘 in the Property Inspector, then verify that the Direct to Stage check box is selected
   The QuickTime tab in the Property Inspector appears, as shown in Figure G-9.

2. Click the **Loop check box** to select it in the QuickTime tab of the Property Inspector
   The Blastoff video is set to continuously repeat.

3. Click the **Rewind button** ⏮ on the toolbar, click the **Play button** ▶ on the toolbar, then click **Videos** on the Stage

Trouble?
If the video delivery speed is slow, the controller bar might flicker.

4. Click the **Show Controller check box** to select it in the QuickTime tab of the Property Inspector, then click the **Play Sound check box** to clear it
   The controller bar appears at the bottom of the video on the Stage, and the sound stops, as shown in Figure G-10.

5. Click the **Show Video check box** to clear it in the QuickTime tab of the Property Inspector, then click the **Show Video check box** again to select it
   The video is hidden and stops as shown or replays.

6. Click the **Play Sound check box** to select it in the QuickTime tab of the Property Inspector, then click the **Show Controller check box** to clear it

7. Click the **Loop check box** to clear it in the QuickTime tab of the Property Inspector

8. When the Blastoff video ends, click the **Stop button** ⏹ on the toolbar, then click the **Rewind button** ⏮ on the toolbar

FIGURE G-9: QuickTime tab in the Property Inspector

QuickTime tab

QuickTime video options

FIGURE G-10: Playing videos directly to the Stage

Play video direct to Stage

Direct to Stage option is turned on

Show Controller option is turned on

Show Controller

Editing a QuickTime video

Director allows you to perform simple editing tasks, such as deleting or reordering a sequence of video frames, in a QuickTime video. Before you can edit a QuickTime video, you need to first open the video in the QuickTime video window of Director. To open the video in Director, double-click the QuickTime video sprite in the Score, or the cast member in the Cast window. Once you open the QuickTime video, you can select a single video frame or a range of frames, and then use the Cut or Clear commands on the Edit menu to delete the selected video frames, or the Copy and Paste commands on the Edit menu to reorder the selected video frames. To select a range of video frames, hold down [Shift] and drag the slider until you reach the last video frame you want to select. The selected range of video frames appears in a dark shade of gray.

Director 8

Cropping and Scaling a Video

When you place a video on the Stage, the shape and size of the video might not look the way you want. In Director, you can crop, or trim, any unwanted areas around the edge of the video, or resize the video to better fit the Stage. When you crop a video, the edges you trim are not removed from the video; they are just hidden. You can restore the cropped area of a video at any time. The Scale option allows you to change the size, or dimension, of a video. When you scale a video, hold down [Shift] to maintain a proportional playback area which ensures the best results. However, any large-scale changes can dramatically reduce the quality of the video display. Jean crops and scales a video in the Journey II movie.

Steps

1. Click the **Blastoff video sprite** in the Score, then click the **QuickTime tab** in the Property Inspector, if necessary
   The QuickTime tab in the Property Inspector appears.

2. Click the **Crop option button** in the QuickTime tab of the Property Inspector, then click the **Center check box** to clear it, if necessary
   The option to crop a video is set.

3. Drag the **right-middle sizing handle** of the Blastoff video sprite on the Stage to the **left** to match Figure G-11
   When you position the pointer over a sizing handle, the pointer changes to black (Win) or white (Mac). The Blastoff video is cropped on the Stage.

QuickTip

To undo the action you just performed, click the Undo button on the toolbar.

4. Drag the **right-middle sizing handle** of the Blastoff video sprite to the **right** until the video is restored to its original display
   The previously cropped area of the Blastoff video is redisplayed.

5. Click the **Earthvenus video sprite** on the Stage, then click the **AVI tab** (Win) or **QuickTime tab** (Mac) in the Property Inspector, if necessary

6. Click the **Scale option button** in the AVI tab (Win) or QuickTime tab (Mac) of the Property Inspector, if necessary
   The option to scale a video is selected.

7. Press and hold **[Shift]**, then drag the **upper-right-corner sizing handle** of the Earthvenus video sprite **inward** slightly to match Figure G-12
   The video is slightly reduced in size on the Stage.

8. Click the **Rewind button** on the toolbar, then click the **Play button** on the toolbar

9. Click **Videos** on the Stage, click the **Stop button** on the toolbar when the Blastoff video ends, then click the **Rewind button** on the toolbar

FIGURE G-11: **Cropping a video**

Click button to select Crop option

Drag sizing handle here to crop video

FIGURE G-12: **Scaling a video**

Drag sizing handle here to scale video

Click button to select Scale option

Director 8

Unit G
Director 8

Synchronizing Media

You can synchronize, or match, sounds and videos with other actions in a Director movie. For example, you can synchronize points in a sound file to make text appear in time with the narration. You can use the Wait for Cue Points option to synchronize points in a sound or video file with specific frames in a Director movie. A common use for the Wait for Cue Point option with sound and video files is to wait for the end of the sound or video before you continue to the next frame. If you want Director to identify the cue points anywhere inside a sound or video file, you need to insert the points in the file using another program, such as SoundEdit 16 (Mac), Peak LE 2 (Mac), Sound Forge 4 (Win), or Cool Edit 96 (Win). To help eliminate delays in loading video files during the playback of a Director movie, you can preload the video into RAM at the beginning of the movie, so it's ready to play at any time, instead of playing it from disk. 🖋 Jean creates navigation between different points in the Journey movie, using markers and scripts.

Steps

1. Click the **Earthvenus video sprite** in the Score, then click the **AVI tab** 🎬 (Win) or **QuickTime tab** 🎬 (Mac) in the Property Inspector, if necessary
   The AVI tab in the Property Inspector appears, as shown in Figure G-13.

2. Click the **Preload check box** to select it in the AVI tab (Win) or QuickTime tab (Mac) of the Property Inspector
   The option to preload the video is set.

3. Click the **Blastoff video sprite** on the Stage, then click the **QuickTime tab** 🎬 in the Property Inspector, if necessary
   The QuickTime tab in the Property Inspector appears.

4. Click the **Preload check box** to select it in the QuickTime tab of the Property Inspector
   The option to preload the video is set.

5. Double-click **frame 100** in the **Tempo channel**
   The Frame Properties: Tempo dialog box opens.

6. Click the **Wait for Cue Point option button**, click the **Cue Point list arrow** 🔽, then click **{End}**
   The Cue Point is set to end, as shown in Figure G-14.

7. Click **OK**
   A wait for the end of the Blastoff video is applied to frame 100.

8. Click the **Rewind button** ⏮ on the toolbar, click the **Play button** ▶ on the toolbar, then click **Videos** on the Stage

9. Click the **Stop button** ⏹ on the toolbar when the Blastoff video ends, then click the **Save button** 💾 on the toolbar
   Director saves the program.

FIGURE G-13: AVI tab in the Property Inspector

AVI tab

AVI video check boxes

FIGURE G-14: Frame Properties: Tempo dialog box

Click arrow to
select sound
or video

Click arrow
to select
cue point

CLUES TO USE

Importing Flash movies in Director

You can import Flash movies into Director movies and save them as Shockwave movies for use on the Web. Flash movies are vector-based animations and media that you can scale, rotate, and modify without losing any degree of sharpness or quality. Director can import Flash files, version 2.0 or later, and support new features in Flash 4. To import a Flash movie as a cast member, click Insert on the menu bar, point to Media Element, then click Flash Movie. In the Flash Asset Properties dialog box, click Browse to select the Flash movie (.SWF extension) you want to import. Once you select the Flash movie, you can set options to link the movie to an external file on your hard disk or network drive, or to a URL; preload the movie into memory before playing; control movie playback in Director, a projector, or a Shockwave movie; specify a quality rating for anti-aliasing; specify a scale mode for the size of the movie; and specify the tempo to play the movie at a rate consistent with the movie.

Director 8

Importing a PowerPoint Presentation

If you have a PowerPoint version 4 or later presentation, you can import the presentation into a Director movie, play the presentation as a slide show, and save the movie as a stand-alone projector file or as a Shockwave movie for the Web. Director imports the graphics, transitions, and text as cast members and converts each slide into a section in the Score. In cases where there is not an exact match for a PowerPoint feature in Director, Director uses the closest matching feature. Director cannot import PowerPoint animation effects, unique fonts, or special formatting, such as shadows. See Director Help for a complete comparison of PowerPoint and Director features. Jean imports a PowerPoint presentation as the basis for a new movie.

Steps

1. Click **File** on the menu bar, point to **New**, then click **Movie**
   A blank movie appears in the Director window.

2. Click the **Movie tab** in the Property Inspector, double-click the **Stage size width box**, type **720**, double-click the **Stage size height box**, type **540**, then press **[Enter]** (Win) or **[Return]** (Mac)
   The Movie tab in the Property Inspector appears with a new Stage size, 720 × 540, the size of a PowerPoint slide.

3. Click **Xtras** on the menu bar, then click **Import PowerPoint File**
   The Please select a PowerPoint to open dialog box opens.

4. Open the file **MD G-2** (Win) or **MD G-2m** (Mac) from the drive and folder where your Project Files are located
   The PowerPoint Import Options dialog box opens with default settings, as shown in Figure G-15. You can set import options for Slide Spacing, the number of blank lines between slides in the Score; Minimum Slide Duration, the minimum number of frames a slide takes up in the Score; Item Spacing, the number of frames used for each item in a PowerPoint build effect; and Fly Transition Item Spacing, the number of frames between keyframes in the Score.

5. Click **Import**, then click **OK**
   A progress meter appears as Director imports the presentation media. Upon completion, the Import Results dialog box appears, indicating that the import process has been successful.

6. Click the **Save button** 🖫 on the toolbar, type **PPT Pres** in the File name text box, click the drive and folder where your Project Files are located, then click **Save**

7. Click the **Score Window button** 🖳 on the toolbar, then click the **Cast Window button** 🏣 on the toolbar, if necessary
   The Score window and Cast window appear with the conversion of the PowerPoint features for Windows or Macintosh in Director, as shown in Figure G-16.

8. Click the **Stage button** 🗔 on the toolbar, click the **Play button** ▶ on the toolbar, then click the **Stop button** ■ on the toolbar at the first slide
   The first PowerPoint slide appears on the Stage, as shown in Figure G-17.

9. Click the **Play button** ▶ on the toolbar, then click the **Rewind button** ⏮
   Director plays the rest of the movie.

Trouble?
If Director can't open the PowerPoint file, open the presentation in PowerPoint, click File on the menu bar, click Save As, click the Files of Type list arrow, click PowerPoint 4.0, then click Save.

Trouble?
Director might play the movie slowly.

FIGURE G-15: PowerPoint Import Options dialog box

FIGURE G-16: Score window and Cast window

Slide 1   Slide 2   Slide 3   Score window and Cast window will be
different on the Macintosh

FIGURE G-17: Slide 1 on the Stage in Director

Director 8

Exporting a Movie to Video

You can export all or part of a movie as a digital video or a series of frame-by-frame bitmaps. You can use the digital video or series of bitmaps in other applications or import it back into Director. Exporting a movie to digital video is recommended only for straightforward linear animations or presentations. When Director exports any interactivity, such as button scripts and frame scripts, the information is not included after the exporting process. When Director exports animation as a digital video, it takes snapshots of the entire Stage moment by moment and turns each snapshot into a frame in the video. Director allows you to export a movie as an AVI (Win) or QuickTime (Mac) video, or as a BMP (Win), PICT (Mac), Scrapbook (Mac), or PICS (Mac) graphic. Before you can export a movie as a QuickTime digital video, QuickTime must be installed on the computer. Jean exports the PowerPoint presentation in Director to a QuickTime digital video.

Steps

1. Click File on the menu bar, then click Export

The Export dialog box opens, as shown in Figure G-18. The options in the Export dialog box are determined by the file format you choose.

2. Click the Format list arrow ▼, then click QuickTime Movie (.MOV)

The next step is to choose the range of frames you want to export and the method of selecting frames within that range.

3. Click the All Frames option button

All the frames in the presentation movie are selected for export to QuickTime.

4. Click Options

The QuickTime Options dialog box opens with a set of parameters specific to QuickTime, as shown in Figure G-19.

5. Click the Tempo Settings option button, if necessary

This option translates the tempo settings in Director to a frames-per-second rate for the export to video. The other alternative is Real Time, which records the video movie exactly as the Director movie plays on the computer.

6. Click the Compressor list arrow ▼, then click Video (scroll as necessary)

The Video compressor setting is a standard for QuickTime video. The compressor is optimized for cross-platform use and 16-bit and 24-bit color images. The average compression ratio is about 5 to 1. See Table G-1 for a description of the Compressor options; different options appear in the list depending on the video hardware and software on your computer.

7. Click OK, then click Export

The Save File(s) as dialog box opens.

8. Click the drive and folder where your Project Files are located, click Save, then click OK

The QuickTime movie is exported to a file (PPT Pres.mov), plays on the screen, then returns to the main Director window.

9. Click File on the menu bar, then click Exit (Win) or Quit (Mac)

Director closes.

> **QuickTip**
>
> For an export to AVI, the Options dialog box only contains an option to set the export rate in frames per second. In addition, when you export to AVI, sounds in the movie are not included.

> **Trouble?**
>
> If a Ready to Export dialog box appears, follow the instructions.

> **Trouble?**
>
> If Director asks you to save the movie, click Yes (Win) or Save (Mac).

FIGURE G-18: **Export dialog box**

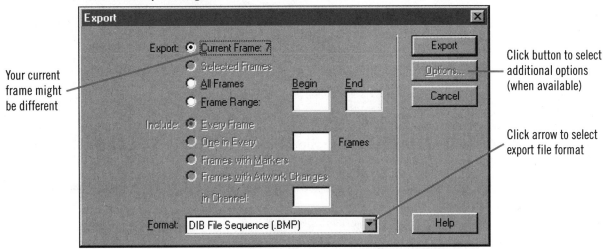

Your current
frame might
be different

Click button to select
additional options
(when available)

Click arrow to select
export file format

FIGURE G-19: **QuickTime Options dialog box**

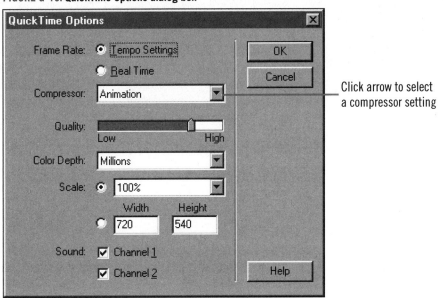

Click arrow to select
a compressor setting

TABLE G-1: **Compressor options**

option	description
Animation	Optimized for simple sprite motions, minimal transitions, and sound play instructions
Cinepak	A standard for high-quality video; recommended for transferring the digital video to traditional video tape; the compression ratio is 10 to 1
Component Video (Mac)	Optimized for capturing raw video footage; the compression ratio is 2 to 1
Graphics	Optimized for 8-bit color; the compression ratio is 11 to 1; files take longer to decompress
None	No compression
Photo-JPEG	A standard for digitized images, such as scanned photographs; the compression ratio is between 10 to 1 and 20 to 1
Video	A standard for QuickTime video; optimized for cross-platform use and 16-bit and 24-bit color images; the compression ratio is 5 to 1
Intel Indeo Video	Optimized for the Intel Indeo video chip

Director 8

Director 8 Practice

► Concepts Review

Label each of the elements of the screen shown in Figure G-20.

FIGURE G-20

Match each of the terms with the statement that describes its function.

8. Compression
9. Mono
10. Sampling rate
11. QuickTime
12. Streaming
13. MP3
14. Bit depth

a. The process of continuously loading a sound or video as it plays
b. A video format common to Macintosh and Windows
c. The process of reducing the size of a file
d. The measure of how much data space is available to store a sound
e. A sound quality channels type
f. The frequency with which sounds are taken per second
g. A format that Director streams to reduce the delay time in playing

Select the best answer from the following list of choices.

15. Which is NOT an import sound format?
    a. AIFF   b. WAV   c. SWA   d. MP3

16. Which video format needs an Xtra installed to import a video?
    a. QuickTime   b. MPEG   c. AVI   d. None of the above

17. Audio and video files are:
    a. A frame-based medium.   c. Linked to the Cast window.
    b. A time-based medium.   d. None of the above

18. Which is the common sampling size for compact discs?
    a. 5.5125 kHz   b. 11.025 kHz   c. 22.050 kHz   d. 44.100 kHz

19. A GIF is a:
    a. Movie.   b. Sound.   c. Video.   d. Animation.

20. Which is NOT a limitation of using the Direct to Stage option?
    a. Prevents the use of ink effects   c. Appears in front of all sprites on Stage
    b. Plays every frame of the video   d. All of the above

21. Cue points are used in Director to:
    a. Synchronize sound or video with other actions.   c. Animate sound or video.
    b. Change the tempo in a sound or video.   d. None of the above

22. Which QuickTime export compressor option is optimized for cross-platform use?
    a. Animation   b. Cinepak   c. Graphics   d. Video

▶ Skills Review

1. **Import audio and video media.**
   a. Start Director, open the file MD G-3 from the drive and folder where your Project Files are located.
   b. Save the file as *Animal Life* in the drive and folder where your Project Files are located.
   c. Select cast member 19.
   d. Import all the sound files, except Eagle and Lion, from the Media SR folder.
   e. Select cast member 25, then import all the video files from the Media SR folder.
   f. If the Select Format dialog box appears, import AVI files in the AVI format.

2. **Control audio in the Score.**
   a. Add the Birds sound to frames 26 through 45, then loop the sound.
   b. Add the Dog sound to frames 106 through 120, and Dog video to frames 105 through 120 in channel 8.
   c. Add the Monkey sound to frames 66 through 80, and Monkey video to frames 65 through 80 in channel 8.
   d. Add the Tiger sound to frames 146 through 160, and Tiger video to frames 145 through 160 in channel 8.
   e. Add the Wolf sound to frames 126 through 140, and Wolf video to frames 125 through 140 in channel 8.
   f. Add the Zebra sound to frames 86 through 100, and Zebra video to frames 85 through 100 in channel 8.

3. **Create and stream Shockwave Audio.**
   a. Convert the Birds sound to an SWA (Win).
   b. Insert the Birds (Win) or Birdsm (Mac) SWA sound in the Cast.
   c. Add the Birds sound to frames 46 through 60 in channel 8.
   d. Play the Birds sound.

4. **Control video in the Score.**
   a. Loop the Wolf video.
   b. Play the Wolf video.

5. **Play video direct to Stage.**
   a. Verify that all the videos are set to Direct to Stage.
   b. Show the controller on the Monkey video.
   c. Play the Monkey video.

6. Crop and scale a video.

   a. Crop the edges of the Tiger video.

   b. Scale the Zebra video slightly larger.

   c. Play the Tiger video and the Zebra video.

7. Synchronize media.

   a. Select the Preload check box for all the videos.

   b. Set the wait for cue point at frame 45 for the end of the Birds sound.

   c. Save the movie.

8. Open a new movie and import a Microsoft PowerPoint presentation.

   a. Import the file MD G-4 (Win) or MD G-4m (Mac) from the drive and folder where your Project Files are located.

   b. Set minimum slide duration to 15 frames per slide, then use the default import settings.

   c. Import the sound files from the Media SR folder that correspond to the animals in the movie.

   d. Add the appropriate sound in a Sound channel to frames with the corresponding animal.

   e. Save the file as *Animal Pres* in the drive and folder where your Project Files are located.

   f. Play the movie.

9. Export a movie to video.

   a. Export the PowerPoint presentation movie to video.

   b. Export all the frames using the Real Time option and the Video compressor.

   c. Save the file as *Animal Pres*, using the Quicktime Movie format in the drive and folder where your Project Files are located.

   d. Exit Director.

▶ Independent Challenges

1. You are a media designer at Play It Again Media, a sound and video development company. You have developed a library of custom sounds. Your boss asks you to create a simple sound player that customers can use to play sounds. You use Director to import a variety of sounds and create a Main menu where you click the name of each sound to play it. You use Director to import a variety of sounds and create a Main menu where you click the name of each sound to play it.
  To complete this independent challenge:

   a. Start Director and save the movie as *Play It Again Sounds* in the drive and folder where your Project Files are located.

   b. Create a text cast member with the text **Play It Again Sounds**, and drag it to the top of the Stage.

   c. Connect to the Internet and go to www.course.com. Navigate to the page for this book, click the link for the Student Online Companion, then click the link for this unit.

   d. Download three or four sounds, including at least one Shockwave Audio file. (*Hint*: Right-click a sound, click Save Target As, navigate to the drive and folder where your Project Files are located, then click Save.)

   e. Import the sounds into Director.

   f. Create a Main menu with the names of the sounds.

   g. Add the sounds to the Score.

   h. Add markers to the frames with each sound, and create scripts to jump to each marker from the Main menu.

   i. Play each sound, save the movie, then exit Director.

2. You are a media designer at Play It Again Media, a sound and video development company. You have developed a library of custom videos. Your boss asks you to create a simple video player with controls to start, stop, and replay the video, which customers can use to preview the material. You use Director to import a variety of videos, create a Main menu where you click the name of each video to play it, and display controls to start, stop, and replay the videos.

To complete this independent challenge:

a. Start Director and save the movie as *Play It Again Videos* in the drive and folder where your Project Files are located.

b. Create a text cast member with the text **Play It Again Videos**, and drag it to the top of the Stage.

c. Connect to the Internet and go to www.course.com. Navigate to the page for this book, click the link for the Student Online Companion, then click the link for this unit.

d. Download two or three videos. (*Hint*: Right-click a video hyperlink, click Save Target As, navigate to the drive and folder where your Project Files are located, then click Save.)

e. Import the videos into Director.

f. Create a Main menu with the names of the videos.

g. Add the videos to the Stage.

h. Add markers to the frames with each sound, and create scripts to jump to each marker from the Main menu.

i. Play the videos directly to the Stage and show controls for each video.

j. Play each video, save the movie, then exit Director.

3. You are the owner of World Travelers, Inc., an international travel tours company. You package and promote customized tours to unique destinations around the world. A client wants to book a travel tour to Israel. The client developed a promotional presentation in PowerPoint, but you need the presentation in digital video. You use Director to import the PowerPoint presentation and export the movie to a digital video.

To complete this independent challenge:

a. Start Director, then set the Stage size to 720×540, if necessary.

b. Import the file MD G-5 (Win) or MD G-5m (Mac) from the drive and folder where your Project Files are located.

c. Use the default import settings.

d. Save the movie as *World Travelers* in the drive and folder where your Project Files are located.

e. Export the PowerPoint presentation movie to video.

f. Export all the frames, using the Tempo Settings option and the Video compressor.

g. Save the file as *World Travelers*, using the QuickTime Movie format in the drive and folder where your Project Files are located.

h. Exit Director.

4. You are the publisher of *Animal Fun*, an online Web magazine for kids. For the anniversary issue, you want to create a fun story about an animal that includes sound and video. You use Director to insert an animal sound and video and control the playback of the media.

To complete this independent challenge:

a. Connect to the Internet and go to www.course.com. Navigate to the page for this book, click the link for the Student Online Companion, then click the link for this unit.

b. Download a sound and video for a bird. (*Hint*: Right-click a sound or video hyperlink, click Save Target As, navigate to the drive and folder where your Project Files are located, then click Save.)

c. Start Director, then save the movie as *Animal Fun* in the drive and folder where your Project Files are located.

d. Change the background of the Stage to a color appropriate to colors in the video.

e. Create a text cast member with the text **Animal Fun**, and drag it to the top of the Stage.

f. Create a text cast member with text for the story title and drag it to the top of the Stage.

g. Create a text cast member with text for the body of the story and drag it below the story title.

h. Drag the animal sound and video on the Stage.

i. Set the Hold on Current Frame behavior for the animal sound and video to the Stage at the story.

j. Set a rollover cursor effect for the story title.

k. Set the video and sound to play when you click the story title.

l. Play the movie, save the movie, then exit Director.

Director 8

► Visual Workshop

Recreate the screen shown in Figure G-21. Your marine animal video and sound might be different. (*Hint*: Search the Web for videos, and download them to your hard drive; see Independent Challenge 4.) Print the screen. (For Windows, use the Windows Paint program. Press the Print Screen key to make a copy of the screen, start the Paint program by clicking Start, pointing to Programs, pointing to Accessories, then clicking Paint, click Edit on the menu bar, click Paste to paste the screen into Paint, then click Yes to paste the large image if necessary. Click File on the menu bar, click Print, click Print or OK in the dialog box, then exit Paint. For the Macintosh, use the SimpleText program. Hold and press the Command, Shift, and 3 keys to make a copy of the screen, double-click the document Picture 1 located on your hard drive, click File on the menu bar, click Print, then click Print in the dialog box. *Note*: When you create a new document with a copy of the screen, and a document Picture 1 already exists, the Macintosh names the new document Picture 2.)

FIGURE G-21

Unit
H

Preparing
and Delivering Movies

Objectives

- ► **Embed fonts in movies**
- ► **Manage Xtras for distributing movies**
- ► **Understand distribution methods**
- ► **Set movie playback options**
- ► **Set projector options**
- ► **Create a projector movie**
- ► **Launch the movie in a projector**
- ► **Create a Shockwave movie**
- ► **Create a protected movie**

Once you create and fine-tune a movie, you are ready to prepare and deliver it. This unit introduces you to basic skills for optimizing and preparing movie-related files, such as external sounds and movies, and a Director movie for delivery on a playback computer. First, you'll learn how to embed fonts in a movie for playback use on all computers, and how to manage Xtra files for movie distribution. Then, you'll learn about the different distribution methods for a movie in Director. Finally, you'll learn how to protect external movie files, set movie playback and projector options, and create a projector movie and a Shockwave movie for delivery. ✐ After completing the Journey movie, Jean wants to prepare and deliver the movie as a projector movie and Shockwave movie for Spaceworks Interactive management.

Director 8

Embedding Fonts in Movies

If you like to use unique fonts in your movies, the fonts need to be installed on the playback computer in order for the font to display properly; otherwise, Director will use a substitute font. You can embed fonts in a Director movie so that the font will display properly even if it is not installed on the playback computer. When you embed a font in a movie, Director stores the font information in the movie file. You can only embed a font in a movie that is also installed on your computer. The embedded fonts are available only to the movie itself, so there are no legal infringements to distributing fonts in Director movies. Embedded fonts appear in a movie as cast members and work on both Windows and Macintosh computers. Once you embed a font in a movie, the font appears on all of the movie's font menus, and you can use it as you would any other font. Director compresses embedded fonts, so they usually only add 14–25K to a file. Jean embeds a font in a movie.

1. **Start Director, open the file MD H-1** from the drive and folder where your Project Files are located, then save it as **Journey Final**
   Director opens, displaying the movie. Your initial settings in Director can vary, depending on previous usage.

2. **Double-click the Journey text** cast member in the Cast window, then select **all the text** in the Text window
   The Text window opens with the Journey text cast member.

Trouble?
If the Impact font is not available on your computer, select another font.

3. **Click the Font list arrow** ▼, scroll down, click **Impact**, then click the **Close button**
   The font type is changed to Impact.

4. **Click Insert** on the menu bar, point to **Media Element**, then click **Font**
   The Font Cast Member Properties dialog box opens.

5. **Click the Original Font list arrow** ▼, then click **Impact**
   The font name appears in the Original Font box and the New Font Name box with an asterisk, as shown in Figure H-1. When you create embedded fonts using the original font name followed by an asterisk, Director uses the embedded font for all the text in the movie that uses the original font. This saves you the trouble of manually reapplying the font to all the text in existing movies.

6. **Click the Sizes option button**, click the **box to the right**, then type **9, 10, 12, 14**
   Only the 9, 10, 12, and 14 point sizes are included in the movie file. If you only plan to use a few font sizes, you do not need to embed all the font sizes; you can only embed the ones you need. When you specify specific font sizes, you reduce the size of the movie file.

7. **Click the Bold check box**, then click the **Italic check box** to select them
   The bold and italic versions of the font sizes are included in the movie file. The text set to Impact bold and Impact italic in the movie display properly on the screen; a substitute font is not used. When you include the bold and italic versions of a font, you increase the size of the movie file.

QuickTip
To include specific font characters in a movie, click the Other check box to select it, then type the characters (a, b, d, s, t, and so on) in the text box to the right.

8. **Click the Partial Set option button**, then click the **Roman Characters check box** to select it
   Only the roman characters (for example, A, a, B, b, and so on) are included with the embedded font type and sizes selected.

9. **Click OK**, then scroll down the Cast window to display the font cast member
   The embedded Impact font appears in the Cast window, as shown in Figure H-2.

FIGURE H-1: Font Cast Member Properties dialog box

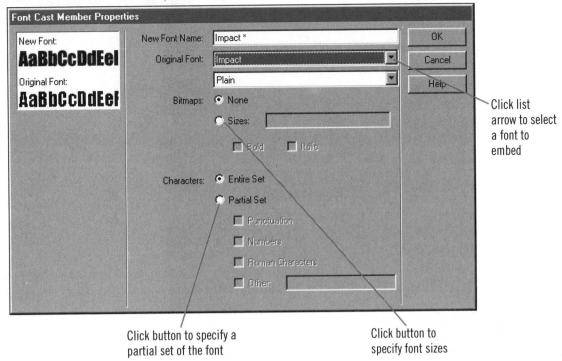

Click list arrow to select a font to embed

Click button to specify a partial set of the font

Click button to specify font sizes

FIGURE H-2: Embedded font in the Cast window

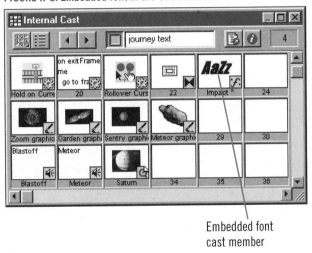

Embedded font cast member

CLUES TO USE

Optimizing font embedding

For the best display at smaller sizes, include bitmap versions of a font when you embed it. For small font sizes, usually from about 7 to 12 points, bitmap fonts often look better than anti-aliased outline fonts. If you add a set of bitmap characters to the movie, you increase the size of the file. To speed up movie downloading, you can keep file size small by specifying a subset of characters to be included. You can also specify which point sizes to include as bitmaps and which characters to include in the font package. If you do not embed fonts in a movie, Director substitutes available system fonts.

Managing Xtras for Distributing Movies

Many important features in Director are controlled by Xtras, such as creating text and vector shapes, importing different media types, or adding third-party transition effects. Like fonts, Xtras in a movie need to be installed on the playback computer so that the movie will run properly. When you distribute a movie, you either need to include the Xtras in the file or provide the end user with the opportunity to download them. You can use the Movie Xtras dialog box, which includes a list of the most commonly used Xtras, to specify the Xtras you want to include and the ones you want the end user to download. If you are not using an Xtra listed in the Movie Xtras dialog box, it is a good idea to remove it in order to reduce the file size and increase the speed of the movie. If you don't package Xtras with the movie, you need to create an Xtras folder in the folder with the projector file, copy the Xtras to the folder, select the Xtras in the Movie Xtras dialog box, and then deselect the Include in Projector check box. The Movie Xtras dialog box also includes the ability to access information about a specific Xtra on the Macromedia Web site, which requires Internet access. Jean adds an Xtra to the movie, gets more information about it from the Internet, and then decides to remove it.

1. Click **Modify** on the menu bar, point to **Movie**, then click **Xtras**
   The Movie Xtras dialog box opens, displaying the currently installed Xtras, as shown in Figure H-3.

2. If you have access to the Internet, click **QT3Asset.x32** (Win) or **QuickTime Asset** (Mac), then click the **Download if Needed check box** to select it
   Director accesses the Macromedia Web site and downloads the QuickTime Xtra. When you use the Download if Needed option, the movie prompts the end user to download the required Xtra.

3. Click **Add**
   The Add Xtras dialog box opens, displaying a list of commonly used Xtras.

4. Scroll if necessary, click **Flash Asset.x32** (Win) or **Flash Asset PPC** (Mac), then click **OK**
   The Xtra is added to the list.

5. Scroll to the bottom of the list, then click **Flash Asset.x32** (Win) or **Flash Asset PPC** (Mac)
   The Xtra appears in the installed list, as shown in Figure H-4. The Include in Projector check box becomes available, and the option is selected. This indicates that the Xtra is included when Director creates a projector file.

6. If you have access to the Internet, click **Info**, then read the Web site information
   Your Web browser opens, displaying the Macromedia Web site with information about the Xtra.

7. Click **File** on the menu bar, then click **Close** (Win) or **Quit** (Mac)
   Your Web browser closes. The Flash Xtra remains selected in the Movie Xtras dialog box.

8. Click **Remove**
   The Xtra is removed from the list, which reduces the size of the movie.

9. Click **OK**

FIGURE H-3: Movie Xtras dialog box

List of currently installed Xtras; your list might be different

Click button to add network-related Xtras

Click button to add the standard Director Xtras

FIGURE H-4: Adding an Xtra to a movie

Select check box to include Xtra in the projector movie

Select check box to prompt for Xtra downlaod (if needed)

Click button to add an Xtra

Click button to get Xtra information from the Macromedia Web site

Working with third-party Xtras

You can use six types of Xtras in Director: image filters, importing, transition, cast member, Lingo or scripting, and tool, all of which are external authoring aids. Image filter Xtras allow you to modify bitmapped images in the Paint window; importing Xtras allow you to insert additional external media not standard to Director; transition Xtras allow you to add transition effects, such as a wipe left or fade right, not built into Director; cast member Xtras allow you to add new media types, such as a spreadsheet or database, to a movie; and Lingo or scripting Xtras allow you to add new Lingo language elements, such as a new command, to Lingo. Director comes with a set of third-party Xtras on the Director installation CD. You can incorporate these and many other Xtras, which you can find on the Macromedia Web site (www.macromedia.com), into your movies. To use these Xtras, you need to install them first. To install an Xtra, find the Xtras folder in the Director program folder, place the new Xtra in the Xtras folder, then restart Director. You can place the Xtra in a folder that is nested inside the Xtras folder no deeper than five folder levels. Xtras are used in Director in different ways. The transition Xtras appear in the Transition dialog box, and the cast member Xtras appear in the Cast window, while other Xtras appear as menu commands on the Xtras menu or the Media Element submenu on the Insert menu.

Understanding Distribution Methods

Director provides several different formats to save a movie for distribution to end users. You can save your Director movie as a projector movie, a Shockwave movie, a Shockwave projector movie, a protected movie, or a Java applet. You can also distribute a movie in the Director movie format, but this method is not recommended because end users will be able to change the movie using Director. Before you save a movie in any of the distribution formats, it's important to understand how Director plays movies in each of the methods. Jean takes some time to familiarize herself with some of the distribution methods available in Director.

Details

Distribution methods:

 A **projector movie** is a stand-alone program that end users can play on their computers without having Director installed. A projector movie can include one or more movies, the standard player, Xtras, multiple casts, and linked media in a single file. The standard player is a self-contained Director movie player that the projector uses to play the Director movie. A projector movie is intended for play in a window or on the full screen without a Web browser, as shown in Figure H-5.

 A **Shockwave movie** is a compressed movie that does not include the standard player. A Shockwave movie is intended for play over the Internet in a Web browser, as shown in Figure H-6. End users must have the Shockwave player installed on their computers in order to play the movie. You can download the Shockwave player for free from the Macromedia Web site at www.macromedia.com.

 A **Shockwave projector movie** is another compressed movie that end users can play on their computers without a Web browser. Shockwave projector movies also use the Shockwave player instead of the standard player, and are much smaller versions of an equivalent projector movie.

 A **protected movie** is an uncompressed Director movie that end users cannot open and modify in Director. Protected movies do not include any player software to play the movie. They can be played only by a projector, as a movie in a window (a Lingo operation), or by using the Shockwave player.

 A **Java applet** created in Director is a movie converted to Java, a programming language. Java applets created in Director provide extended functionality to play simple movies in a Web browser where plug-ins, such as the Shockwave player, are not allowed. When you convert a movie to Java, not all Director features are available, so you need to be aware of the authoring issues involved in the process.

FIGURE H-5: Projector movie in a window

FIGURE H-6: Shockwave movie in a Web browser

CLUES TO USE

Distributing a movie on a disk, to a local network, or to the Internet

When you distribute a movie on a disk, local network, or the Internet, all linked media, such as bitmaps, sounds, and videos, need to be in the same relative location as they were when you created the movie. To make sure you don't forget any linked media, it is a good idea to place linked files in the same folder as the projector or in a folder inside the projector folder. If you plan to place a movie on the Internet for playback in a Web browser, the linked media need to be at the specified URL when the movie plays. If you plan to link media

on a local disk only to a Shockwave movie, you need to place the media in a folder named dswmedia. To test movies in a Web browser, place the movie, linked casts, and linked media in folders within a dswmedia folder, and use relative links instead to refer to them. If you plan to place a movie on a local network, all files must be set to read-only, so that other users cannot change the movie file, and end users must have read/write access to their system folder, so that the movie player can access system files.

Director 8

Setting Movie Playback Options

You can use the Movie Playback Properties dialog box to set General and Streaming playback options for the movie. In the General area, you can select options to lock the movie to its current tempo settings and make the movie pause when its window is deactivated. In the Streaming area, you can set the movie to stream, and then specify the number of frames downloaded before the movie begins to play. If you have an introductory scene that plays while other media are downloading, you need to set the download value so that all of the required media for the introductory scene are loaded before the movie begins to play. To help you determine when media elements appear in a movie, you can make the movie display placeholders (a rectangle with diagonal lines) for media elements that have not downloaded yet. The playback option can be set or changed at any time before you create the projector or Shockwave movie. Jean sets movie playback options for the projector and Shockwave movies.

1. **Click Modify on the menu bar, point to Movie, then click Playback**
   The Movie Playback Properties dialog box appears, as shown in Figure H-7.

2. **Click the Pause When Window Inactive check box to select it**
   This option makes the movie pause when its window is deactivated.

3. **Double-click the Download box to select the current value**
   The Download box allows you to specify the number of frames downloaded before the movie begins to play.

QuickTip

Setting a higher download value is useful for streaming movies that were not created for streaming.

4. **Type 30**
   The download value is set to 30 frames.

5. **Click the Show Placeholders check box to select it**
   This option displays placeholders for media elements that did not completely download in time to display in the movie.

6. **Click OK**
   The options set in the Movie Playback Properties dialog box take effect when you create a projector or Shockwave movie, or preview the movie in a Web browser.

Movie Playback Properties ⊠

General: ☐ Lock Frame Durations

☐ Pause When Window Inactive

Streaming: ☑ Play While Downloading Movie

Download 1 Frames Before Playing

☐ Show Placeholders

OK

Cancel

Help

Select check box to
stream the movie

Setting up a movie to stream

A streaming movie starts to play as soon as Director downloads the Score information and the cast members for the first frame. After the movie starts to play, Director continues to download cast members and any linked media in the background as they appear in the Score. When you create a movie to stream, you need to make sure all cast members have been downloaded by the time the movie needs them; otherwise, the cast member will not appear in the frame. To set up a movie to stream, you use the Movie Playback Properties dialog box. To turn on the streaming option, click Modify on the menu bar, point to Movie, click Playback, click the Play While Downloading Movie check box to select it, then click OK. If the streaming option is deselected, Director downloads all cast members before the movie starts to play.

Director 8

Director 8

Setting Projector Options

Before you create a projector movie, it's important to set the options that will affect the Director movie. Some of the options are specific to the computer on which you create the projector. You can set projector options to play back one or more movies in the foreground or the background, determine the screen size and Stage size for one or more movies, compress the projector file, and select the player to use. Director retains the options settings once you define them, so you don't have to set them each time. You can include only Director 8 movies in projectors. You can use the Update Movies command on the Xtras menu to convert older movies to the latest version of Director. ✐ Jean sets options for the projector movie.

Steps

1. Click **File** on the menu bar, then click **Save and Compact**
   The movie is saved and compressed to create a faster projector file.

2. Click **File** on the menu bar, then click **Create Projector**
   The Create Projector dialog box appears.

QuickTip
If you want to include more than one movie in the projector, click the Play Every Movie check box to select it.

3. Click **Options**
   The Projector Options dialog box appears, as shown in Figure H-8.

4. In the Playback area, click the **Animate in Background check box** to select it
   This option plays the movie even when the end user switches to another program. If you clear this option, the projector pauses when the end user switches to another program and resumes playing when the end user selects the projector. Notice that it is similar to selecting the Pause When Window Inactive check box in the Movie Playback Properties dialog box.

QuickTip
To automatically switch the color depth of your monitor to the color depth of each movie in the projector play list, click the Reset Monitor to Match Movie's Color Depth check box to select it (Mac).

5. In the Options area, click the **Full Screen option button** (Win) or click the **Full Screen check box** to select it, if necessary (Mac)
   The movie is set to fill the entire screen when playing. This option hides the computer's desktop. If a menu bar is used in the movie, it appears at the top of the Stage.

6. In the Stage Size area, click the **Center check box** to select it
   This option plays the movie in the center of the screen, which is convenient when the Stage is smaller than the full screen size. In Windows, projectors are always centered.

7. In the Media area, click the **Compress (Shockwave Format) check box** to select it
   This option compresses the movie in the Shockwave format, which reduces the projector file size but increases the time needed to load the movie. It is important to note that this option does not create a Shockwave movie; it only uses Shockwave technology to compress the projector movie.

QuickTip
To make Director use available system memory when its own partition is full, click the Use System Temporary Memory check box to select it (Mac).

8. In the Player area, click the **Compressed option button**
   This option includes a compressed version of the standard player in the projector file. See Table H-1 for a description of the player options.

9. Click **OK**, then click **Cancel**
   The projector options are set, even though you did not create a projector movie. These settings remain in effect until you change them.

Click option to select
player type in projector

TABLE H-1: Player options in the Options dialog box

player option	description
Standard	Includes the uncompressed player in the projector file. This option starts the movie faster than other options but creates the largest projector file.
Compressed	Includes a compressed version of the standard player in the projector file. The compressed version significantly reduces the projector file size, but decompressing the player adds a few seconds to the startup time of a movie.
Shockwave	Makes the projector use the Shockwave player installed on the end user's computer instead of including the standard player in the projector file. If the Shockwave player is not available when the movie plays, the movie prompts the end user to download it.

Director 8

Creating a Projector Movie

A projector is a stand-alone play-only version of your movie. You can include as many movies as you want in a projector. When you create a projector, Director embeds all files (such as Internal and External Casts and Xtras), except linked media, into a single program file. If you have linked media, you need to place the files in the same folder as the projector to make sure the movie plays properly. To create a projector for Windows or on the Macintosh, you need to use Director for Windows or Macintosh, respectively. In other words, you cannot create a projector for Windows using Director for Macintosh, or vice versa. If you want to create a cross-platform movie using either Director for Windows or Director for Macintosh, you must create a Shockwave movie. The end user can play the movie created in either platform in their Web browser. Once you create a projector movie, you cannot modify it; you need to change the original movie in Director, and then create a new projector file. Jean creates a projector of the Journey movie.

Steps

1. Click **File** on the menu bar, then click **Create Projector**
   The Create Projector dialog box appears.

2. Click the **Look in list arrow** ▾, then click the drive and folder where your Project Files are located
   A list of the files and folders appears, as shown in Figure H-9 (Win) or Figure H-10 (Mac). You can select files individually or together in the file list to add into the projector.

   QuickTip
   You can click Move Up or Move Down to change the order of multiple movies in the projector.

3. In the list of files and folders, click **Journey Final**, then click **Add**
   The movie file appears in the File List.

4. Click the **Files of type list arrow** ▾, then click **Movie Cast Xtra**, if necessary (Win)
   This option includes the movie, cast, and Xtra files in the projector file.

5. Click **Create**
   The Save projector as dialog box appears.

6. In the File name box, type **Take the Journey**

   QuickTip
   To avoid problems with linked media, create the projector file in the same folder as the linked media.

7. Click the **Save in list arrow** ▾, then click the drive and folder where your Project Files are located, if necessary

8. Click **Save**
   A progress meter appears as Director saves the movie, cast, and included Xtras into a single projector file.

FIGURE H-9: **Create Projector dialog box (Windows)**

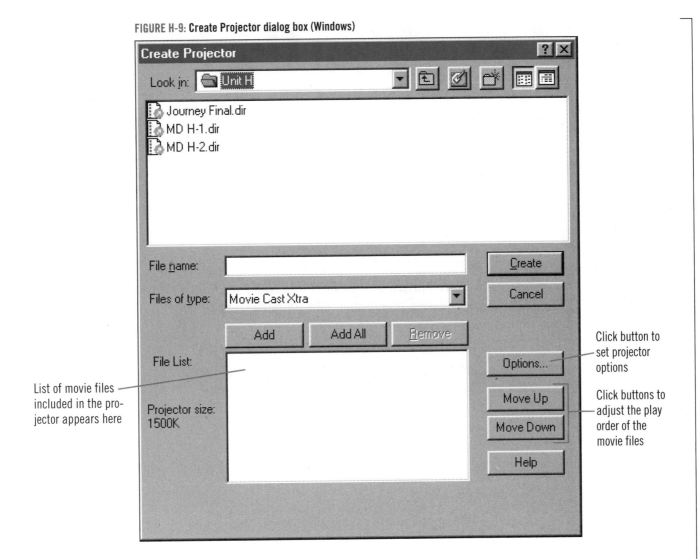

List of movie files included in the projector appears here

Click button to set projector options

Click buttons to adjust the play order of the movie files

FIGURE H-10: **Create Projector dialog box (Macintosh)**

Click button to set projector options

List of movie files included in the projector appears here

Click button to adjust the play order of the movie files

Launching the Movie in a Projector

After you create a projector movie, it's a good idea to test the projector, especially if it includes linked media, to make sure the movie plays properly. A projector movie can be identified by a distinctive icon. Unless you linked files to the projector, everything the movie needs to play is included in the stand-alone program. As long as the end user's computer meets the minimum hardware requirements, the system can play the projector movie. If you include a player in the projector movie, the end user doesn't need to install Director or any other player. ▰▰▰ Jean launches the projector movie.

Steps 1 2 3 4

1. Click the **Start button** on the taskbar, point to **Programs**, then point to **Accessories** (if necessary), then click **Windows Explorer** (Win) or double-click the **hard drive icon** (Mac)
   The Windows Explorer window (Win) or the hard drive window (Mac) appears.

2. Double-click the drive and folder where your Project Files are located
   The projector file appears in Windows Explorer, as shown in Figure H-11, or on the Macintosh, as shown in Figure H-12.

3. Double-click the **Take the Journey icon**
   The movie plays.

4. Click **Exit** on the Stage
   The projector closes.

5. Click the **Windows Explorer program icon** on the taskbar (if necessary), then click the **Close button** (Win) or click the **Finder menu** (Mac), click the **Close button** in the Windows Explorer window (Win), then click the **Director 8 program icon** on the taskbar (Win) or click the **Finder menu**, then click **Director 8** (Mac) (if necessary)
   Windows Explorer closes (Win) and the Director program window appears.

6. Click **File** on the menu bar, click **Create Projector**, then click **Options**
   The projector options remain in effect until you change them. It's a good idea to restore them.

7. Click the **Animate in Background check box** to clear it, click the **In a Window option button** (Win) or click the **Finder menu** and click **Director 8** (Mac), then click the **Show Title Bar check box** to select it

8. Click the **Compress (Shockwave Format) check box** to clear it, then click the **Standard option button**

9. Click **OK**, then click **Cancel**

FIGURE H-11: **Projector icon in Windows Explorer (Windows)**

Your folder location might be different

Your list of files might be different

Projector icon

FIGURE H-12: **Projector icon in a window (Macintosh)**

Projector icon

Testing a movie

Before you release your movie, it's important to test the final product on a variety of computer systems to make sure it plays properly in different conditions. During the testing process, check to make sure that all linked media and fonts appear correctly on the screen, and that the movie plays properly on all computers (such as Windows 95, 98, NT, 2000, Me, or later and Mac OS 8.x, 9.x, or later) and monitor display settings (8-, 16-, and 32-bit color) that end users are likely to use. If you plan to play the movie over the Internet, you need to check to make sure the movie plays fast enough over a slow Internet connection.

Director 8

Creating a Shockwave Movie

You can convert a Director movie and all its linked media to a Shockwave movie that you can play back in a Web browser on the Internet or on an intranet. Unlike a projector movie, a Shockwave movie cannot include the player in the file. The end user needs to have the Shockwave player installed on his or her computer to play the Shockwave movie. Before you create a Shockwave movie, you can preview and test it in your Web browser. When you create a Shockwave movie, you also need to create an HTML file (a standard Web page format) so that a Web browser can play it. After you create the HTML file, you can use other Web page editing programs, such as Macromedia Dreamweaver, to further customize the HTML file. Once you create a Shockwave movie, you cannot modify it; you need to change the original movie in Director, and then create a new Shockwave file. ✎ Jean previews the Journey movie in a Web browser, then creates a Shockwave movie.

Trouble?

If a warning dialog box about missing an Xtra appears, click OK, then see the "Managing Xtras for Distributing Movies" lesson earlier in this unit to install the missing Xtras.

1. Click **File** on the menu bar, click **Preview in Browser**, then click **Yes**, if necessary, to save the movie
   Your Web browser appears, loads the movie, and plays it, as shown in Figure H-13. Director creates a temporary Shockwave file and HTML file to preview the movie in the Web browser. Notice that some Director functions and commands, such as Exit, do not function in a Web browser.

2. Click **Videos** on the Stage to play the Saturn QuickTime movie, then click **Menu** on the Stage
   The movie plays properly in a Web browser.

3. Click **File** on the menu bar, then click **Close**
   The Web browser closes. Now you are ready to save your Director movie as a Shockwave movie.

4. Click **File** on the menu bar, then click **Publish Settings**
   The Publish Settings dialog box appears, displaying the Formats tab, as shown in Figure H-14.

5. Click the **HTML File button** , click the **Look in list arrow** , click the drive and folder where your Project Files are located (if necessary), then click **Select Folder** (Win) or click **Folder "Unit H"** (Mac)

6. Click the **Shockwave File button** , click the **Look in list arrow** , click the drive and folder where your Project Files are located, then click **Select Folder** (Win) or click **Folder "Unit H"** (Mac)

7. Click **OK**
   The file locations for the HTML and Shockwave files are set to the folder where your Project Files are located.

8. Click **File** on the menu bar, click **Publish**, then click **Yes** (Win) or **Save** (Mac), if necessary, to save the movie
   Director publishes the Shockwave file with the .dcr extension (Win) and the HTML file with the .htm extension (Win) in the folder where your Project Files are located, and then the movie plays in a Web browser.

9. Click **File** on the menu bar, then click **Close**
   The Web browser closes.

FIGURE H-13: Previewing the movie in a Web browser

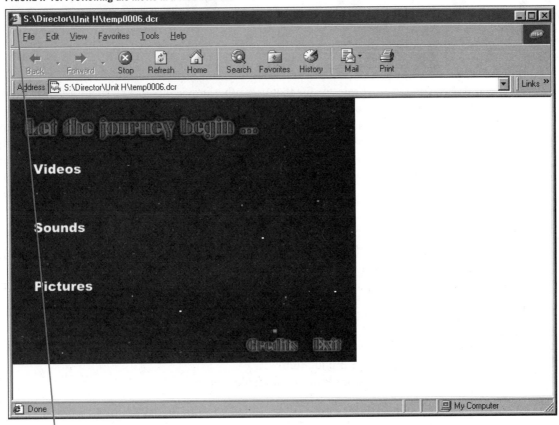

Your browser might
be different

FIGURE H-14: Publish Settings dialog box

Click tabs to set
Shockwave publishing
options

Click buttons to
select the location
to store the file

CLUES TO USE

Playing a Shockwave movie

If you don't have the latest version of Shockwave player installed on your computer, you can download it from the Macromedia Web site and install it. The Shockwave player works with Netscape Navigator 3.0 and later versions on Windows and Macintosh, and with Internet Explorer 3.0 and later versions on Windows and 4.01 and later on the Macintosh. It also works with browsers that are compatible with Netscape Navigator 3.0 plug-in architecture. To play a Shockwave movie on your computer system, start your Web browser, click File on the menu bar, click Open, click Browse (if necessary), select the HTML file (.htm extension on Windows) that plays the Shockwave movie, then click Open. The HTML file should be in the same location as the Shockwave movie and any External Casts or linked media that is used.

Unit H

Director 8

Creating a Protected Movie

When you create a projector file that uses other movie files or External Casts, you might want to protect those external files from being modified. When you protect external files, Director sets a flag that prevents end users from opening and editing the files in Director. Before you create a protected movie, make sure you have backup copies of the original. Once you create a protected movie, no one will be able to open it in Director. While it is important to protect your external files, there is one disadvantage: Director does not compress the movie into a smaller size. Jean creates a protected movie of the Journey movie for internal office review.

Steps

1. Click **Xtras** on the menu bar, click **Update Movies**, then click **Yes**, if necessary, to save the movie
   The Update Movies Options dialog box opens, as shown in Figure H-15.

QuickTip

To overwrite the originals with the new protected files, click the Delete option button. Make sure you have backup copies.

2. Click the **Protect option button**

3. Click **Browse**, click the **Look in list arrow**, then click the drive and folder where your Project Files are located
   A list of files for your Project Files folder appears.

4. Click the **Create New Folder button** (Win), or **New** (Mac), type **Originals**, press **[Enter]** (Win) or **[Return]** (Mac), then double-click the **Originals folder** (Win)

5. Click **Select Folder** (Win) or **Folder Originals** (Mac), then click **OK**
   The Choose Files dialog box opens.

6. Click the **Look in list arrow**, then click the drive and folder where your Project Files are located

QuickTip

To include folders in addition to files, click the "Add All" Includes Folders check box to select it.

7. In the file list, click **Journey Final**, then click **Add**
   The protected file appears in the File List at the bottom of the dialog box.

8. Click **Proceed**, then click **Continue**
   Director closes the movie file and creates a protected movie and adds the .dxr extension (Win) to the protected movie files, and a .cxt extension (Win) to any protected casts. Director creates a new Untitled movie file.

QuickTip

To play a protected movie, right-click the protected movie file, click Open with, click your Web browser (for example, iexplore), then click OK (Win).

9. Click **File** on the menu bar, then click **Exit** (Win) or **Quit** (Mac)
   Director closes.

Click option to create
a protected movie

Click button to select the
location for the original
movie files

Converting multiple movies to Shockwave files

You can use the Convert to Shockwave Movie option in the Update Movies dialog box to create compressed Shockwave movies. Once a movie is compressed into the Shockwave format, you cannot edit it. You need to change the original Director movie and then reconvert the movie to Shockwave. The conversion creates a movie file with the .dcr extension and a cast with the .cxt extension, which the end user cannot modify (Win). If you have multiple Director movies and casts, you can convert them to Shockwave files all at once, instead of converting each one individually. You can convert the files while preserving the original files or convert the files and delete the original files. To convert multiple movies to Shockwave files, click Xtras on the menu bar, click Update Movies, click the Convert to Shockwave Movie option button, click the Backup into Folder option button, click Browse, select the folder where you want to put the original files, click Open, click OK, select the movie(s) you want to convert, click Add for each individual file or Add All, then click Proceed. Director does not automatically save linked External Casts; you need to add each External Cast that you want to convert.

Practice

▶ Concepts Review

Label each of the elements of the screen shown in **Figure H-16**.

FIGURE H-16

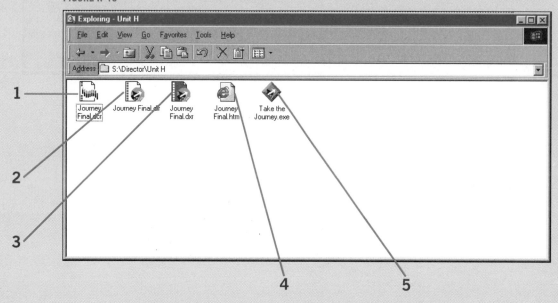

Match each of the terms with the statement that describes its function.

6. Projector movie
7. Java applet
8. Protected movie
9. Shockwave projector movie
10. Shockwave movie

a. An uncompressed movie that end users cannot open and modify
b. A stand-alone program that end users can play without Director installed
c. A compressed movie that end users play in a Web browser
d. A movie that end users can play in a Web browser without a plug-in
e. A compressed movie that end users can play independently of a Web browser

Select the best answer from the following list of choices.

11. Embedded fonts appear in a movie as a(n):
    a. Xtra.
    b. Cast member.
    c. Sprite.
    d. Behavior.

12. Which is NOT an Xtra type?
    a. Importing
    b. Transition
    c. Cast member
    d. Sprite

13. Which distribution method includes a player in the file?
    a. Shockwave movie
    b. Projector movie
    c. Protected movie
    d. Java applet

14. Which is NOT a projector player option?
- **a.** Shockwave
- **b.** Compressed
- **c.** Protected
- **d.** Standard

15. Which extension (Win) identifies a Shockwave movie file?
- **a.** .exe
- **b.** .dir
- **c.** .dcr
- **d.** .dxr

16. Which extension (Win) identifies a protected movie file?
- **a.** .exe
- **b.** .dir
- **c.** .dcr
- **d.** .dxr

17. When Director creates a Shockwave file, it also creates a(n):
- **a.** HTML file.
- **b.** Java file.
- **c.** External Cast file.
- **d.** Xtra file.

18. Which menu command creates a protected movie file?
- **a.** Publish
- **b.** Update Movie
- **c.** Protected
- **d.** Create Projector

▶ Skills Review

1. Embed fonts in movies.
- **a.** Start Director, open the file MD H-2 from the drive and folder where your Project Files are located.
- **b.** Save the file as Animal Life Final in the drive and folder where your Project Files are located.
- **c.** Change the font for the Welcome text and to text cast members to Lucida Bright or one available on your computer, and add bold to the text.
- **d.** Embed the Lucida Bright font or the one you selected for the 22- and 36-point sizes and Bold.

2. Manage Xtras for distributing movies.
- **a.** Add the SWAStrm.x32 (Win) or SWA Streaming PPC Xtra (Mac) Xtra to the movie. If the Xtra is not available, then add SwaCmpr.x32 (Win) or SWA Compression Xtra (Mac).
- **b.** Read the Web site information about the Xtra.
- **c.** Remove the SWAStrm.x32 (Win) or SWA Streaming PPC Xtra (Mac) Xtra.

3. Explain distribution methods.
- **a.** List and describe the differences among the five types of distribution methods.

4. Set movie playback options.
- **a.** Change the number of frames downloaded before the movie plays to 15.
- **b.** Select the option to pause the movie when the window is inactive.
- **c.** Select the option to show placeholders.

5. Set projector options.
- **a.** Save and compact the movie.
- **b.** Select the projector option to play in a window (Win) and show the title bar (if necessary).
- **c.** Select the projector option to play the movie in the center of the Stage.
- **d.** Select the projector option to compress the movie with the Shockwave format.
- **e.** Select the projector option for the compressed player.

6. Create a projector movie.
- **a.** Create a projector movie for the Animal Life Final movie.
- **b.** Name the projector file Wild Animal Life.
- **c.** Save the projector file in the drive and folder where your Project Files are located.

Director 8

7. **Launch the movie in a projector.**
   a. Display the folder where your Project Files are located in Windows Explorer (Win) or Finder (Mac).
   b. Start the Wild Animal Life projector movie.
   c. Switch back to Director.
   d. Clear the projector option to compress the movie with the Shockwave format.
   e. Select the projector option for the standard player.
8. **Create a Shockwave movie.**
   a. Save the movie.
   b. Preview the Animal Life Final movie in a browser.
   c. Select the folder location for the HTML and Shockwave files to the drive and folder where your Project Files are located. Close the Web browser.
   d. Publish the Shockwave movie file and save the movie, if necessary.
9. **Create a protected movie.**
   a. Protect the Animal Life Final movie.
   b. Back up the original movie file in the Originals folder located in the drive and folder where your Project Files are located.
   c. Exit Director.

▶ Independent Challenges

1. You are the marketing manager at Font Mania, a font development company. You have developed two new fonts for a client. You want to create a simple font viewer for the client to review the fonts. You use Director to display two fonts, embed them in a movie, and create a projector.

To complete this independent challenge:

a. Start Director and save the movie as *Font Catalog* in the drive and folder where your Project Files are located.
b. Create a text cast member with the text **Font Mania**, and drag it to the top of the Stage.
c. Create a text cast member with the entire alphabet and numbers 0 to 10, using a font, and drag it to the left side of the Stage. (*Hint*: Select a unique font on your computer.)
d. Create a text cast member with the entire alphabet and numbers 0 to 10, using another font, and drag it to the right side of the Stage.
e. Embed the fonts in the movie.
f. Create a compressed projector file as *Font Mania Catalog*, with the movie centered in a window.
g. Save the movie, then exit Director.

2. You are a multimedia instructor at a local college. You are teaching a class on Macromedia Director and want to explain and demonstrate Director's movie distribution method. You use Director to create a movie with definitions of each distribution method and save the movie in each format.

To complete this independent challenge:

a. Start Director and save the movie as *Movie Delivery* in the drive and folder where your Project Files are located.
b. Create a text cast member with the text **Director Movie Distribution Methods**, and drag it to the top of the Stage.
c. Create a text cast member with the text **Projector** and its definition, then drag it on the Stage.
d. Create a text cast member with the text **Shockwave** and its definition, then drag it on the Stage.
e. Create a text cast member with the text **Protected** and its definition, then drag it on the Stage.
f. Create a text cast member with the text **Java applet** and its definition, then drag it on the Stage.
g. Create a projector movie as *Movie Delivery*, Shockwave movie, and protected movie.
h. Play the projector movie and the Shockwave movie.
i. Save the movie, then exit Director.

3. You are the campaign manager of a candidate for a local state senate race. You want to create a movie to promote the candidate for distribution through e-mail. Use Director to create a movie about a fictitious candidate and save the file as a Shockwave projector movie to reduce the file size and provide Web browser independence.

To complete this independent challenge:

a. Start Director and save the movie as *Senate Race* in the drive and folder where your Project Files are located.

b. Create a text cast member with the name of the candidate and drag it to the top of the Stage.

c. Create a text cast member with brief biographical information about the candidate, then drag it on the Stage.

d. Create a Shockwave projector movie as *Senate Race.*

e. Play the Shockwave projector movie with the Shockwave player, not in a Web browser.

f. Save the movie, then exit Director.

4. You are the publicist for a space documentary, *Earth Unveiled*. The producer of the documentary has given you a clip of the movie in the MPEG format. You want to create a Director movie with the documentary movie clip and package it for audiences to view on the Web. You use Director to install an Xtra, called DirectMedia Xtra, to import the MPEG movie, then create a Shockwave movie. *Note*: For Macintosh, skip Steps a through c. The Macintosh does not need an Xtra to import an MPEG movie.

To complete this independent challenge:

a. Connect to the Internet and go to www.course.com. Navigate to the page for this book, click the link for the Student Online Companion, then click the link for this unit.

b. Download the free DirectMedia Xtra from the Web site, or use the DirectMedia Xtra in the drive and folder where your Project Files are located. (*Hint*: For instructions on downloading and installing the DirectMedia Xtra, see the "Installing an Xtra" in the Appendix.)

c. Install the DirectMedia Xtra.

d. Start Director, then save the movie as *Earth Unveiled* in the drive and folder where your Project Files are located.

e. Change the background of the Stage to black.

f. Create a text cast member with the text **Earth Unveiled**, and drag it to the top of the Stage.

g. Import the Earth.mpeg movie from the drive and folder where your Project Files are located. (*Hint*: Use the DirectMedia Xtra command on the Tabuleiro Xtras submenu on the Insert menu (Win) or the Import command on the File menu (Mac) to import an MPEG movie.)

h. Preview the movie in a browser.

i. Create a Shockwave movie.

j. Save the movie and exit Director.

Director 8

▶ Visual Workshop

Recreate the projector shown in Figure H-17. Your animal video and sound might differ. Print the screen. (For Windows, use the Windows Paint program. Press the Print Screen key to make a copy of the screen, start the Paint program by clicking Start, pointing to Programs, pointing to Accessories, then clicking Paint, click Edit on the menu bar, click Paste to paste the screen into Paint, then click Yes to paste the large image, if necessary. Click File on the menu bar, click Print, click Print or OK in the dialog box, then exit Paint. For the Macintosh, use the SimpleText program. Hold and press the Command, Shift, and 3 keys to make a copy of the screen, double-click the document Picture 1 located on your hard drive, click File on the menu bar, click Print, then click Print in the dialog box. Note: When you create a new document with a copy of the screen, and a document Picture 1 already exists, the Macintosh names the new document Picture 2.)

FIGURE H-17

Appendix

Objectives

► **Import file types**
► **Identify cast members**
► **Use the Paint window tools**
► **Choose a Paint ink effect**
► **Use sprite keyboard shortcuts**
► **Choose a sprite ink effect**
► **Install the QuickTime player**
► **Install an Xtra**

This appendix provides a quick reference for using Director more effectively. You can quickly find out options and descriptions for import file types, cast member types, paint window tools, paint ink effects, sprite keyboard shortcuts, and sprite ink effects. Director uses other external programs to help you extend the functionality and capabilities of your movies. This appendix also includes instructions for installing external programs, such as QuickTime and an Xtra.

Importing File Types

If you already have developed animations and multimedia content, images, sounds, video, or text in other programs, you can import these media elements into the active Cast window. Importing media elements is an important part of creating a movie with Director. Before you can import a media element into Director, you need to know the different types, or formats, Director can import, as shown in Figure AP-1. Table AP-1 summarizes formats you can import into Director. If you have a media element in a format not included in the supported list of formats, you need to convert the media element to one of the supported formats, or use an Xtra to insert the media element. Director comes with built-in Xtras, on the Media Element submenu on the Insert menu, as shown in Figure AP-2, or you can install third-party Xtras developed by other companies. For more information on installing a third-party Xtra, see the topic "Installing an Xtra" in this appendix.

TABLE AP-1: Import file types

type of file	supported formats
Animation and multimedia	Animated GIF, Flash movies, PowerPoint 4.0 presentations, Director movies, Director External Cast files
Image	BMP, GIF, JPEG, LRG (xRes), Photoshop 3.0 (or later), MacPaint, PNG, TIFF, PICT, Targa
Multiple-image file	FLC, FLI (Win); PICS, Scrapbook (Mac)
Sound	AIFF, WAV, MP3 audio, Shockwave Audio, Sun AU uncompressed, IMA compressed (Win); System 7 sounds (Mac)
Video	QuickTime 2, 3, 4; AVI (Win)
Text	RTF, HTML, ASCII (often called Text Only), Lingo scripts
Palette	PAL, Photoshop CLUT

FIGURE AP-1: Import Files into "Internal" dialog box

Click arrow to select import file type

FIGURE AP-2: Insert Media Element submenu

Click menu command to insert a media element

Identifying Cast Members

When you create cast members in Director or import media elements created in other programs, a small icon in the lower-right corner of each cast member identifies its type, as shown in Figure AP-3. Table AP-2 summarizes formats and objects you can import into Director. You can turn off or on the display of cast member icons in Thumbnail view and change the Cast window display. To change the Cast window display preferences, click Choose File on the menu bar, point to Preferences, then click Cast. To specify whether Director displays an icon in the lower-right corner of each cast member, indicating the cast member's type, click the Media Type Icons list arrow, then click All Types, All but Text and Bitmap, or None, as shown in Figure AP-4. To display a script indicator icon in the lower-left corner of each cast member that has a script attached, click the Script check box to select it.

TABLE AP-2: **Cast member symbol type**

symbol	type	symbol	type
	Animated GIF		Palette
	Behavior		PICT
	Bitmap		QuickTime video
	Button		Radio button
	Check box		Script
	Custom cursor		Shape
	Digital video		Shockwave Audio
	Field		Sound
	Film loop		Text
	Flash movie		Transition
	Font		Vector shape
	Linked bitmap		Xtra
	OLE		

FIGURE AP-3: Internal Cast window

Cast member identification symbol

FIGURE AP-4: Cast Window Preferences for "Internal" dialog box

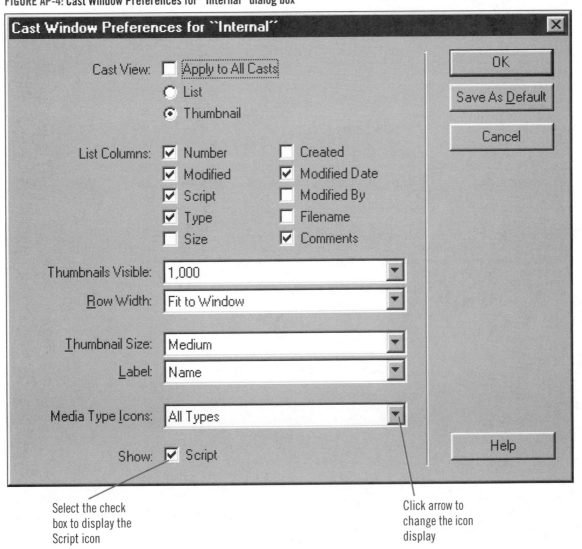

Select the check box to display the Script icon

Click arrow to change the icon display

Director 8

App

Director 8

Using the Paint Window Tools

Director includes a simple paint program to make it easier for you to create and edit bitmapped cast members without having to open another program, such as Adobe Photoshop. You create and modify a bitmapped cast member by using the tools on the Tool Palette. Table AP-3 describes the paint tools. A small arrow in the lower-right corner of a tool indicates that pop-up menu options are available for that tool. To display the pop-up menu, click a tool, then press and hold the mouse button. The toolbar at the top of the Paint window contains buttons you can use to apply effects to bitmapped cast members. Table AP-4 describes the buttons on the Paint toolbar. Before you can apply an effect, you need to select all or part of the bitmap with the Lasso or Marquee tool. Effects that change the shape of the selection, such as flip, rotate, skew, warp, and perspective, work only when you make the selection with the Marquee tool. Effects that change colors within the selection work with both the Marquee and the Lasso tools.

TABLE AP-3: Paint tool palette

tool	name	function
	Lasso	Selects an irregular area
	Marquee	Selects a rectangular area
	Registration Point	Changes the location of the registration point
	Eraser	Erases pixels or cast member
	Hand	Moves the view of the Paint window
	Magnifying Glass	Zooms in or out on an area
	Eyedropper	Selects a color in a cast member
	Paint Bucket	Fills all adjacent pixels of the same color with the foreground color
	Text	Enters bitmap text
	Pencil	Draws a 1-pixel line in the current foreground
	Air Brush	Sprays variable dots of the foreground color
	Brush	Brushes strokes of the foreground color
	Arc	Paints an arc shape
	Line	Paints a line
	Filled Rectangle	Paints a filled rectangle shape with the foreground or gradient color
	Rectangle	Paints a rectangle shape
	Filled Ellipse	Paints a filled ellipse shape with the foreground or gradient color
	Ellipse	Paints an ellipse shape
	Filled Polygon	Paints a filled polygon shape with the foreground or gradient color
	Polygon	Paints a polygon shape
	Gradient Colors	Blends from one color to another color

TABLE AP-3: Paint tool palette (continued)

tool	name	function
	Foreground Color	Default color in single color shapes and primary color in multicolor patterns (top color box)
	Background Color	Secondary color in multicolor patterns (lower color box)
	Pattern	Fills a shape with a pattern or tile
4 pixels	Other Line Width	Selects thickness of a line
16 bits	Color Depth	The number of colors a graphic can display

TABLE AP-4: Paint toolbar buttons

button	name	function
	Flip Horizontal	Flips artwork along the horizontal axis; left to right
	Flip Vertical	Flips artwork along the vertical axis; top to bottom
	Rotate Left	Rotates artwork 90 degrees to the left
	Rotate Right	Rotates artwork 90 degrees to the right
	Free Rotate	Rotates artwork freely in one-degree increments
	Skew	Slants the artwork while maintaining a parallelogram shape
	Warp	Bends and stretches artwork
	Perspective	Makes one part of the artwork appear closer than the other
	Smooth	Softens the edges of artwork
	Trace Edges	Creates an outline around the edges of the artwork
	Invert	Flips the color palette and reassigns all the colors
	Lighten	Increases brightness
	Darken	Decreases brightness
	Fill	Fills the selected area with the foreground color and pattern
	Switch Colors	Switches between the current foreground color and destination color

App

Director 8

Choosing a Paint Ink Effect

You can use Paint window inks to create color effects for bitmap cast members. You can select an ink effect from the Ink list arrow at the bottom of the Paint window, as shown in Figure AP-5. The result of the ink you choose depends on whether you are working in color or black and white. Also, some inks work better when you paint with patterns, and others work better when you paint with solid colors. Table AP-5 describes the different ink effects. To apply a Paint ink effect, select the bitmap in the Paint window, click the Ink pop-up menu, then click an ink effect.

TABLE AP-5: Paint ink effects

Paint ink effect	works with	description
Normal	Solids and patterns; B&W and Color	Uses the current foreground color and any selected patterns
Transparent	Patterns; B&W and Color	Makes the background color in patterns transparent; you can see any artwork behind the pattern
Reverse	Solids and patterns; B&W	Changes any color to its mirror color at the opposite end of the color palette; a color 10 spaces from the top of the palette changes to the color 10 spaces from the bottom of the palette
Ghost	Solids (B&W) and patterns (Color)	Paints with the current background color
Gradient	Brush, Bucket, shape tools; B&W and Color	Paints a blend of colors, starting with the foreground color and ending with the destination color
Reveal	Brush, shape tools; B&W and Color	Reveals a previous cast member in its original foreground color
Cycle	Solids and patterns; Color	Cycles through all the colors in the color palette between the foreground color and the destination color
Switch	Brush; Color	Changes any pixels in the foreground color to the destination color
Blend	Solids and patterns; Color	Blends with the background color to create transparent artwork
Darkest	Patterns; Color	Replaces pixels with the artwork color anywhere the foreground color is darker than the pixels of the artwork
Lightest	Patterns; Color	Replaces the pixels with the foreground color anywhere the foreground color is lighter than the pixels of the artwork
Darken	Brush; Color	Reduces the brightness of artwork
Lighten	Brush; Color	Increases the brightness of artwork
Smooth	Brush; Color	Blurs artwork; useful for smoothing out jagged edges
Smear	Brush; Color	Causes the paint of your artwork to spread or smear in the direction you drag
Smudge	Brush; Color	Causes the paint of your artwork to spread; like smear, except that the colors fade faster
Spread	Brush; B&W and Color	Uses the artwork under the brush as the shape for the paintbrush
Clipboard	Brush; B&W and Color	Uses the contents of the clipboard as the pattern for the paintbrush

FIGURE AP-5: Applying Paint ink effects

Click arrow to
change ink effects

Director 8

Using Sprite Keyboard Shortcuts

Sometimes, it is easier and faster to use the keyboard than the mouse. You can use key combinations, also called **keyboard shortcuts**. The most common keyboard shortcuts appear on the right side of menus, as shown in Figure AP-6 and Figure AP-7, while all others appear in Director Help. Table AP-6 lists commonly used sprite keyboard shortcuts.

TABLE AP-6: Sprite keyboard shortcuts

shortcut	Windows	Macintosh
Move 1 pixel in a direction	Arrow keys	Arrow keys
Move 10 pixels in a direction	[Shift][Arrow key]	[Shift][Arrow key]
Open the source cast member	Double-click a sprite	Double-click a sprite
Access the Inks pop-up menu	[Ctrl][Click a sprite]	[Command][Click a sprite]
Display a pop-up menu	Right-click a sprite	[Control][Click a sprite]
Exchange cast members in the Score	[Ctrl][E]	[Command][E]
Delete a sprite	[Backspace]	[Delete]
Find selected cast member in the Score	[Ctrl][H]	[Command][H]
Apply Extend Sprite	[Ctrl][B]	[Command][B]
Join sprites	[Ctrl][J]	[Command][J]
Move playback head to beginning of Score	[Shift][Tab]	[Shift][Tab]
Jump to next marker comment	[Ctrl][Right arrow]	[Command][Right arrow]
Jump to previous marker comment	[Ctrl][Left arrow]	[Command][Left arrow]

FIGURE AP-6: Sprite keyboard shortcuts on the Edit menu

Keyboard shortcuts

FIGURE AP-7: Sprite Keyboard shortcuts on the Modify menu

Keyboard shortcuts

Choosing a Sprite Ink Effect

Sprite inks change the display of a sprite's colors. Inks are most useful to hide white backgrounds, but they can also create useful and dramatic color effects. Inks can reverse and alter colors, make sprites change colors depending on the background, and create masks that obscure or reveal portions of a background. Unlike Paint ink effects, which are applied in the Paint window and are permanent, sprite ink effects are applied in the Score and can be changed at any time. Table AP-7 describes the different sprite ink effects. To apply a sprite ink effect, select the sprite in the Score window, click the Ink list arrow in the Sprite tab of the Property Inspector, then click an ink effect, as shown in Figure AP-8. For many ink effects, you can also apply a blend percentage to lighten or darken an ink effect. To apply a blend, click the Blend list arrow, then click a blend percentage.

TABLE AP-7: Sprite ink effects

sprite ink effect	description
Copy	Displays all the original colors in a sprite with a white background; copy is the default ink and animates faster than sprites with any other ink
Matte	Removes the white bounding box around a sprite; artwork within the boundaries is opaque
Background Transparent	Makes the background color of a sprite transparent; you can see the background color on the Stage behind it
Transparent	Makes all light colors of a sprite transparent; you can see any lighter colors behind it
Reverse	Reverses overlapping colors; changes any color to its mirror color at the opposite end of the color palette; a color 10 spaces from the top of the palette changes to the color 10 spaces from the bottom of the palette
Ghost	Reverses overlapping colors; nonoverlapping colors are transparent
Not Copy	Reverses all colors to create a negative of the original
Not Transparent, Not Reverse, Not Ghost	Reverses the foreground color of a sprite, then applies the Not Transparent, Not Reverse, or Not Ghost ink
Mask	Defines the transparent or opaque parts of a sprite
Blend	Blends with the background color to create transparent artwork
Darkest	Compares RGB colors in the foreground and background and uses whichever color is darkest
Lightest	Compares RGB colors in the foreground and background and uses whichever color is lightest
Add	Creates a new color by adding the RGB color values of the foreground and background colors; if the value of the two colors exceeds the maximum RGB color value, Director determines the new color from the color palette
Add Pin	Creates a new color by adding the RGB color values of the foreground and background colors, but the new color value cannot exceed the maximum RGB color value
Subtract	Creates a new color by subtracting the RGB foreground color value from the background color value; if the value of the two colors is less than zero, Director determines the new color from the color palette
Subtract Pin	Creates a new color by subtracting the RGB foreground color value from the background color value, but the new color value cannot be less than zero
Darken	Changes the foreground and background properties of a sprite to darken and tint it on the Stage
Lighten	Changes the foreground and background properties of a sprite to lighten it on the Stage

FIGURE AP-8: Applying a sprite ink effect

Ink effect   Blend percentage

App

Director 8

Installing the QuickTime Player

In order to play QuickTime movies in Director, you need to install the QuickTime player on your computer. The QuickTime player is a software product developed by Apple Computer, Inc. for Macintosh and Windows computers. Director 8 supports QuickTime version 3 or later, but recommends version 4. The QuickTime software comes in two versions: QuickTime player, a basic movie player, and QuickTime Pro, a movie creator, editor, and player. You can download the latest version of the QuickTime player for free and QuickTime Pro for a price, from the Apple Computer Web site at www.apple.com. To download the QuickTime player, you need a connection to the Internet.

Steps

1. Start your **Web browser**, connect to the Internet, and go to www.course.com. Navigate to the page for this book, click the link for the Student Online Companion, then click the link for the Appendix
   The Web browser appears, displaying the Web page to download the QuickTime player, as shown in Figure AP-9. The location and look of the Web page for QuickTime may vary.

2. Scroll as necessary, fill out the required information, click the **QuickTime for Macintosh** or **QuickTime for Window option button**, click the **Language list arrow** ▼, then click **Download QuickTime**
   The Download dialog box opens.

3. Click the **Save this program to disk option button**, click **OK**, click the **Look in list arrow** ▼, select a location on your hard disk, then click **Save**
   The QuickTime software is downloaded to the location on your hard disk.

4. Close your Web browser, start **Windows Explorer** (Win) or open **Finder** (Mac), then open the folder with the downloaded QuickTime software
   The QuickTime installation program appears in the window.

5. Double-click the **QuickTimeinstaller icon**, then follow the instructions to download the Minimum QuickTime installation, view the QuickTime README file, and view the Sample Movie
   A window opens with the QuickTime software, the QuickTime README file, and the Sample Movie, as shown in Figure AP-10.

6. Close the QuickTime movie window, QuickTime window, Windows Explorer (Win), and the README file

FIGURE AP-9: Apple Computer's QuickTime Web page

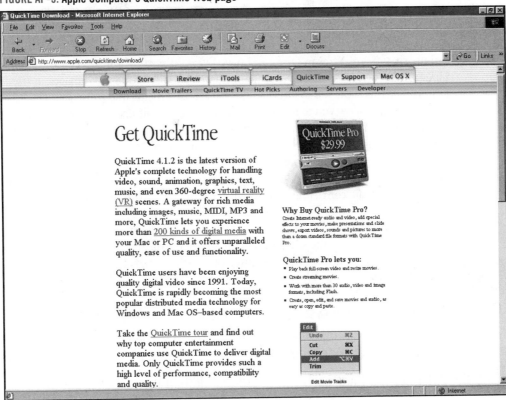

FIGURE AP-10: QuickTime player installation

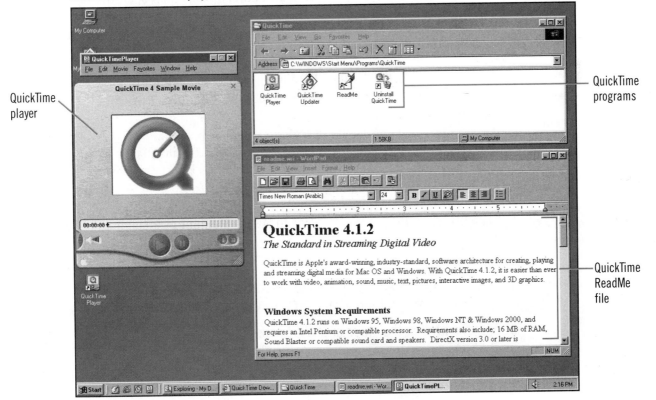

QuickTime player

QuickTime programs

QuickTime ReadMe file

Installing an Xtra

An Xtra is a software module you can add to Director, which extends the capabilities of Director. You can use six types of Xtras in Director: image filters, importing, transition, cast member, scripting or Lingo, and tool. Image filters Xtras allow you to modify bitmapped images in the Paint window; importing Xtras allow you to insert additional external media into a movie not standard to Director; transition Xtras allow you to add transition effects not built into Director; cast member Xtras allow you to add new media types, such as a spreadsheet or database, to a movie; scripting Xtras allow you to add new Lingo language elements to Lingo; and tool Xtras allow you to add external authoring aids. Director comes with a set of third-party Xtras on the Director installation CD. You can incorporate these and many other Xtras, which you can find on the Macromedia Web site (www.macromedia.com), into your movies. To use these Xtras, you need to install them first. Xtras are used in Director in different ways. The transition Xtras appear in the Transition dialog box, and the cast member Xtras appear in the Cast window, while other Xtras appear as a menu command on the Xtras menu or the Media Element submenu on the Insert menu. For this example, you install the Fireworks Import Xtra for Director, which imports Fireworks layers, rollovers, and slices, or the DirectMedia Xtra (Win), which plays MPEG movies, by Tabuleiro da Baiana Prod. e Ed Ltda.

1. Start your Web browser, connect to the Internet, and go to www.course.com. Navigate to the page for this book, click the link for the Student Online Companion, then click the link for the Appendix

QuickTip

You can insert a CD or floppy disk with the third-party Xtra folder.

2. Locate the third-party Xtra, read installation instructions, and download the third-party Xtra from the Internet to a location on your hard disk, as shown in Figure AP-11

For this example, you don't have to download a third-party Xtra. Xtras are included where your Project Files are located.

3. Start **Windows Explorer** (Win) or open **Finder** (Mac), then open the folder with the third-party Xtra

The third-party Xtra folder appears. For this example, you can find the DirectMedia Xtra in the Xtras folder where your Project Files are located.

QuickTip

You can place the Xtra in a folder nested inside the Xtras folder no more than five folder levels.

4. Double-click the installation program and follow the instructions, or drag the third-party Xtra folder in the Xtras folder in the Director program folder, as instructed on the Web site

For example, you can double-click the installation programs (fw3_import_xtra.exe for Windows; fw_import_xtra_for_director for Macintosh) to install a Fireworks import Xtra or (DirectMediaXtra150.exe for Windows) to install the DirectMedia Xtra.

5. Start Director

Trouble?

The menu location of the third-party Xtra command might vary. Read installation information for more details.

6. Click **Insert** on the menu bar, point to **Media Element** or a command related to the Xtra's product name, then click the Xtra command

The Xtra dialog box appears with options.

7. Select the options or files related to the Xtra

In most cases, the Xtra appears in the Cast window, as shown in Figure AP-12.

8. Drag the **Xtra** on the Stage or in the Score

The Xtra works just like any other cast member.

FIGURE AP-11: File Download dialog box

Downloading Xtra from the Internet

Click option button to save Xtra to local hard disk or network

FIGURE AP-12: Director window with a DirectMedia Xtra

Drag DirectMedia Xtra on the Stage or in the Score

DirectMedia Xtra in the Cast window

Click button to change DirectMedia movie properties

CLUES TO USE

Inserting an ActiveX control

In Director for Windows, you can insert ActiveX controls that let you take advantage of the technology, and adapt ActiveX controls to make them function as sprites in Director. The range of uses for ActiveX in Director is as limitless as the variety of ActiveX controls available. Before you can insert an ActiveX control, you need to use the manufacturer's installation utility to install the ActiveX control in Director on your computer. To insert an ActiveX control on the Stage, click Insert on the menu bar, point to Control, click ActiveX, select the ActiveX control you want to insert, then click OK. The ActiveX Control Properties dialog box appears, which lets you edit the ActiveX control and view information related to its properties, functionality, and support. Set the values for each property in the ActiveX control, then click OK. The ActiveX control appears in the Cast window. Drag the ActiveX control from the Cast on the Stage, and then it can be repositioned and resized just like any other sprite Xtra. When you pause the movie, the ActiveX control stays in authoring mode and does not react to mouse or keyboard events. When you play the movie, the control responds to user input.

Project Files List

To complete many of the lessons and practice exercises in this book, students need to use a Project File that is supplied by Course Technology. Once obtained, students select where to store the files, such as to the hard disk drive, network server, or Zip disk. Depending on where students store the files, you might need to relink any external files, such as a QuickTime (.mov) or AVI (.avi) video file, associated with a Director project file. When you open a project file, Director will ask you the location of the external file. Below is a list of the files that are supplied, and the unit or practice exercise to which the files correspond. For information on how to obtain Project Files, please see the inside cover of this book. The following list only includes Project Files that are supplied; it does not include the files students create from scratch or the files student create by revising the supplied files. Note that Unit G contains files that are Macintosh-specific.

Unit	File or Folder supplied	Folder File supplied	Location file is used in unit
Director Unit A	MD A-1.dir		Lessons/Skills Review
Director Unit B	MD B-1 Media folder	Space Background.gif Blue Earth.jpg Mwm Logo.tif	Lessons/Skills Review
Director Unit C	MD C-1.dir		Lessons/Skills Review
Director Unit D	MD D-1.dir Media folder	Colorful Star.gif Jupiter.gif Space Background.gif 4 Planets.jpg 9 Planets.jpg Blue Earth.jpg Mostly Space.jpg Saturn.jpg Space Planet.jpg Uranus.jpg	Lessons Lessons/Skills Review
Director Unit E	MD E-1.dir MD E-2.dir		Lessons Skills Review
Director Unit F	MD F-1.dir MD F-2.dir		Lessons Skills Review

Unit	File or Folder supplied	Folder File supplied	Location file is used in unit
Director Unit G	MD G-1.dir MD G-2.ppt MD G-2m.ppt (Mac) Media folder		Lessons
		Blastoff.mov Blastoff.wav Blastoffm.swa (Mac) Earthvenus.avi Meteor.wav	
	MD G-3.dir MD G-4.ppt MD G-4m.ppt (Mac) Media SR folder		Skills Review
		Birds.wav Birdsm.swa (Mac) Dog.aiff Dog.mov Eagle.wav Lion.au Monkey.au Monkey.mov Tiger.au Tiger.avi Wolf.au Wolf.mov	
	MD G-5.ppt MD G-5m.ppt (Mac)		Independent Challenge 3
Director Unit H	MD H-1.dir Saturn.mov		Lessons
	MD H-2.dir Monkey.mov Tiger.mov Wolf.mov		Skills Review
	Earth.mpeg		Independent Challenge 4
Director Appendix	Xtras	DirectMediaXtra150	Lessons
		fw3_import_xtra (Win) FW3 Import Xtra for Director (Mac)	

Glossary

Director 8

Active A window with a blue title bar, indicating any actions you perform will take place in this window.

Actual tempo Documents the real speed of playback.

Align window Moves sprites not to a specific location on the Stage, but to positions relative to one another.

Anti-aliasing Blends the bitmap's colors with background colors around the edges to make the edge appear smooth instead of jagged.

Authoring tool A software program, also known as a development platform, that allows you to create your own software.

Background color The secondary color in multicolored patterns.

Behavior channel A place to write frame scripts, also known as the script channel.

Bézier curve A type of vector shape curve.

Bit depth A measure of how much data space is available to store a given moment of sound. The higher the bit depth, the higher the sound quality.

Bitmap A pixel-by-pixel representation of a graphic.

Blend The transparency level of a sprite.

Blend list arrow Selects a blending percentage.

Blend value Makes a sprite more or less transparent. A blend value of 100% makes a sprite completely opaque and a blend value of 0% makes a sprite completely transparent.

Bullet mark An identifying feature indicating that an option is enabled.

Cast Library A special type of unlinked External Cast. Libraries are useful for storing any type of commonly used cast members, especially behaviors.

Cast members Media elements in the Cast window.

Cast window The storage area that contains media elements, such as graphics, images, digital videos, sounds, animations, text, color palettes, film loops, and scripts.

Channels Rows in the Score window.

Check mark An identifying mark indicating that a feature is currently selected.

Closed shape A shape in which the points do connect.

Color depth The number of colors a graphic or a computer system can display.

Command A directive that accesses a program's feature.

Compression Reduces the size of a file. The higher the compression ratio, the smaller the file size.

Context-sensitive help A help function that specifically relates to what you are doing.

Control handles Vector shape components that determine the degree of curvature between the vertices.

Control Panel A way to control the playback of a movie using VCR-type controls, including rewind, stop, and play buttons.

Cue point A marker in a sound or video that you can use to trigger an event in Director.

Destination color The ending color of gradient blends that start with the foreground color.

Development platform A software program, also known as an authoring tool, that allows you to create your own software.

Dialog box An onscreen display, indicated by an ellipsis, used to enter or select information.

Dithering Blends the colors in the new palette to approximate the original colors in the bitmap.

Editable button Sets a text sprite's editable property.

Editable property Allows users to enter text on the Stage while the movie is playing.

Editable sprites Allows end users to enter text (in a field or text sprite) on the Stage while the movie is playing.

Effects channels The upper channels in the Score window.

End frame The last frame in a sprite, denoted in a sprite by a small bar.

External Cast A cast that is saved in a separate file outside of the movie.

Field text The text created using the field tool or field window.

File A collection of information stored together as an individual unit.

File extension A three-letter extension at the end of a filename that identifies the file type for the operating system.

First line indent marker Sets the indent for only the first line of the text in a paragraph.

Flip Flips a sprite horizontally or vertically.

Flip horizontal button Flips a sprite horizontally.

Flip vertical button Flips a sprite vertically.

Floppy disk Removable media that you insert into the disk drive of your computer.

Foreground and Background color The color or tint of a sprite.

Foreground color The default color used with the painting tools, the fill color for solid patterns, and the primary color in multicolored patterns.

Foreground or Background color box Used to select a color from the color palette.

Frame channel The shaded channel, also known as the timeline, which contains the numbers that identify the frame number.

Frame scripts One way to add interactivity and extended functionality to a movie.

Frames Columns in the Score window.

Frames per second (fps) A measurement of a movie's tempo in frames per second.

Gradient blend Shading from one color to another color.

Grid A set of rows and columns of a specified height and width that are used to help place sprites on the Stage.

Guides Horizontal or vertical lines you can either drag around the Stage or lock in place to help you align sprites in a straight line.

Handlers Respond to messages triggered by a specific event during the movie's playback. A handler starts in the Behavior Script window with the word *on* followed by the name of a trigger message.

Hanging indent Indent where the first line left margin starts at 0" while the margin for the remaining lines starts at 1".

Hard disk The storage media that is built into the computer.

Highlight White text on a black background indicating that the text has been selected.

Indent markers Displayed on the ruler, they show the indent settings for the paragraph that contains the insertion point in the text window.

Ink effect Changes the display of a sprite's colors.

Ink list arrow Sets an ink effect for a sprite.

Interactive multimedia Software produced with Director that combines the elements of interactivity and multimedia.

Interactivity A software program that includes user feedback and navigation.

Internal Cast An internal storage area for cast members that is saved as part of the movie.

Irregular shape A freeform object.

Java applet A movie converted to Java, a programming language. Java applets created in Director provide extended functionality to play simple movies in a Web browser where plug-ins, such as the Shockwave player, are not allowed.

Keyboard shortcuts Keyboard combinations that you use to perform commands and functions instead of clicking the mouse. The most common keyboard shortcuts appear on the right side of menus.

Kerning A specialized form of spacing between certain parts of characters, kerning improves the appearance of text in large sizes but does very little to improve small text.

Keyframe The first frame in a sprite, denoted in a sprite by a circle.

Lasso tool Tool in the Paint window that selects anything that is surrounded with it.

Left indent marker Sets the indent for entire text in a paragraph.

Library behaviors Adds navigation controls and interaction to a movie using a built-in behavior from the Library palette with a prewritten Lingo script.

Linear gradient Shading from one color on one side to another color on the other side.

Lingo scripts Creates simple scripts that can be attached to sprites or frames to navigate to a specific location in a movie. You can create a script by double-clicking a frame in the Behavior channel, and then typing one or more Lingo instructions.

Lock button Used to set a sprite's locking property.

Locking property Locks a sprite on the Stage to prevent any changes made to the sprite.

Marker A number or a distinctive icon at the beginning of each channel.

Marquee tool Tool in the Paint window that selects everything within its rectangle bounds.

Menu A list of commands that you use to accomplish certain tasks.

Menu bar Organizes commands into groups of related operations. You can choose a menu command by clicking it or by pressing [Alt] plus the underlined letter in the menu name (Win), or by pressing [Command] plus the designated letter (Mac).

Moveable button Sets a sprite's moveable property in the Sprite tab of the Property Inspector.

Moveable property Allows users to drag a sprite on the Stage while the movie is playing.

Movie A Director file.

Multimedia A combination of graphics, images, digital video, sound, text and animation.

Open shape A shape in which the starting point and the ending point do not connect.

Palette channel Sets the available colors for the movie.

Pixel An individual point in a graphic with a distinct color.

Playback head The object in the frame channel that moves through the Score, indicating the frame that is currently displayed on the Stage.

Postscript A common graphics format.

Preload value Determines when cast members are loaded into memory as the movie plays.

Projector movie A stand-alone program that end users can play on their computers without having Director installed.

Property Inspector A way to view and change attributes of any selected object or multiple objects in a movie.

Protected movie An uncompressed movie that end users cannot open and modify in Director. Protected movies do not include any player software to play the movie.

QuickDraw graphics Shapes created with the tool palette.

Radial gradient Shading from one color in the center to another color on the outside.

RAM (random access memory) A temporary storage space that is erased when the computer is turned off.

Registration point Adjusts the location of a sprite on the Stage by entering a horizontal (X) and vertical (Y) value measured from the top left corner of the Stage.

Regular shape An oval, rectangle, or rounded rectangle.

Regular text The text created using the text tool or text window.

Remapping Replaces the original colors in the bitmap with the most similar solid colors in the new palette, which is often the preferred option.

Removable media Portable media that you insert into the disk drive of your computer.

Resize Adjusts the size of a sprite by dragging a resize handle on the Stage or by entering width (W:) and height (H:) dimensions in the Sprite tab of the Property Inspector.

Restore Re-establishes the height and width to the cast member by using the Restore All button.

Right indent marker Sets the indent for the text from the right margin in a paragraph.

Rotate Rotates a sprite by entering a number of degrees; a positive number rotates the sprite clockwise in degrees and a negative number rotates it counterclockwise.

Sampling rate The frequency with which samples are taken per second, measured in kilohertz, or kHz.

Scale button Proportionately resizes a sprite.

Score window The window that organizes and controls media elements over a linear timeline.

ScreenTip A feature that displays the name of a button on the toolbar.

Script channel A place to write frame scripts, also known as the behavior channel.

Seconds per frame (spf) Seconds per frame, a more accurate measure of a movie's tempo.

Select Text that has been highlighted.

Server A computer on a network.

Shockwave movie A compressed movie that does not include the standard player. A Shockwave movie is intended for play over the Internet in a Web browser.

Shockwave projector movie A compressed movie that end users can play on their computers independent of a Web browser.

Skew Tilts a sprite. Entering a positive value skews the sprite to the right; entering a negative value skews it to the left.

Sound channels Used to add music, sound effects, and voice-overs.

Span duration A default duration of 28 frames that each new sprite contains.

Spread value Controls whether the gradient is weighted more toward the start color or end color. Values greater than 100 weight the gradient toward the starting color and vice versa.

Sprite A representation of a cast member that has been placed on the Stage or in the Score.

Sprite bar The line that connects the circle and the small bar.

Sprite channels The numbered channels at the bottom of the Score window used to assemble and synchronize all the cast members in the Cast window.

Sprite label The text that identifies the sprite in the Score window.

Sprite Overlay Panel Displays important sprite properties directly on the Stage.

Sprite span The range of frames in which the sprite appears.

Stage window Serves as the viewing area for the visual elements of a Director movie.

Standard player A self-contained Director movie player that the projector uses to play the Director movie.

Start frame The first frame in a sprite.

Stereo or mono encoding Two types of sound quality. Stereo encoding produces high-quality sound, but the file size associated with a stereo file is twice the size of a mono sound.

Stroke width Determines the thickness of lines and outlines.

Tab Used to position text at a specific location in the text window.

Tab stop A predefined position in the text to which you can align tabbed text. By default, tab stops are located every ½" from the left margin.

Tempo The speed of a movie.

Tempo channel Used to adjust the speed or time of the movie as it plays.

Tempo mode Displays the playback rate that Director is currently attempting to achieve.

Tempo settings Sets the speed of the movie and pauses the movie at a specific frame.

Tile A graphic used to repeat in a pattern to create backgrounds, textures, or fillers.

Timeline The shaded channel, also known as the frame channel, which contains the numbers that identify the frame number.

Title bar Displays the filename of the open file.

Tool palette Contains a set of tools used to create shapes, such as lines, rectangles, rounded rectangles, and ellipses.

Toolbar Contains buttons for the most frequently used commands.

Trail property Leaves a trail of images on the Stage.

Trails button Sets a sprite's trail property in the Sprite tab of the Property Inspector.

Transition channel Sets screen transitions, such as fades, wipes, dissolves, and zooms.

Transition settings Select a transition effect used to move smoothly from one scene to another, and set the duration and smoothness of a transition.

Tweening A way to make a sprite move from one position to another.

Unload value Determines which cast members stay in memory and which ones are removed when the movie plays.

Vector shape A mathematical description of a geometric form.

Vertices Fixed points of a vector shape.

Windoid A window that can be moved but not resized.

Xtra A software module you can add to Director, which extends the capabilities of Director.

Index

Index

Index